T0366945

APOLLOS OLD TESTAMENT
COMMENTARY

7B

RUTH

APOLLOS OLD TESTAMENT
COMMENTARY
7 B

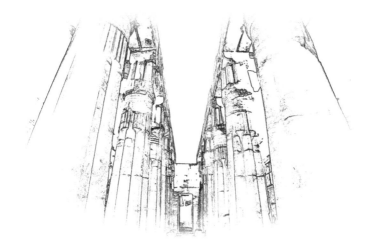

RUTH

Series Editors
David W. Baker and Gordon J. Wenham

L. DANIEL HAWK

SPCK Group
London

InterVarsity Press, USA
P.O. Box 1400
Downers Grove, IL 60515-1426, USA
www.ivpress.com
email@ivpress.com

SPCK Group (an imprint of Inter-Varsity Press, England)
Studio 101, The Record Hall
16-16A Baldwin's Gardens, London EC1N 7RJ
www.ivpbooks.com
ivp@ivpbooks.com

InterVarsity Press®, USA, is the book-publishing division of InterVarsity Christian Fellowship/USA® and a member movement of the International Fellowship of Evangelical Students. Website: intervarsity.org.

Inter-Varsity Press, England, is closely linked with the Universities and Colleges Christian Fellowship, a student movement connecting Christian Unions throughout Great Britain, and a member movement of the International Fellowship of Evangelical Students. Website: uccf.org.uk.

First published 2015

USA ISBN 978-0-8308-2525-7
UK ISBN 978-1-78359-307-1

Set in Sabon 10/12pt

Typeset in Great Britain by CRB Associates, Potterhanworth, Lincolnshire

Printed and bound in the UK CPI Group (UK) Ltd, Croydon CR0 4YY

green press INITIATIVE As a member of the Green Press Initiative, InterVarsity Press is committed to protecting the environment and to the responsible use of natural resources. To learn more, visit greenpressinitiative.org.

Library of Congress Cataloging-in-Publication Data
A catalog record for this book is available from the Library of Congress.

British Library Cataloguing in Publication Data
A catalogue record for this book is available from the British Library.

| P | 21 | 20 | 19 | 18 | 17 | 16 | 15 | 14 | 13 | 12 | 11 | 10 | 9 | 8 | 7 | 6 | 5 | 4 | 3 | 2 |
| Y | 33 | 32 | 31 | 30 | 29 | 28 | 27 | 26 | 25 | | | | | | | | | | | |

CONTENTS

To David and Morven Baker

'A person with many companions may find them at odds,
but a devoted friend holds on tighter than kin.'
(Proverbs 18:24)

EDITORS' PREFACE

The Apollos Old Testament Commentary takes its name from the Alexandrian Jewish Christian who was able to impart his great learning fervently and powerfully through his teaching (Acts 18:24–25). He ably applied his understanding of past events to his contemporary society. This series seeks to do the same, keeping one foot firmly planted in the universe of the original text and the other in that of the target audience, which is preachers, teachers and students of the Bible. The series editors have selected scholars who are adept in both areas, exhibiting scholarly excellence along with practical insight for application.

Translators need to be at home with the linguistic practices and semantic nuances of both the original and target languages in order to be able to transfer the full impact of the one into the other. Commentators, however, serve as interpreters of the text rather than simply its translators. They also need to adopt a dual stance, though theirs needs to be even more solid and diversely anchored than that of translators. While they also must have the linguistic competence to produce their own excellent translations, they must moreover be fully conversant with the literary conventions, sociological and cultural practices, historical background and understanding, and theological perspectives of those who produced the text as well as those whom it concerned. On the other side, they must also understand their own times and culture, able to see where relevance for the original audience is transferable to that of current readers. For this to be accomplished, it is not only necessary to interpret the text, but one must also interpret the audience.

Traditionally, commentators have been content to highlight and expound the ancient text. More recently, the need for an anchor in the present day has also become more evident, and this series self-consciously adopts this approach, combining both. Each author analyses the original text through a new translation, textual notes, a discussion of the literary form, structure and background of the passage, as well as commenting on elements of its exegesis. A study of the passage's interpretational development in Scripture and the church concludes each section, serving to bring the passage home to the modern reader. What we intend, therefore, is to provide not only tools of excellence for the academy, but also tools of function for the pulpit.

David W. Baker
Gordon J. Wenham

AUTHOR'S PREFACE

It has been a privilege to live with, ponder and write about this remarkable little book, which, like a finely cut gemstone, glitters with many facets when held up to the light. My thanks are due first of all to the faculty, president and seminary board of Ashland Theological Seminary, who approved a study leave during which the bulk of this commentary was written. I am grateful to be a part of the diverse community of theological educators gathered at Ashland, and for the commitment to Christ, Scripture and the spirit of enquiry that unites us.

I also want to express my appreciation to Inter-Varsity Press for the collegial and supportive relationship I have enjoyed at every stage of this project. I am indebted to Drs Philip Duce, David Baker and Gordon Wenham for approving the publication of this commentary as a stand-alone volume. I have been encouraged throughout by Dr Duce's congenial spirit, and the finished product has been significantly improved by the seasoned editorial feedback I received from Drs Baker and Wenham. I have likewise benefited from the superlative copy-editing work of Eldo Barkhuizen, whose attention to detail is second to none.

I thank my wife, Linda, for her remarkable forbearance and love, especially during times when I should have been focused on things other than thinking through the complexity of a literary trope or the implications of a linguistic turn.

Finally, I owe a debt of gratitude, over and above his editorial role, to my colleague David Baker. David invited me to contribute to this series and encouraged me throughout the writing process. He has been a kindred spirit and confidante, whose wisdom in matters both scholarly and personal I have often sought and always benefited from. He and his wife, Morven, have been gifts to Linda and me. As this manuscript has reached completion while they are preparing to leave Ashland for a new home, where children and grandchildren await, it is both fitting and a pleasure to dedicate this volume to David and Morven. May Yahweh indeed grant them full reward for their kindness.

L. Daniel Hawk
December 2014

ABBREVIATIONS

TEXTUAL

Gen. R.	*Genesis Rabbah*
HB	Hebrew Bible
K	Kethibh (the written Hebrew text)
LXX	Septuagint
MS(S)	Manuscript(s)
MT	Masoretic Text
OL	Old Latin
Q	Qere (the Hebrew text to be read out)
Ruth R.	*Ruth Rabbah*

HEBREW GRAMMAR

cohort.	cohortative
com.	common
const.	construct
f.	feminine
hiph.	hiphil
imp.	imperative
impf.	imperfect
juss.	jussive
m.	masculine
pf.	perfect
pi.	piel
pl.	plural
pr.	pronoun
prep.	preposition
sg.	singular

MISCELLANEOUS

ANE	Ancient Near East(ern)
Aram.	Aramaic
ESV	English Standard Version
gal	gallons

Hebr.	Hebrew
JPS	The Jewish Publication Society TANAKH
km	kilometres
lit.	literally
mi.	miles
NASB	New American Standard Bible
NJB	New Jerusalem Bible
NLT	New Living Translation
NRSV	New Revised Standard Version
p. (pp.)	page(s)
TNIV	Today's New International Version
tr.	translated by
v. (vv.)	verse(s)
vs.	versus

JOURNALS, REFERENCE WORKS, SERIES

AB	Anchor Bible
ACCS	Ancient Christian Commentary on Scripture
AcT	*Acta theologica*
AJT	*Asia Journal of Theology*
ASB	*Austin Seminary Bulletin*
ASOR	American Schools of Oriental Research
ATD	Das Alte Testament Deutsch
BETL	Bibliotheca ephemeridum theologicarum lovaniensium
BHHB	Baylor Handbook on the Hebrew Bible
BHS	K. Elliger and W. Rudolph (eds.), *Biblia Hebraica Stuttgartensia*, 2nd ed., Stuttgart: Deutsche Bibelstiftung, 1977
Bib	*Biblica*
BibInt	*Biblical Interpretation*
BibIntSer	Biblical Interpretation Series
BJS	Brown Judaic Studies
BLS	Bible and Literature Series
BN	*Biblische Notizen*
BSac	*Bibliotheca sacra*
BST	The Bible Speaks Today
BT	*Bible Translator*
BTB	*Biblical Theology Bulletin*
BZ	*Biblische Zeitschrift*
BZAW	Beihefte zur Zeitschrift für die alttestamentliche Wissenschaft
CBQ	*Catholic Biblical Quarterly*
CBR	*Currents in Biblical Research*

CC	Continental Commentary
DOTHB	B. T. Arnold and H. G. M. Williamson (eds.), *Dictionary of the Old Testament: Historical Books*, Downers Grove: InterVarsity Press; Leicester: Inter-Varsity Press, 2006
DOTP	T. D. Alexander and D. W. Baker (eds.), *Dictionary of the Old Testament: Pentateuch*, Downers Grove: InterVarsity Press; Leicester: Inter-Varsity Press, 2003
DOTWP&W	T. Longman III and P. Enns (eds.), *Dictionary of the Old Testament: Wisdom, Poetry & Writings*, Downers Grove: InterVarsity Press; Nottingham: Inter-Varsity Press, 2008
DSBS	Daily Study Bible Series
EvQ	*Evangelical Quarterly*
FAT	Forschungen zum Alten Testament
FCB	Feminist Companion to the Bible
GCA	*Gratz College Annual*
HBT	*Horizons in Biblical Theology*
HS	*Hebrew Studies*
HTKAT	Herdes theologischer Kommentar zum Alten Testament
HTR	*Harvard Theological Review*
IBC	Interpretation: A Bible Commentary for Teaching and Preaching
IBS	*Irish Biblical Studies*
Int	*Interpretation*
ISBL	Indiana Studies in Biblical Literature
ITC	International Theological Commentary
JAAR	*Journal of the American Academy of Religion*
JAOS	*Journal of the American Oriental Society*
JBL	*Journal of Biblical Literature*
JJS	*Journal of Jewish Studies*
JNSL	*Journal of Northwest Semitic Languages*
JPSBC	Jewish Publication Society Bible Commentary
JSOT	*Journal for the Study of the Old Testament*
JSOTSup	Journal for the Study of the Old Testament Supplement Series
JSS	*Journal of Semitic Studies*
JTSA	*Journal of Theology for South Africa*
LAI	Library of Ancient Israel
LBC	Library of Biblical Studies
LCBI	Literary Currents in Biblical Interpretation
LHB/OTS	Library of the Hebrew Bible / Old Testament Studies
LSTS	Library of Second Temple Studies
NAC	New American Commentary
NCB	New Century Bible
NCBC	New Cambridge Bible Commentary

NIB	L. E. Keck and D. Petersen (eds.), *The New Interpreter's Bible*, 12 vols., Nashville: Abingdon, 1994–2004
NICOT	New International Commentary on the Old Testament
NIDOTTE	W. A. VanGemeren (ed.), *New International Dictionary of Old Testament Theology and Exegesis*, 5 vols., Carlisle: Paternoster; Grand Rapids: Zondervan, 1996
NIVAC	The NIV Application Commentary
OBO	Orbis biblicus et orientalis
OBT	Overtures to Biblical Theology
Or	*Orientalia*
OTE	*Old Testament Essays*
OTG	Old Testament Guides
OTL	Old Testament Library
PIBA	*Proceedings of the Irish Biblical Association*
PMLA	*Publications of the Modern Language Association of America*
R&T	*Religion & Theology*
ResQ	*Restoration Quarterly*
SBLSP	*Society of Biblical Literature Seminar Papers*
SBS	Stuttgarter Bibelstudien
SemeiaSt	Semeia Studies
SHE	*Studia Historiae Ecclesiasticae*
SJOT	*Scandinavian Journal of the Old Testament*
SJT	*Scottish Journal of Theology*
SPHS	Scholars Press Homage Series
SWR	Studies in Women and Religion
TynB	*Tyndale Bulletin*
UBS	United Bible Societies
UBSMS	United Bible Studies Monograph Series
USQR	*Union Seminary Quarterly Review*
VT	*Vetus Testamentum*
VTSup	Vetus Testamentum Supplement Series
WBC	Word Biblical Commentary
WTJ	*Westminster Theological Journal*
WW	*Word and World*
ZAW	*Zeitschrift für die alttestamentliche Wissenschaft*
ZBK	Zürcher Bibelkommentar

INTRODUCTION

1. READING RUTH

Ruth is a tale of disarming charm. The story it tells – of small-town life, family values, an outcast woman's marriage to a noble man and coming home – articulates motifs attested in literature around the world. Told with an air of nostalgia and a hint of romance, it evokes the sense of an idyllic, bygone past, when life was simple and relationships unadorned. A closer look, however, also reveals a world of hardship: of calamity, suffering, death and loss; of impoverished widows struggling to survive; of immigration driven by necessity; and of a vulnerable immigrant trying to find a secure place in a new land and society.

It is little wonder, then, that interpreters hold diverse opinions on what kind of narrative Ruth is. From ancient times the book has been read as a story of conversion, with Ruth playing the role of the archetypal convert (Brady 2013: 133–146) and, in Christianity, as a prefiguring of the gathering of nations into the church (Franke 2005: 181–192). Historical-critical scholarship has attempted to classify the book within modern literary taxonomies. Ruth has been variously classified as an idyll (Gunkel 1913), a short story (Campbell 1975; Hubbard 1988a; Block 1999), a novella (LaCocque 2004) and a folk tale (Sasson 1989). Many modern interpreters, taking a cue from the concluding genealogy, also see broader social and political agendas at play. Some read Ruth as an apology for the Davidic monarchy (e.g. Hubbard 1988a) and as an ancestral narrative for the

Davidic dynasty, corresponding to the patriarchal narratives in Genesis (e.g. Nielsen 1997). Others view Ruth as a document of resistance, written to counter the exclusive, inflexible notion of Jewish identity promulgated by Nehemiah and Ezra during the post-exilic era (e.g. LaCocque 2004; Eskenazi and Frymer-Kensky 2011).

Notions of what kind of narrative Ruth *is* have much to do with a particular reader's sense of what kind of narrative Ruth is *like*. The texts that readers associate with Ruth, in other words, both confirm and influence the way such readers interpret the book and its message. Ruth's location within various biblical canons demonstrates the point. In the Christian canon Ruth is nestled between Judges and 1 Samuel. So situated, it offers a short respite from the paroxysms of violence, division and ethnic conflict that infuse the stories of judges and kings, presenting instead an idyllic and peaceful portrait of everyday life. Ruth tells a story of devotion, fullness and hospitality to the ethnic other in counterpoint to the inveterate turning to foreign gods that provokes divine wrath in Judges (2:11–23; 3:7, 12; etc.). It also looks forward to 1 Samuel and particularly to Hannah, the childless outcast who begins 1 Samuel with a song about a king (1 Sam. 2:10; cf. Ruth 4:22). Ruth's faithfulness anticipates Hannah's, linking the two women as models of exemplary devotion and revealing God's grace to the outcast through the births of favoured sons. Ruth's placement in the Christian canon thus prompts the reader to read the book within the larger narrative and in the light of the themes of devotion and faithfulness that configure it. It renders a brief, peaceful interlude between the turbulent events of Judges and 1 Samuel and a portrait of the lives of ordinary people in the spaces between crisis and transformation.

Different associations are suggested by Ruth's location in Jewish canons. The modern Jewish canon situates Ruth in the Writings, the last of its three divisions, and with the Megillot, the five scrolls associated with the festivals of the Jewish liturgical calendar. Ruth, by virtue of its connection to Shavuot (Pentecost), stands second in the sequence and follows the Song of Songs, which is associated with Passover. The sequence accentuates the theme of romance in Ruth and its celebration of life and love. The association prompts the reader to see marriage as the main thread of the book and the fruit of marriage as a gift of God. An alternative placement in the Megillot is attested in the Leningrad Codex, the oldest extant copy of the HB (early eleventh century AD). There Ruth stands first among the five scrolls and follows Proverbs. The sequence suggests still another way to view the book. Proverbs concludes with a paean to 'a noble wife' (31:10–31), who exemplifies the initiative, diligence and devotion to family prized by the sage. Boaz refers to Ruth with the same Hebr. phrase (*'ēšet ḥayil*, 3:11; cf. Prov. 31:10) as the two speak on the threshing floor, and in so doing invites the reader to see Ruth as the embodiment of the sage's ideal.

Thematic associations elicit more ways to understand what kind of story the book tells. Ruth is one of two books in the Old Testament in which women are the main characters, the other being Esther. The two books present complementary reflections on Israelite identity in the context of interactions with other peoples. Ruth utilizes story as a vehicle to think through how Israel should relate to foreigners living in its midst. Esther, on the other hand, takes the opposite tack: how to live as a minority within a dominant and sometimes hostile culture. Read together, the books comprise a narrative diptych on the topic of Jewish identity, one from the vantage point of the outsider who enters the community and the other from the perspective of the outsider living within a larger and more powerful society.

The form of Ruth – a migration narrative with a genealogical attachment – evokes associations with the ancestral narratives of Israel's patriarchs. As an ancestral narrative, Ruth provides the backstory of the Davidic monarchy, corresponding to the roles that the stories of Abraham, Isaac and Jacob play with respect to the formation of Israel as a covenant people. Ruth looks forward to the establishment of monarchical Israel and Yahweh's promise to David, much like the patriarchal narratives look to the establishment of tribal Israel in its land. The latter share an impressive catalogue of motifs with Ruth, including migration due to famine, immigration to a foreign land, the initiative of women, a son with a great destiny born of a childless woman, and the integration of foreigners into a new family and homeland. (For a detailed list, see Hubbard 1988a: 39–41.)

The people of Bethlehem associate Ruth with Rachel and Leah, as well as Tamar, the mother of Perez, and thus acknowledge her as an ancestral matriarch in her own right (4:11–12). Tamar's story (Gen. 38:1–30) shares the motifs of widowhood and dead sons and of an outsider who is driven to extraordinary means to secure her place within the community. These means include a carefully planned sexual advance, explicit in the story of Tamar but suggestive and ambiguous in Ruth's story (Nielsen 1997: 12–17). Ruth is also like Hagar the Egyptian, another outsider who becomes an ancestral mother blessed by God (Gen. 16:7–16; 21:15–21). Ruth's story reverses key elements of Hagar's. Hagar is abused by her mistress, with the acquiescence of Abraham, and driven away from the family she is attached to. Ruth, however, enters the community from the outside and stays. Boaz, the patriarch at the centre of the village community, provides for her and sees to it that she does not suffer abuse (2:9, 16, 22). The women of Bethlehem receive her with acclamation (4:15).

The narrative's many allusions to Deuteronomic commandments (notably the exclusion of Moabites, 23:3–6; the levirate commandment, 25:5–10; the provision for widows, orphans and aliens through gleaning, 24:19–22) cast Ruth as a narrative reflection on how these and other commandments are to be interpreted and implemented (Goulder 1993; Braulik 1999; Berman 2007). Her story, like that of Rahab the harlot (Josh. 2:1–24; 6:22–25), challenges a rigid interpretation of the commandments. Rahab is Ruth's alter ego in the conquest narrative, a woman from a despised ethnic group that is condemned and excluded by Mosaic command, one of the peoples of the land who are to be exterminated without mercy (Deut. 7:1–4; 20:16–18). Ruth is a Moabite, a member of a people permanently banned from the Israelite congregation (Deut. 23:3–6). Both women symbolize the threat of idolatry. Rahab is a prostitute and so embodies the threat of 'prostituting oneself' by following other gods (Exod. 34:15–16; Lev. 17:7; Deut. 31:16), while Moabite women are associated in Israel's memory with sexual and spiritual entrapment. Rahab's and Ruth's stories, however, override the commandment that excludes them. Rahab becomes the beneficiary of a forbidden agreement and is spared from the fate meted out to the other people of Jericho. The people of Bethlehem welcome Ruth with enthusiasm and unanimity, and her great-grandson becomes the founder of Israel's dynastic monarchy. In Joshua Rahab shows hospitality to Israelites, while in Ruth Israelites show hospitality to the foreigner. Finally, like Rahab, Ruth confesses the God of Israel (Josh. 2:11; Ruth 1:16), displays faithfulness (ḥesed) to Israelites (Josh. 2:12–14; Ruth 1:8; 3:10) and receives a place for herself and her descendants among the people of God.

As the foregoing discussion indicates, Ruth resists classification and invites readers to understand its story in conversation with a variety of other texts in the biblical canon. Reading Ruth alongside other texts therefore opens important trajectories for interpretation; all such readings contribute to a richer understanding of the meaning of the book. Those themes, however, that raise the issue of collective identity run deep within the book and deserve particular attention.

2. ETHNICITY AND IDENTITY

Ruth's Moabite ethnicity generates the energy that drives the plot of the story. Her identity becomes a problem only at the point of departure, when Ruth decides to leave her own land and family and follow her Israelite mother-in-law to a village in Judah (1:16–17). By doing so, Ruth steps across the spatial and social boundaries that differentiate Israelites from Moabites, and the people of God from all other peoples. Ruth the Moabite enters Israel's social and geographical space, uninvited and probably unwanted. The ensuing drama grapples with the import of the foreigner's presence among the descendants of Jacob. How should Israelites deal with outsiders who attach themselves to the nation and its God? On what basis or for what reasons may non-Israelites be incorporated into the covenant community? Is it right to allow Moabites to live together with Israelites in the land Yahweh promised to Abraham and his descendants? What, in essence, makes one a member of the covenant community that has been chosen, established and blessed by Yahweh?

Ethnicity may be understood as a complex of classifications that a particular group observes to differentiate itself from others. While genealogical descent may feature largely in the way an ethnic group defines who belongs within it, and the group itself may employ family terms to signify the bonds that bind it, the factors that configure and maintain ethnic identity constitute a dense fabric of shared experiences, perspectives and values. Ethnicity is not so much a biological given as a complex of sentiments that constructs a sense of collective identity. John Hutchinson and Anthony D. Smith (1996: 6–7) identify six criteria by which ethnic groups configure and sustain their identity: (1) a common proper name that identifies and expresses the 'essence' of the group; (2) a myth of common ancestry – a shared story of origins that creates a sense of kinship; (3) shared memories of definitive events and heroes; (4) elements of a common culture, usually expressed through common beliefs, customs, dress or language; (5) connection to a homeland, either by occupation or, in the case of diaspora groups, to a land of ancestry; (6) a sense of solidarity in whole or part.

Ethnicity is not an essential, natural or permanent phenomenon. Rather, an ethnic group constructs a sense of solidarity, belonging and identity by ascription. That is, groups unify and define themselves by ascribing to themselves attributes they consider to be definitive of who they are and of what makes them different (Barth 1969: 9–38). Ascriptions, practices and dispositions comprise the internal boundaries that mark group identity and differentiate insiders from outsiders. Group cohesion and identity consequently depend on the maintenance of these internal boundaries.

Groups commonly express attributes as dichotomies, defining themselves by characteristics they consider distinctive and often projecting the opposite attributes onto particular out-groups. The opposing attributes are reinforced through stereotypes. For example, a group that considers itself as industrious, intelligent and civilized might attribute laziness, stupidity and savagery to another opposing group. The practice of stereotyping can tend towards the extreme in relation to 'near others', that is, those out-groups that are close to the subject group or that share significant sectors of interaction. Near others constitute a constant threat to the ethnic group and its internal boundaries, because their proximity and the frequency of social exchanges expose the ascribed attributes and stereotypes as fictions (Cohn 1994: 74–90). Consider for example a member of a group that regards compassion as a distinctive attribute and constructs an opposing group as callous or cruel. Frequent interactions with members of the out-group inevitably lead to encounters that reveal the kindness of the others and the callousness of group members. Ethnic tensions may therefore be greatest between groups that are close to each other in any number of ways, as face-to-face encounters threaten the internal boundaries that constitute the basis for group cohesion. For this reason intermarriage, which provokes the highest and most intimate levels of interaction, is viewed as a practice to be avoided at all costs in societies around the world. Intermarriage violates the internal boundaries of the group and challenges them by humanizing the stereotypical 'them'.

A survey of biblical texts referring to Moabites reveals images and attributes that signal a high degree of ethnic antagonism. In opposition to Israel's self-understanding as a covenant people in submission to God stand depictions of Moab as the epitome of arrogant human defiance. Jeremiah and Isaiah declare, 'We have heard about the pride of Moab, of his extreme sense of superiority, of his haughtiness, arrogance and conceit, and of his lofty disposition' (Jer. 48:29; cf. Isa. 16:6; Zeph. 2:8, 10). The wilderness narrative depicts the Moabites as an aggressive people and devotes considerable attention to relating the measures a Moabite king took to curse and destroy the Israelites (Num. 21:1 – 24:25). Deuteronomy casts Moab as a callous and inhospitable nation, demonstrated pointedly by the fact that they did not greet the Israelites with food and water when they arrived in the region but rather tried to curse them (23:4).

Moabites are subject to degrading imagery. For one thing, they are associated with excrement. When Ehud assassinates the Moabite king Eglon, the narrator includes the grotesque but unnecessary detail that the king's bowels emptied as Ehud plunged the knife into his fat belly (Judg. 3:22). Isaiah envisions proud Moab flailing about in a latrine (25:10–11). Moabite women constitute particular threats and are portrayed as sexual predators. Moab's origin narrative, as Israel tells it, centres on daughters getting their father drunk and then sleeping with him (Gen. 19:30–38). At Baal-Peor, in the wilderness, Moabite women seduce Israelite men and draw them to worship their gods (Num. 25:1– 5). Moabite women, in short, epitomize the dangerous seductiveness of all foreign women. Strident declarations therefore proscribe intermarriage with them and all foreign women as, in a strain of thinking prominent in the Old Testament, intermarriage leads inevitably to apostasy, the transgression of the nation's internal boundaries and the eventual dissolution of the nation (Deut. 7:1–4; Josh. 23:6–13; 1 Kgs 11:1–8; 16:31–33; Ezra 9:10–15).

These sentiments, however, exist alongside others that acknowledge a degree of interaction and proximity. The Transjordanian territories settled by Reuben and Gad appear to have been home to a mixed population of peoples and were thus an arena for substantial social exchanges (Dearman 2005: 705–707). The tradition that Israel shares a common ancestor with the Moabites and Ammonites through Terah acknowledges a certain level of kinship, albeit in a belittling manner (Gen. 11:31 – 12:4; 19:30), and biblical texts record instances where one people gave refuge to the other. The king of Moab gave refuge to David's family when the latter was being pursued by Saul (1 Sam. 22:3–4), and Isaiah calls on the people of Judah to give refuge to the Moabites in their time of trouble (16:1–4). The book of Ruth also attests to times of peaceful coexistence. Elimelech evidently finds sufficient provision and welcome to live in Moab for ten years and find Moabite wives for his sons.

A complex of relationships, memories of conflict and ethnic stereotypes thus infuses the story of Ruth, suggesting that Moabites functioned as near others in Israel's world and thus as a perceived threat to national identity. Deuteronomy codifies these sentiments by singling out Moabites and Ammonites as peoples who are never to be admitted into the Israelite assembly (Deut. 23:3–6[4–7]). The reasons given for this radical exclusion are, first, that they did not greet Israel with food and water when they came out of Egypt and, secondly, that they hired Balaam to curse the nation. The legislation reveals a reciprocal antagonism between the peoples ('they do not want us and we do not want them'). It concludes with an emphatic flourish: 'you shall never seek their welfare or their benefit all of your days!' (v. 6[7]).

The book of Ruth plays directly off these sentiments and turns them on their heads. In Ruth the reader encounters a Moabite who joins the Israelite community and devotes herself to Israel's God. She personifies the faithfulness (*ḥesed*) that defines the heart of ideal Israel. She marries an upstanding Judean male and becomes the great-grandmother of Israel's greatest king. Although she is 'Ruth the Moabite' throughout the narrative, the final mention of her name does not include the ethnic signifier. In the end she is only 'Ruth' (4:13), fully identified with the covenant community (Glover 2009: 294, 302–303).

The author of Ruth takes aim not only at the Deuteronomic legislation that forbids the inclusion of Moabites but also at the ascriptions that lie behind it. This is nowhere more apparent than in Ruth's nocturnal visit to Boaz on the threshing floor (3:6–15). The scene evokes the archetypal image of the Moabite menace: the Moabite woman stalking an unsuspecting Judean male in the middle of the night. In Ruth, however, the scene results not in disobedience and apostasy but rather in an act of devotion that leads to the incorporation of separated widows into the community, to the continuation of an endangered patriarchal lineage and ultimately to the establishment of Israel's dynastic monarchy.

3. METAPHOR AND NARRATIVE

The dichotomized thinking that configures identity formation appears in Ruth in the form of bipolar constructions of space and character. The story associates Moab with death and loss but Bethlehem with life and fullness. Naomi travels with her family to Moab, and all her men die there. In her own words she was 'full' when she left Bethlehem but comes back 'empty' from Moab (1:21a). She loses her sons in Moab (1:5) but gains a son in Bethlehem (Obed, 4:17), not to mention a daughter-in-law worth more than seven sons (4:15). Departing from Bethlehem brings woe and separation. Returning to Bethlehem brings fulfilment and restoration.

'Field' functions as a mediating metaphor, that is, a metaphor that signifies both oppositions and thus facilitates a transformation in the symbolic matrix of the story. Associated with Moab, 'field' signifies emptiness and loss. Associated with Bethlehem, it signifies fullness and well-being. 'The Field of Moab', the outside space from which Ruth and Naomi journey, is a place of death and emptiness (1:1–2, 6, 22). The fields of Bethlehem (2:2–3; 4:4–5) – the one in which Ruth gleans and the one that Naomi ostensibly sells – bring sustenance and connection. The narrator, at the beginning, carefully preserves this symbolic construction, by conceptually distancing Bethlehem from the famine that opens the book. The famine strikes 'the land'. Bethlehem, on other hand, is intro-duced with reference to Elimelech (1:1a). 'Field', then, is directly associated with 'Moab', where Elimelech travels with his family and which – in the straightforward prose of the narrator – becomes a place of death (1:1b–3). The women's journey from 'the Field of Moab' subsequently signals a change of affairs (1:6). A final reference, which comments on Ruth and Naomi's arrival at Bethlehem, then confirms the new trajectory. Ruth's declaration of her intent to glean in 'the field' (2:2), which opens the next act, signals the women's entry into a new space and thus into a new life of provision and security.

The narrative also situates the main characters on opposite ends of the basic axes that define human beings within social systems: gender, ethnicity and social status. Boaz is a noble Judean male. Naomi and Ruth are poor women from Moab. Boaz occupies the centre of the society from whose perspective the story is told. He has power and influence, owns property, employs workers and knows how to orchestrate events to accomplish his objectives. Ruth and Naomi, on the other hand, inhabit the periphery, close to the social boundary. They are destitute, isolated and apparently without access to property or livelihood. Ruth's Moabite ethnicity casts her as a radical outsider, a person banned by the law of Moses. Naomi is the mother-in-law of Moabite wives. Boaz and the women thus stand on opposite ends of fundamental social axes: a powerful Israelite male versus two impoverished women with Moabite connections.

The journey of the two women from Moab to Bethlehem is therefore not just a journey home in the geographical sense. It is in a more profound sense a journey from the social periphery to the communal centre, from dislocation towards a place of belonging in the fullest sense. In the course of the story Naomi and Ruth travel from isolation and exclusion to re-integration and incorporation. In the end they find a place within the patriarchal network that configures their world (1:9b; 4:18–22) and among the town's women (1:8; 4:14–17).

The thematic polarities and inversions that configure the narrative of Ruth point to the working out of concerns that run beneath the story's surface. Because it addresses myth as a system of tensions and oppos-itions, the structuralist approach of Claude Lévi-Strauss, as it has been applied to the interpretation of literary texts, offers an effective way to excavate the story's subsurface. 'Myth' in this sense can be understood as the distillation of all that a culture thinks life is or should be. The purpose of myths, according to Lévi-Strauss, is to mediate the contradictions in a culture's belief system, that is, to reconcile the oppositions that humans see in the world and that must be explained in order to make them acceptable as part of the basic structure of reality. Myths mediate oppositions by rendering them through metaphorical and symbolic equivalents, and reforming and reorganizing them into their own structures. (See e.g. the discussion in The Bible and Culture Collective 1995: 70–118.)

Ruth is not a myth in the sense that it focuses on other-worldly beings or places. It is instead firmly tethered to human experience in space and time. It is mythic, however, in the sense that it mediates opposing visions of identity and utilizes metaphors and deep structures to transform and reconfigure the nation's self-understanding. Identifying and elaborating the narrative's mythic infrastructure, by identifying its dense fabric of interlocking codes, symbols and oppositions, therefore provides an important orientation to the book. The tight symmetries and imagery that interpreters have long admired signify more than stylistic panache. They are the marks of an author of remarkable sophistication, who configures the narrative with symmetries, polarities and symbols in order to address the difficult and contested question of the nation's identity. Is Israel, at the core, a people who can trace genetic descent back to common ancestors, or a people constituted by devotion to the covenant with Yahweh? The former view defines Israel as a closed community, the latter as a community open to all who enter, confess Israel's God and live faithfully. Through the adroit and subtle use of various devices and motifs the author aims for a transformation in the way the community looks at itself, away from the first view (Israel as defined by patriarchal descent) to the second (Israel as defined by devotion to Yahweh and others). To grasp how the narrator facilitates this transformation in vision and identity we must therefore read Ruth on two levels, with attention not only to the *content* of the story but also to the *way* the narrator configures it.

The story opens by presenting the exclusive perspective through Naomi, specifically her insistence that Orpah and Ruth would be better off with their own kind (1:6–18). The central section of the book's first act revolves around a conversation in which Naomi tries to persuade her daughters-in-law to go back to Moab, with the rationale that they will be better off among their own people (1:6–18). Specifically, she urges them to find security in the home of a husband back in Moab (v. 9). Her words thus endorse marriage to members of one's own group (endogamy) as the preferred state of affairs.

The book concludes, however, with the community's blessing of a Moabite wife as better than seven (Israelite) males (4:15), articulating the conviction that faithful foreigners can become valued members of the covenant community. The central section of the book's last act endorses marriage to outsiders (exogamy) as an even better scenario (4:7–17). Here too the message is conveyed by direct speech, this time through Boaz and the people of Bethlehem. Boaz presents marriage to a Moabite as a means of restoring a broken patriarchal line (v. 10), the village elders equate the outsider with Israel's ancestral mothers (vv. 11–12) and the women of the village acclaim the outsider as bringing a restorative benefit worth more than seven men (v. 15).

The book of Ruth thus opens with a single character commending in-group marriage but ends with the entire community praising the benefits of out-group marriage. The intervening narrative skilfully facilitates the transformation through a sequence of carefully crafted events. In the narrative space between the beginning and ending, Ruth the outsider is gradually drawn from the periphery of the community and into its centre through the agency of Boaz, a figure who occupies the centre, to the acclaim of one and all. In the process the main characters undergo their own transformations in identity. Ruth the Moabite woman enters Israelite space and becomes the mother of Israel's dynastic monarch. Boaz, the upstanding Israelite male who occupies Israelite space, breaks the Deuteronomic commandment, acquires a Moabite wife and fathers a son of mixed heritage. Naomi, an Israelite woman who has lived in Moabite territory, re-enters Israelite space and re-enters the community.

Marriage opens a significant metaphorical arena for addressing in-group versus out-group views of identity. It can be conceived as an institution that joins an in-group (kin) with an out-group (in-laws) to create a new social unit. Two forms of marriage – endogamy (in-group marriage) and exogamy (out-group marriage) – can represent opposite ends of the deeper polarity: on the one hand, by a concern to preserve ethnic purity and, on the other, a concern to open the covenant community to faithful foreigners. By telling a tale about marriage in these two forms, the author thus aims at a shift in the reader's point of view on Israelite identity: beginning with an affirmation of homogeneity (through Naomi's speech endorsing endogamy) and ending with an affirmation of heterogeneity as even better (through the acclaim of the village elders and neighbourhood women of Bethlehem).

Narratives shape the way we see things. By using story as the medium, and metaphor as the method, the author of Ruth is able to address the contentious issue of Israelite identity in a subtle but effective way. By exploiting narrative's capacity to draw readers in and to identify with characters and situations, the author changes the way readers view their world and the issues they face in it. By identifying with Naomi and Ruth, the reader sees the world through the eyes of a destitute widow and an ostracized other. By identifying with Boaz, the reader sees the world through the eyes of a man who has the power to organize the affairs of

the community. Entering into the lives of the characters invites readers to
see their own world, and those who populate it, in a new way. Ruth
addresses an issue of fundamental import, the complexity of which can
be conveyed only via deep structures and symbols.

The author constructs the narrative along five symbolic axes: (1) the
world of women versus the world of men; (2) familiar space (Bethlehem)
versus foreign space (Moab); (3) ethnic insider (Judean) versus ethnic
outsider (Moabite); (4) private versus public; and (5) life and fullness versus
death and emptiness. The polarities are juxtaposed in various combin-
ations so as to facilitate the desired transformation in perspective. This is
accomplished in two ways: first, through symmetrical plot devices, and,
secondly, through the names and interrelationships of the characters.

First, the symmetries. The book begins and ends by evoking the world
of men through references to fathers and sons. Elimelech and his family
leave Bethlehem and travel to Moab, where they live as immigrants (1:1–5).
Residency in Moab, however, brings death for the men and the end of
Elimelech's line. The book concludes with another reference to fathers
and sons in the form of a genealogy that confirms the birth of a son and
the continuation of a patriarchal lineage (4:18–22). To put it another
way, the world of men constitutes a bracket around the story of women,
mirroring how the lives of women are lived out within the frame of Israelite
patriarchy.

While the narrator begins and ends with males, the first and last characters to speak in the story are women. Naomi, in the first scene of the
story proper, utters the first words, which reinforce the narrator's association of Moab with death and no sons. As she leaves Moab, she speaks
of the dead (1:8) and makes pointed reference to the fact that she no longer
has sons. Moab, she laments, has robbed her of her sons and now, as
she departs, she has lost her capacity to bear more (1:11b–12a). Upon
returning to Bethlehem, she reiterates the symbolic meaning of Moab,
declaring that she was 'full' when she left Bethlehem but now returns
'empty' (1:21).

As the story nears its conclusion, on the other hand, the women of
Bethlehem acclaim the birth of a son to Naomi (4:17) and, like a mother,
Naomi places the son at her bosom (4:16). At the story's beginning Naomi
leaves Moab aged and without sons, but at the end the women of Bethlehem
celebrate the birth of the son to her, who will restore life and sustenance.
And they praise her daughter-in-law as being worth more than seven sons
(4:15). Moab signifies death, emptiness and no sons. Bethlehem signifies
life, fullness and sons.

Structural symmetries connect Ruth 2 with the previous chapter. Ruth 1
concludes with a reference to the beginning of the barley harvest in
Bethlehem, reinforcing the association of Bethlehem with life and fullness
and portending the restoration of the same for Naomi (v. 22). The events
that unfold in Ruth 2 confirm the restoration of fullness. They begin, as

in the previous chapter, with destitute women and a decision by one of them to go to a place that promises food, in this case Ruth's determination to seek a field in which to glean (v. 2; cf. 1:6–7). They conclude with a tangible confirmation of provision when Ruth returns to Naomi with a copious yield for her gleaning and a gift of parched grain (v. 18). The narrator then sums up with a concluding comment that mentions both the barley and wheat harvests (v. 23). The narrator's summary comment in 1:22 thus signals Bethlehem's promise of sustenance, while that in 2:23 confirms the realization of the promise.

The narrator also unites the events in the field of Boaz (Ruth 2) with those on the threshing floor (Ruth 3) by rendering the two chapters according to the same pattern. Both chapters begin and end with conversations between Ruth and Naomi, with conversations between Ruth and Boaz intervening (see the table below).

Ruth 2	*Ruth 3*
Ruth plans to glean (2:2)	Naomi plans an encounter (3:1–5)
Boaz welcomes Ruth (2:3–13)	Ruth approaches Boaz (3:6–13)
Boaz gives Ruth grain (2:14–18a)	Boaz gives Ruth grain (3:14–15)
Ruth tells Naomi about Boaz (2:18b–23)	Ruth tells Naomi about Boaz (3:16–18)

The plot of chapters 2 and 3 follows a simple sequence: (1) Ruth departs to a public place associated with the harvest; (2) Ruth meets Boaz; (3) Boaz responds kindly to Ruth; (4) Ruth returns to Naomi with an abundant supply of grain and reports; and (5) Naomi talks about Boaz. These chapters, furthermore, oppose the public to the private. Ruth's conversation with Boaz at the place of reaping takes place during the light of day and with many observers and witnesses, comprising the male and female field hands employed by Boaz (Ruth 2). Ruth's conversation with Boaz at the place of threshing, however, takes place in secret and in the middle of the night, with a pronounced concern that no one see Ruth there (Ruth 3).

Naomi's comment that Boaz will not rest until he resolves matters (3:18) leads back into the public sphere at the city gate, the locus of male interaction and decision-making. Here the men ratify Boaz's plan to marry Ruth, bless their union and articulate the fundamental concern of men: the continuation of the patriarchal lineage and the enhancement of reputation and status (4:1–12). The story proper, however, concludes in the space women occupy (4:13–17). Here the speeches centre on caring for, sustaining and connection to a male advocate.

The narrative oscillates between the worlds of men and women and between the public and private spheres through blocks of dialogue between the main characters, each of which is situated at the centre of the respective chapters (primary dialogue block italicized).

Exposition: Elimelech and his family (1:1–5)
Private: Naomi and her daughters-in-law in transit (1:6–18)
Public: the women of Bethlehem and Naomi (1:19–22)
Private: Ruth and Naomi at home (2:2)
Public: Boaz and the overseer in Boaz's field (2:4–7)
Public: Boaz and Ruth in the field (2:8–18)
Private: Ruth and Naomi at home (3:1–5)
Private: Ruth and Boaz at the threshing floor (3:6–15)
Private: Ruth and Naomi at home (3:16–18)
Public: Boaz and the men at the town gate (4:1–12)
Public: Naomi and the women of Bethlehem (4:13–17)
Conclusion: genealogy from Perez to David (4:18–22)

The four main dialogues intersect and complement each other in various ways. The first conversation (1:6–18) takes place between women (Ruth and Naomi), the last (4:1–12) takes place between men (Boaz and the elders), and the middle two (2:8–18; 3:6–15) take place between a woman and a man (Ruth and Boaz). In the course of the second dialogue Boaz commends Ruth publicly for her devotion to Naomi (2:11), while in the third he commends Ruth privately for her devotion to himself (3:10).

The four named characters who carry the plot personify the various configurations of land and kinship that comprise the core of national identity:

Boaz: Israelite ethnicity; remains in Judah
Naomi: Israelite ethnicity; 'returns' from Moab to reside in Judah
Ruth: Moabite ethnicity; 'returns' from Moab to reside in Judah
Orpah: Moabite ethnicity, remains in Moab

Boaz and Orpah signify opposing and homogeneous identities. Boaz is a Judean living in Judah, Orpah a Moabite living in Moab. Naomi and Ruth, however, mix ethnic and geographical identities. Both leave the land that defines their people and travel to another. Both 'return', Naomi back to the land of her people, Ruth to the land of the opposing people. The participial form of the verb for turning or returning (*haššābâ*) defines both women (Naomi: 1:22; 4:3; Ruth: 2:6) and facilitates a mediating wordplay: Naomi's journey to Bethlehem is a returning to her people and land, while Ruth's is a turning to a new people and land. Returning or turning to a land thus both unites and differentiates the two women. For Naomi, returning brings a restoration of connection to community and land, but for Ruth turning brings connections to a new community and a new space.

Naomi and Ruth thus signify hybrid identities that bridge the opposing identities signified by Boaz (inside) and Orpah (outside). They are mediating characters, that is, vehicles through which the author works to change perspectives on core elements of community identity. Can people with mixed identities become integral members of the Israelite community? If so, how can they be incorporated so that the community's internal boundaries remain intact? What, in essence, *are* the internal boundaries that define the nation? Kinship ties? Land? The devotion to Yahweh and others called for by Israel's covenant with Yahweh?

Naomi and Ruth enter Bethlehem from the outside but, at the story's end, find themselves fully embraced by the men and women of the community. Ruth in particular receives the honour of association with Israel's and Judah's ancestral mothers (4:11–12). It is a remarkable transformation. Ruth the Moabite, the quintessential outsider and an archetype of threat, apostasy and ethnic hostility, becomes, in the course of the story, Ruth the matriarch and progenitor of kings.

The narrator brings about the transformation in Ruth's identity through a series of relational associations that draw Ruth incrementally from the outside of village society to its centre. Ruth enters Bethlehem under a cloak of invisibility; the women who greet Naomi on her return say nothing about or to the woman who accompanies her. When Ruth does speak, it is to announce her intention to glean anywhere she can find a place (2:2). Gleaning marks her as an individual inhabiting the outer rung of Israelite society, someone with no land and thus no viable bond to others. When this woman from 'the Field of Moab' (1:22; 2:6), however, enters the field of Boaz, things change. The field of Boaz is a microcosm of village society, and Boaz, whom the narrator has introduced as 'an eminent and powerful man' (2:1), occupies its centre.

As events occur, Boaz draws the Moabite woman from the outer rung to the inner circle. The narrator initially situates Ruth at the edge of the community through the speech of the overseer, who identifies her only as 'the Moabite who returned with Naomi from the Field of Moab' and reports that she has asked to follow 'behind the harvesters' (2:6–7). Boaz thereupon directs Ruth to join his young women and stay in his field (2:8), pulling her socially and spatially into the web of associations that configures the community. He then invites her to benefit from the water his young men have drawn (2:9). Boaz later issues a third invitation to join the harvesters at suppertime and so draws her into the circle of all the workers (2:14) and thus further into the community. Finally, Boaz singles Ruth out for special treatment, instructing his young men to pull out sheaves for her (2:15–16).

The concluding scene, in which Ruth returns with the grain and left-over food, then carefully reiterates the social space she has traversed. She tells Naomi of Boaz's invitation but makes a subtle change. While Boaz invited her initially to 'join my young women' (2:8), Ruth reports that he invited her to 'join my young men' (2:21). Naomi, on the other hand, affirms Ruth's association with 'the young women' (v. 22) and names Boaz as 'a close relative of ours, one of our family redeemers' (v. 20). In the field of Boaz Ruth therefore travels, through a series of associations, from a position outside the community and its work into the outer ring (the young women), then to the circle of young men, and finally to a privileged status, as the beneficiary of special treatment.

The scene at the threshing floor completes Ruth's journey to the centre. Here there are only Ruth and Boaz. By identifying Boaz as a kinsman redeemer (3:9), Ruth the Moabite claims a family tie to this powerful man of means. By affirming her claim (3:12a), Boaz in turn acknowledges Ruth as family and so confirms she belongs with him at the centre of village society. His declaration that she is 'an admirable woman' (3:11b) consolidates the association by conferring on her a status approximating his own (3:1). From this point on, all that remains is for the community to agree to Ruth's change of status, a matter that Boaz deftly facilitates at the city gate.

Marriage thus becomes not only the end point of Ruth's quest for security but also, in a deeper sense, a metaphor for the inclusion of outsiders into the Israelite community. The narrator begins the story with a speech that lifts up marriage to one's own kind as the most desirable situation (1:8–9). The story concludes with an entire town extolling the marriage of a poor Moabite widow to an upstanding member of the community (4:11–12, 15). The message? That marriage to a Moabite woman brings about restoration, blessing and a glorious future. Intermarriage becomes laudable and ensures the continuity and well-being of the people. Embracing the faithful foreigner opens up new possibilities and, perhaps, a glorious and unimagined future.

4. COMPOSITION

Although Ruth is set 'in the days when the judges ruled' (1:1), there is very little to go on to determine when the book was written. Early Christian and Jewish traditions name the prophet Samuel as the author of Ruth. Critical study of the book has shown this to be unlikely, however, and modern scholars have proposed a number of scenarios for the composition of the book. Generally speaking, the proposals derive from evaluations of the book's linguistic and stylistic features, as well as speculation about the purpose of the concluding genealogy.

One scenario places the composition of Ruth in or around the reign of Solomon. Proponents note the presence of archaic linguistic forms in the Hebr. text and references to arcane practices. The linguistic forms include the paragogic nun (2:8–10; 3:4, 18) and instances of a putative early 2 sg. impf. verbal form (3:3–4; 4:5; see Campbell 1975: 25–28). The reference to the custom of removing the sandal to formalize transactions (4:8) is deemed noteworthy not only because the narrator comments on it (4:7) but also because, it is argued, the practice presumes a time before written documentation became the norm for formalizing agreements (as would be the case in a monarchy). Setting the book's composition during this period assumes that the early monarchy generated a flourishing literary culture and that Ruth was written to support the establishment of the monarchy.

If Ruth was written during the early monarchy, the links to the patriarchal narratives of Genesis elevate and legitimate David's dynasty. The character Ruth functions as the matriarchal precursor to the Davidic promise and the monarchy, corresponding to the patriarchs' role as precursors to the Sinai covenant and the constitution of the nation. Ruth thus would provide an important theological framework in support of the Davidic dynasty by showing that providence was at work well before David appeared on the scene, just as it was at work in the patriarchs long before the time of Moses (e.g. Hubbard 1988a: 39–42). So conceived, Ruth would serve the ends of a new monarchy concerned with unifying the nation and consolidating popular support. Alternatively, Ruth could have been composed for apologetic reasons. Here the genealogy assumes primary significance. Nielsen (1997: 21–29), for example, proposes that Ruth was written to deflect the troublesome problem of David's Moabite ancestry, which was probably raised by the family of Saul or prophetic circles opposed to David or perhaps, at a later time, by Jeroboam I and his supporters. She regards Ruth's association with Tamar to be particularly significant because of the message Tamar's story conveys: Yahweh chose a foreigner as ancestral mother and blessed her progeny.

The reign of Josiah has been proposed as another plausible scenario. Sasson (1989: 250–251) suggested that the book's glorification of David through the valorization of Ruth and Boaz would fit well in support of the reforming programmes of Hezekiah or Josiah. Block (1999: 590–598; see also 2008: 673–676) has fleshed out the proposal by positing literary allusions to Josiah in the characterization of Boaz and oblique references to the reform. He raises the possibility of an author from the north and suggests that Ruth was composed in the light of northern Israel's return to the Davidic kingdom under Josiah. In a twist on the idea of Ruth as an apology, he suggests that the book answered northern detractors who questioned David's legitimacy by raising his Moabite ancestry.

On the basis of an exhaustive linguistic analysis Bush (1996: 17–31) posits that Ruth was written during a transitional phase in biblical Hebr., between standard biblical Hebr. (SBH, the pre-exilic form of the language) and late biblical Hebr. (LBH, the post-exilic form). He identifies ten linguistic features that align Ruth with the former (SBH) and eight that align it with the latter (LBH). This linguistic mix indicates a transitional phase in the development of the language that, he argues, is attested also in the book of Ezekiel. In his view the linguistic features are decisive and point to a composition during the late pre-exilic period (at the earliest) or early post-exilic era (at the latest). Since the time frame does not lend itself to the view that Ruth was written in support of the Davidic monarchy,

Bush concludes that Ruth is a short story written to lift up and model virtues such as devotion and faithfulness.

To sum up, arguments that place the authorship of Ruth in pre-exilic contexts rest on three pillars. First, considerable weight is placed on the significance of the concluding genealogy, which is taken as evidence that the entire book was written to support the Davidic monarchy, either by associating David with the patriarchs or by countering challenges to David's legitimacy raised in the light of his Moabite ancestry. Secondly, the central problem of Ruth – the marriage of a Moabite woman to an Israelite male – is presumed to address concerns raised by the influx of foreigners into Israel or the extension of Israelite political influence into foreign lands (e.g. foreign mercenaries in David's service, immigrant and hybrid groups in the erstwhile Israelite lands recovered by Josiah). Finally, the story manifests archaic practices and linguistic forms that, while not decisive, support a pre-exilic composition.

As has been widely acknowledged even by those who look to them, the archaic elements of the book are of limited value in ascertaining the time of composition. First, the presence of arcane practices and linguistic forms may be attributed to an archaizing tendency, that is, to a later author's decision to employ older forms of Hebr. to evoke a sense of the olden days, 'when the judges ruled'. In addition, the categorization of forms, expressions and vocabulary into standard and late biblical Hebr. remains a tenuous enterprise, as biblical texts present only snapshots of what was spoken in their times. The dearth of extra-biblical Hebr. texts offers linguists scant resources to discern how, when and where Hebr. was spoken, and therefore what phase of the language any given text may reflect.

The putative apologetic purpose of the book is also speculative. There is little in the biblical literature associated with the early monarchy to suggest Israelite antagonism towards foreigners in general and Moabites in particular (Amalekites excepted). Likewise, there is reason to question the extent to which marriage with foreigners would have brought reproach. The report that Solomon's wives led him into idolatry (1 Kgs 11:1–13) may reflect more the concerns of a later redactor than a general disposition at the time. A similar situation obtains with respect to the reign of Josiah. The account of his reform reports the slaughter of idolatrous priests and the destruction of high places in and around Jerusalem and Samaria, including 'for Chemosh, the abomination of Moab' (2 Kgs 23:13). Yet no invectives are levelled and no actions taken against any specified group. The reform, in other words, focuses on the purification of the cult within the land of Israel, not the suppression of non-Israelites.

There is, however, a direct textual connection between the content and rhetorical agenda of Ruth and anxiety about the threat of foreign women as reflected in Ezra and Nehemiah. The latter book concludes with a report that a public reading of the scroll of Moses led to the discovery of the proscription against Moabites and Ammonites (Deut. 23:3–6) and that, as a result, the community excommunicated those of mixed parentage (Neh. 13:1–3). There follows an account of Nehemiah's removal of Tobiah the Ammonite's furniture from a chamber in the temple and the subsequent cleansing of the space (13:4–9). The book concludes with Nehemiah's discovery of Jews who have married women from Ashdod, Ammon and Moab and a report of his consternation that their children cannot speak the language of Judah (13:23–27). He has some of the men publicly beaten and humiliated, denounces them for not remembering that foreign wives led Solomon astray and asks, 'Should we listen to you, and do this huge, evil thing, commit a sacrilege against our God and marry foreign women?' (v. 27). Nehemiah ends his account with the report that he cleansed the priesthood from all foreign elements and set the order of the Levites and festivals (13:30–31).

For its part the book of Ezra depicts intermarriage as the single most important cause of the exile and a present threat to the survival of the restored community (9:1 – 10:44). The report of his reform, which probably takes place later than Nehemiah's, reveals that the issue of ethnic outsiders in the midst of the community was not easily or quickly resolved, and that agreement and compliance with Ezra's programme was not unanimous. That programme begins when community leaders complain to Ezra (9:1b–2):

> The people of Israel, the priests, and the Levites have not kept themselves separate from the peoples of the land and their abominations, from the Canaanites, the Hittites, the Perizzites, the Jebusites, the Ammonites, the Moabites, the Egyptians, and the Amorites. Rather, they have taken some of their daughters for themselves and their sons. So the holy seed has mingled with the peoples of the land. The leaders and officials have taken the lead in this sacrilege.

Those who approach Ezra have his ear and have an agenda. Their idea of the nation's identity is at odds with what others in the community, and particularly its religious leaders, appear to hold. They appeal to Ezra to intervene. Those who approach Ezra believe that narrow and rigid internal boundaries are essential for the well-being of the community, while those they oppose evidently hold an expansive view that sees no difficulty in incorporating members of the surrounding peoples into the covenant community. The presenting issue is intermarriage, which, as the petitioners see it, threatens the purity of the 'seed'. The way they refer to the surrounding peoples is telling. Canaanites, Hittites, Perizzites, Jebusites and Amorites probably disappeared as discrete ethnic groups long before the post-exilic era. Naming the surrounding peoples in this way therefore appears to be a smear that associates them with ancient enemies who were to be expelled from the land (Exod. 23:23–28; Deut. 7:1–2; Josh. 11:3; 24:11;

cf. 1 Kgs 9:20) and who represented a threat so virulent that the Torah commands their annihilation (Deut. 20:17–19; cf. Josh. 23:11–13).

Ezra is clearly sympathetic to the complaint as well as the view of Jewish identity that informs it. He responds with a dramatic display of dismay (9:3–5) and a public prayer of confession (vv. 6–15). The prayer laments Israel's persistent sinfulness and acclaims God's lavish mercy, before zeroing in on intermarriage as Exhibit A of the disobedience that provoked the exile. The implication is clear: by marrying foreign women the post-exilic community has again broken God's commandments and risks an outpouring of wrath that may bring it to an end (vv. 14–15). The people who have gathered around Ezra respond immediately. They confess that mixed marriages are sinful, resolve to divorce foreign wives and disown the children of those unions, declare their solidarity with him, and appeal to Ezra to take action (10:1–5). The result is a public assembly, which every Jewish male is required to attend (vv. 6–8). When the assembly takes place, Ezra leads the nation in a public confession for the mixed marriages and issues a decree that all such marriages be dissolved (vv. 9–11). The decree is then taken to the villages of Yehud, a tribunal established and a process for identifying the offenders is initiated (vv. 12–44).

Space does not allow a discussion of the complex social and ideological struggles that beset the post-exilic community. Suffice it to say that the books of Ezra and Nehemiah reveal a deep-seated ethnic anxiety about communal identity that fixates on the practice of intermarriage. Ezra in particular casts marriages to outside women as a primal threat to the survival of the community and, along with Nehemiah, appeals to the Torah to authorize and enforce the expulsion of those women and their children from the community.

Restriction of marriage within the in-group, it will be recalled, manifests a signal expression of strict boundary maintenance. The reforms, in short, imposed a rigid and exclusive view of Jewish identity that was expressed by a determination to preserve the continuity and purity of patriarchal lineages. The accounts of the reform, however, also reveal that significant elements of the post-exilic community, which included members of the priesthood, resisted the programme and maintained an expansive view of Jewish identity.

The intensity of the reformist agenda reveals how deeply many in the community resisted its aims. The struggle can be understood as a conflict between competing views of national identity, one that viewed Israelite identity as fixed and immutable, and the other that viewed the nation's identity in terms of adherence to criteria constructed by the group (Eskenazi and Frymer-Kensky 2011: xlii–xlv, following Glover 2009: 293–313). The Ezra–Nehemiah party represented the former view, which held that Israelite identity was determined by genetic descent and therefore fixed. The same by extension was true of outsiders. Moabites could be Moabites only, and therefore never members of the covenant people. We do not know specifically what the opposing side believed. We have only the view of the Ezra–Nehemiah faction, and their account casts the opposing party in the most negative possible light. Yet there is enough to suggest that many within the community, including prominent religious leaders, held an understanding of Israelite identity that made room for the incorporation of others who chose to confess Israel's God and live in covenantal obedience to Yahweh.

Implicit challenges to ethnic antagonism, intermarriage, a strict imple- mentation of commands, and a fixed idea of Israelite identity focused on patriarchal lineage are precisely those concerns that configure the narrative programme of Ruth. The book's rhetorical agenda, in other words, speaks directly and specifically to perspectives and struggles attested in post-exilic literature. I therefore join recent commentators (e.g. LaCocque 2004; Eskenazi and Frymer-Kensky 2011; Matthews 2004) in regarding Ruth as a narrative of dissent probably written in response to the reforms of Nehemiah and Ezra, that is, sometime between the mid-fifth to early fourth century BC. Against Ezra's and Nehemiah's attempts to redefine Israel along the lines of genetic purity, Ruth presents a vision of Israel as a nation that welcomes outsiders and presents the conditions on which they may be incorporated. Although Ruth the Moabite is excluded by a strict inter- pretation of the Deuteronomic commandment, she nevertheless declares her devotion to Israel's God, exemplifies covenant faithfulness and receives the blessing of Yahweh and the acclaim of the community.

The lack of a polemical edge to the book does not weigh heavily against this view (contra e.g. Hubbard 1988a: 36–37). Both Nehemiah and Ezra undertook their reforming agendas as emissaries of the Persian court, probably with an imperial mandate and with the authority to define the polity of the post-exilic community and promulgate its laws (Berquist 1995: 105–127). They possessed, in other words, political as well as religious authority and were backed by the full power of the Persian Empire. One confronts a concerted, determined imposition of imperial authority at one's own peril. Ruth reflects a strategy of dissent that uses the medium of narrative in a subtle and subversive way to persuade community members that the blessing of Abraham extends to all who seek refuge in the shadow of Yahweh's wings.

5. RUTH AND ISRAEL'S PAST

Telling the story of one's past, whether by an individual or a community, is not just an act of remembering; it is a statement of identity, a declaration of what makes that individual unique. This is particularly true of the narratives that define and unite a nation. By assembling, selecting and ordering its memories of the past into a coherent whole, a society articu- lates and reinforces how it views itself and the world around it. This is accomplished by taking up formative events and constructing a pattern of meaning that binds them together. The pattern reinforces the values, convictions and sentiments that differentiate the nation from all others. Historical narratives say in effect, 'These are the experiences that have made us the nation we are today,' and 'Here are the attributes that have carried us through those experiences.' They are a form of what has been called 'cultural memory': the way a society relates the past in its own way and in support of its own identity. 'The truth of memory', writes Jan Assmann, 'lies in the identity that it shapes' (1997: 14). Collective narratives relate the events that have shaped the community and identify the pattern of meaning that binds them together. 'These are the experiences that have made us who we are,' the narratives proclaim, 'and here's the unifying thread that tells us what they mean.'

Consider, on a smaller scale, the sharing of stories that often occurs at family gatherings. Why do families repeat certain stories when they gather? It is probably not because family members have short memories! Rather, sharing stories about family experiences binds the members together and reinforces a common identity. Those stories that are remembered and shared repeatedly over the course of time are the ones that in some way express the family's sense of identity. They exemplify typical family characteristics or practices. The same holds true of larger collectives. Those events and experiences a nation remembers are those that in some way typify the nation's view of itself, and the larger narrative in which they are embedded provides the patterned meaning by which they can be interpreted.

Historical narratives, then, are not simple recapitulations of past events but rather imaginative constructions that are both fixed and fluid: fixed by the core attributes of group identity and fluid in their meaning as the group's perspectives are shaped by new experiences and interactions. The past, then, is a cultural projection (Forget 2010: 4). Consequently, the truth a society tells about itself through its narratives is continually constructed and contested. It 'is subject to time so that it changes with every new identity and every new present. It lies in the story, not as it happened but as it lives on and unfolds in collective memory' (Assmann 1997: 14).

Symbols and structures constitute the system of meaning by which the nation's account of its past is woven into the fabric of the present. They offer available cultural frameworks that can be taken up in the service of the meaning the historian sees in the past. Without the interpretative associations that metaphor and mythic patterning provides, history is devoid of meaning, comprising only a catalogue of events. Human imagination and artistry play a large role, in short, in constructing and interpreting historical narratives (see White 1987).

The role of imagination and perspective in historical narrative can be illustrated by comparing the story of the Israelite monarchy narrated in Samuel to Kings with the story as it is narrated in 1–2 Chronicles. The former presents an ambivalent reflection on monarchy that is attuned to the acquisition and exertion of power within the system, and in coordination with or (more often) opposition to Yahweh's power and sovereignty. It devotes considerable attention to the social forces that gave rise to the monarchy and renders nuanced portraits of Saul and David. Prophets appear prominently throughout the account, which as a whole emphasizes Israel's inveterate waywardness and refusal to abide by the commandments. By contrast, Chronicles displays scarcely any interest in Saul, reports nothing that could in any way cast David in a negative light and foregrounds the role and ministry of the priesthood. Samuel–Kings tells the story of Israel to include the northern kingdom, but Chronicles keeps the focus squarely on the kingdom of Judah. Overall narrative strategies result at points in significantly different presentations and assessments of the reigns of kings (cf. e.g. the account of Manasseh in 2 Kgs 21:1–18 with that in 2 Chr. 33:1–20).

The idea of history as cultural memory clashes with certain modern notions of history. The development of the so-called historical consciousness in Western civilization owes much to the influence of positivism during the nineteenth century, when history was in the process of developing as an academic discipline in European and American universities. Positivism associates truth with facts. As an approach to the past, positivism oriented Western remembering towards discovering, identifying, interpreting and evaluating historical 'facts' and called for the same objective, detached approach to historical facticity that defined scientific enquiry. History writing in the nineteenth and early twentieth centuries thus aspired to present an unembellished account of the past that derived from a critical enquiry of the past and available sources. One consequence of this development, which persists to the present day, was the creation of a false dichotomy that regarded historical narratives, which relate actual events, as 'true', and mythic narratives, which relate fictional events, as 'false'. With respect to biblical narratives this led to a concern to validate the historical facticity of biblical narratives, propelled by the conviction that if biblical narratives were not historical they could not be true.

Modern notions of 'history' and 'historical' therefore represent ways of remembering that are tied to culturally embedded ways of thinking and knowing. A true account of the past, in the modern sense, is one that says 'it happened just this way' and 'here's how you can know that it did'. If we recognize, however, that every culture remembers the past in its own way, we will not expect a book like Ruth to accommodate to our ideas of how to relate the past correctly. What constituted a true memory for Israel was also embedded within a socially embedded matrix of perspectives, values, tropes and understandings that cannot easily be discerned or readily translated into a modern context.

The modern impulse to evaluate the historicity of Ruth, in other words, has much to do with the need to confirm Ruth's historical facticity and thus its truthfulness. The task is daunting. There are no ancient sources outside the Bible that can corroborate whether Ruth, Naomi and Boaz actually existed, leaving the modern historian to make judgments solely on internal evidence. Commentators concerned to do so point to a number of features as indicators of historical narration: the straightforward and unembellished character of the narration; the absence of miracle as an indicator of historical writing; names typical of the late second millennium BC; customs that appear to fit the period of the judges; and the narrator's explanation of the sandal ceremony (4:7). While these aspects have inclined some to classify the book as historiography and not fiction (e.g. Block 2008: 677–678), the most we can affirm with confidence is that the book presents a historically plausible scenario (Campbell 1975: 9–10; Hubbard 1988a: 48). Realistic writing, as the modern-day novels of Steinbeck and Hemingway attest, does not necessarily signal historical content. Furthermore, explanations may function rhetorically to create the sense of antiquity rather than to provide information about an actual past practice.

This is not to say, however, that Ruth does not refer to something that actually happened. Here the concluding genealogy, which links the narrative to the Davidic monarchy, is decisive. The presence of the genealogy has rhetorical impact only if the memory of David's Moabite ancestry was a familiar and incontestable element of Israel's historical traditions. It connects David to the story of Ruth by way of historical reminder. The author of Ruth, writing in opposition to the cleansing programmes of Nehemiah and Ezra, found in this memory a powerful vehicle for countering the reformers' exclusivist hermeneutic and ideology. Here was a remembrance that one of David's ancestors was a Moabite, one of the peoples specifically targeted by the reforms. She was faithful to the people of Israel and the God of Israel, and the result was the blessing of the nation and the beginning of a new chapter in the nation's life. The message of Ruth could not be made if David's Moabite ancestry was not widely known.

The tradition is probably authentic. Because of the negative associations connected to Moabites attested across biblical literature, it is difficult to conceive a reason for fabricating it. Whatever its original form and origin, the presence of such a story in the collective memory of the post-exilic community provided the author of Ruth with a medium to counter those who restricted Israelite identity to an Israelite pedigree – and to offer a vision of Israel as a community defined by devotion to Yahweh and each other.

6. THE THEOLOGY OF RUTH

Although God is mentioned frequently throughout Ruth, the narrator reports only one instance in which God acts. That is the book's final reference, which reports that God bestowed pregnancy to Ruth (4:13). In contrast to God's direct interaction with human beings in the books surrounding Ruth, God does not appear or speak to individuals, nor does the narrator report or comment on his will or involvement as the story develops. God is present in Ruth but only indirectly, through the words of the characters who invoke him through lament, blessing and celebration.

The work of Ronald Hals (1969) has exerted a significant influence on the way many contemporary Protestant interpreters discern the theological message of the book. Hals views the final reference to God (4:13) as the key interpretative statement that signals the basic orientation of the book. He notes that the report immediately follows references to God's gift of children (4:11–12), which bring the story to a close on a note of happiness in counterpoint to its sorrowful beginning. Hals concludes that the singular report of God's involvement at the point of completion signals God's work throughout the narrative. This affirms, in his view, that 'the story is about the providence of God' (6), a distinct expression of what Hals describes as 'the basic Israelite belief in Yahweh's all-causality . . . That which happens comes from the Lord' (9). The narrator of the story, he proposes, refrains from pointing out or commenting on Yahweh's activity in order to convey a sense of the hiddenness of God in human affairs. In contrast to the surrounding books, where God's activity is dramatic and episodic, Ruth's restrained view of divine activity confirms the continuity of God's presence and work within the ordinary events of life. Thus, Hals argues, Ruth offers an important reflection on the vital truth that God is always at work in seen and unseen ways to bring about divine purposes through faithful servants.

Hals's assertion that Ruth presents the 'hiddenness and continuousness' of God's providential guidance has been taken up by many subsequent commentators. Nielsen notes that the plans of the human agents in the book are never fully coordinated; it must therefore be God who carries out a larger plan through the decisions each individual makes. She writes, 'God guides and controls events, but from beneath the surface' (1997: 31). Block declares that Ruth 'must be interpreted as a glorious account of divine providence' (1999: 610) that reveals God's determination to 'orchestrate events so that David could emerge' from the chaotic days of the judges (2008: 682). Bush asserts that 'not only Boaz's faithfulness and Naomi's risky plan (chap. 3) but also Ruth's accidental steps are part of the control God effects over his world behind the scenes and in the shadows' (1996: 47). 'God's all-causality', he adds, 'is implicit, acting through the ordinary hopes, intentions, and purpose of the human protagonists' (55). Hubbard offers a more nuanced reading that sees in Ruth both 'God's continuous, hidden all causality and his cosmic role as rewarder'. He suggests that the narrative's indirectness regarding God does not downplay God's providence but rather heightens the reader's awareness of it. Human deeds are the way God exercises his rule throughout the book, and his hidden activity in human agents 'is presumed to be the implicit, immanent cause of events' (1988a: 69, 70).

The assumption that Ruth depicts God's 'hidden all causality' owes much to the theology of providence that informs the hermeneutic of the commentators. A straightforward reading of the book, on the other hand, suggests a more nuanced and multifaceted theological vision focused instead on human perception and action. In this respect the thematic centrality of *ḥesed* comes to the fore. *Ḥesed* may be understood as passionate devotion, an unqualified decision *for* someone else expressed by specific and tangible actions. The word occurs only three times within the book, but the disposition and practice it signifies pervades the story. Naomi acclaims Yahweh by blessing (1:8) and acclamation (2:20) as a God who bestows *ḥesed*. Boaz, however, affirms Ruth as a human practitioner of *ḥesed* both to him and to Naomi (3:10; cf. 2:11–12). Ruth's devotion to Naomi issues in concrete acts: she forsakes her family, people and land for Naomi's sake and cares for Naomi's needs by gleaning in Boaz's field. Her devotion to Boaz, at least in the latter's eyes, is demonstrated over against more attractive alternatives. The narrator associates these human acts of *ḥesed* with those of Yahweh through a deft wordplay. In the field Boaz invokes the blessing of 'Yahweh, the God of Israel, under whose wings you have come for refuge' (2:12). At the threshing floor Ruth appeals to Boaz to 'spread your wing over your servant' (3:9). Boaz's agreement to do so thus implicitly casts his decision for Ruth as a human expression of Yahweh's *ḥesed*.

Eskenazi and Frymer-Kensky (2011) reflect on the many ways the characters' invocations of divine blessing and intercession are fulfilled by human agents. They comment, 'This narrative pattern typifies this book: what one person wishes for another comes to fruition principally through the actions of the well-wisher. Thus, although people frequently invoke God's intercession, it is they who actually intercede in setting things right' (li). Naomi, for example, looks to God to help her daughters-in-law find a home (1:9) but later orchestrates this outcome for Ruth by directing her to approach Boaz on the threshing floor (3:1–4), just as Boaz becomes the answer to his own prayer for Ruth. They continue, 'it is almost as if human actions and words bring God into the world. God-centred people prompt God to show up, as it were' (2011: li–lii).

Eskenazi and Frymer-Kensky draw attention to an important theological characteristic of Ruth. That is, Ruth focuses the theological lens on human agency rather than divine agency, and human initiative rather than divine initiative. In the ancestral narratives of Genesis Yahweh appears directly to human beings, initiates events through promises and carries them through to fulfilment. In Ruth, however, God remains in the background. Human agents mediate the divine presence through their prayers and actions. Human initiative overcomes the real-life challenges the characters face and propels the story towards a satisfying resolution. Yahweh's sole action, giving Ruth pregnancy, comes in the final scene and can be seen as a divine 'amen' to the magnanimous faithfulness and devotion that members of the human community have displayed towards each other. This story, in other words, portrays Yahweh's acting in response to rather than as the director of what human beings do, as a God who gives 'payment in full' to those who devote themselves to the good of others (2:12).

The mediation of God's presence through the words of others draws attention to the role others play, specifically those of the community, in interpreting his ways and character. Ruth's theology, in short, is constructed not so much by the narrator as by individuals in a God-centred community who speak about God. Native-born residents of Bethlehem speak of Yahweh's blessing: the men by invoking blessing (the field hands and Boaz in 2:4 and 3:10 respectively) and the women by affirming blessing (Naomi and the community women in 2:20 and 4:14). Characters also appeal to Yahweh to bring about particular benefits. Naomi appeals to Yahweh to show devotion to her daughters-in-law and secure a home for them (1:8–9). Boaz invokes Yahweh to reward Ruth and repay her for caring for Naomi (2:12). The council of elders appeals to Yahweh to establish a lineage through Ruth of equal stature to those established through Rachel, Leah and Tamar (4:11–12). Finally, Ruth and Boaz call on Yahweh to oversee and guarantee promises (1:17; 3:13).

On a broader scale Naomi attributes both weal and woe to Yahweh. Three times she speaks of Yahweh as a benefactor (1:8–9; 2:20), and three times as an opponent who brings calamity and loss (1:13, 20–21). Ruth the Moabite, for her part, speaks of Yahweh in a confessional mode, as a contingent object of her devotion to Naomi (1:16–17). It is left to the narrator to portray Yahweh as the source of sustenance (1:6) and life itself (4:13).

The narrator's focus on human agency, in sum, underscores and validates human initiative and actions in relationship to God. Threaded through the book are human deeds of blessing, kindness and hospitality taken voluntarily and for the good of the other. These occur alongside acclamations of divine blessing and kindness. As the story progresses, words of blessing find fulfilment through the acts of ḥesed that people display to others. If one reads the story through a theology of providential 'all-causality', then human agency in the story may be viewed as a demonstration that 'Yahweh moves through human actions which please him because he is sovereignly immanent in them' (Hubbard 1988a: 72). Yet seeing God's presence and work in the story does not necessarily lead to an affirmation of his causality. As reflected by the characters' theological utterances, Ruth seems rather 'to teach that the capacities and actions initially projected upon God by the book's protagonists, in turn, empower people to emulate God' (Eskenazi and Frymer-Kensky 2011: lii).

By foregrounding human agency, Ruth portrays God at work *in response to* rather than *as the cause of* human acts of blessing and ḥesed, played out against the frame of his role as the author of life and provision. Read in this way, Ruth becomes the theological complement of the patriarchal narratives. The ancestral narratives of Genesis portray a God who consistently enters the lives of human beings with promise and direction, and human beings whose response consists of dependence. Ruth, on the other hand, depicts human beings who care for others in the context of a God-oriented community, and a God who blesses human caring with fullness and security. The theology that configures the book equates devotion to others with devotion to Yahweh and suggests that faithful living in the context of ordinary affairs results in well-being, blessing and a glorious future.

TEXT AND COMMENTARY

RUTH 1:1–22

Translation

¹:¹In the days when the judges ruled, a famine struck the land. A man from Bethlehem of Judah migrated to the Field of Moab, accompanied by his wife and two sons. ²The man's name was Elimelech. His wife's name was Naomi, and the names of his two sons were Mahlon and Chilion. They were Ephrathites, from Bethlehem of Judah. They set off for the Field of Moab, and that is where they ended up. ³Then Elimelech, Naomi's husband, died, leaving her and her two sons alone. ⁴The sons took Moabite wives for themselves. The name of one was Orpah, and the name of the other was Ruth. They lived there about ten years. ⁵Then the two sons, Mahlon and Chilion, also died, leaving the woman bereft of her two children and husband. ⁶So she got up and turned her back on the Field of Moab, because she heard, while in the Field of Moab, that Yahweh had visited his people and was providing them food.

⁷She set out from the place where she had been, accompanied by her two daughters-in-law, and travelled on the road that would bring her back to the land of Judah. ⁸'Go! Return, each of you, to her mother's home,' Naomi said to her two daughters-in-law. 'May Yahweh show you the same devotion that you have shown to the dead and to me. ⁹May Yahweh grant that each of you find a place to settle down in her husband's home.'

Then she kissed them, and they cried out loud.¹⁰They said to her, 'No! We are going back with you to your people!'

¹¹But Naomi said, 'Turn around, my daughters. Why should you come with me? Do I still have sons in my womb who could become your husbands? ¹²Turn around, my daughters! Go away. I am too old to have a husband. Even if I had any hope – even if I had a husband tonight and gave birth to sons – ¹³would you wait around for them to grow up? Would you, then, shut yourselves away so that no man could have you? No, my daughters! Things are far more bitter for me than for you, because Yahweh's hand has gone out against me.'

¹⁴They just kept crying. Then Orpah kissed her mother-in-law, but Ruth held on to her. ¹⁵So Naomi said, 'Look, your sister-in-law has turned around to her people and her god. Turn around after your sister-in-law.'

¹⁶But Ruth said, 'Do not keep insisting that I leave you and turn around from following you. Wherever you go, I will go. Wherever you lodge, I will lodge. Your people are my people, and your God is my God. ¹⁷Wherever you die, I will die. And that is where I will be buried. May Yahweh do to me, and even more, if anything but death separates you from me.'

¹⁸When Naomi realized that Ruth was determined to go with her, she stopped talking to her. ¹⁹So the two of them travelled until they arrived at Bethlehem.

Their arrival in Bethlehem set the whole town buzzing. The women said, 'Can this be Naomi?' ²⁰She said to them, 'Do not call me Naomi! Call me Mara, because Shaddai has made things very bitter for me. ²¹I went away full, and Yahweh brought me back empty. Why call me Naomi? Yahweh has laid me low, and Shaddai has brought calamity to me.' ²²So Naomi returned, accompanied by Ruth the Moabite, her daughter-in-law, who returned with her from the Field of Moab. They arrived in Bethlehem at the beginning of the barley harvest.

Notes on the text

1:1. *wayĕhî*, 'and there was', is a transition marker that signifies the beginning of a narrative unit. It signals Ruth's place within the larger canonical narrative. Joshua, Judges and 1 and 2 Samuel also begin with *wayĕhî*. The extended phrase *wayĕhî bîmê*, 'and there was in the days of', however, links Ruth specifically to Esther, the only other biblical book that begins the same way. Another *wayĕhî* follows the reference to the judges, an unusual but not unknown construction. Since the use of the verb in both instances serves primarily as a narrative marker, and for the sake of a smoother reading, neither has been translated.

Lit. 'in the days the judges were judging'; the LXX has simply 'in the days of the judges'.

'A man went from Bethlehem of Judah to sojourn' or 'a man of Bethlehem of Judah went to sojourn' are both appropriate translations. The latter is preferable as it identifies Elimelech in a manner continued in v. 2, where he and his sons are identified as 'Ephrathites, from Bethlehem'.

śĕdê, 'field of', would appear to be a m. pl. const. (fields of), but this is unlikely since the noun is f. (and thus should, if pl., take the form *śādôt*).

It is probably an alternative and perhaps archaic spelling of the sg. const. form (normally *śādeh*, 'field of'). Both spellings occur in Ruth, even within the same verse (1:6). Whether 'the Field of Moab' denotes the whole of Moab or a region within it cannot be determined, although a reference in Num. 21:20 suggests the latter.

2. The LXX has 'Abimelek' instead of 'Elimelech'. The name Abimelek occurs more frequently in the Old Testament and here alludes to the discredited son of Gideon and would-be king in Judges (9:1–57). It is probable that a scribe changed Elimelech to Abimelek to make this allusion and thus cast a negative light on this man who left Israel for Moab.

'eprātîm, 'Ephrathites', designates a member of the tribe of Ephraim in certain contexts (1 Sam. 1:1; Judg. 12:5; 1 Kgs 11:26), although the phrase 'sons of Ephraim' (*bĕnê 'eprātîm*) is more common. (Both are conventionally translated 'Ephraimites'.) The term, however, also signifies an 'Ephrathite'. David is called the son of an Ephrathite man of Bethlehem in Judah (1 Sam. 7:12), suggesting that the name denotes a discrete kinship unit within the tribe of Judah (1 Chr. 2:18–24, 42–50). In other contexts it seems to refer to a geographical area or region. A gloss in Gen. 35:19 equates Ephrath with Bethlehem (cf. 35:16; Mic. 5:2[1]). It is possible that the name may signify a group of Ephraimites who lived in the region of Bethlehem, but this cannot be confirmed.

4. The phrase 'they took wives', *yiś'û . . . nāšîm*, is characteristic of 2 Chronicles and Ezra (Ezra 10:44; 2 Chr. 11:21; 13:21; 24:3); see Campbell 1975: 55.

6. The forms of the first three verbs in the Hebr. text are sg., although the subject is compound. The sg. form keeps Naomi in the narrative foreground.

8. The Q *ya'aś* is juss., 'may he judge', while the K *ya'aśeh* can be either indicative or modal, 'he will judge' or 'let him judge'. There is little difference in meaning (Holmstedt 2010: 73).

The antecedent for the pr. in *'immākem*, 'with you', and *'ăśîtem*, 'you have done', is the two daughters-in-law, yet the pr. is m. These are two instances of seven in the book, in which an apparent m. pl. pr. refers to a f. antecedent (1:9, 11, 13, 19, 22; 4:11). The disjunction has been explained as a truncated form of an archaic dual ending (Campbell 1975: 65) and alternatively as cases of a m. pr. referring to f. substantives (Waltke and O'Connor 1990: §135o). Holmstedt (2010: 73) notes that the majority of instances occur on the lips of Naomi and speculates that the narrator may be using marginal language to lend a foreign or archaic nuance.

9–11. To cry out loud, lit. 'raise one's voice and weep', is a common idiom (Gen. 21:16; 27:38; 29:11; Judg. 21:2; 1 Sam. 24:16; 30:4; 2 Sam. 3:32; 13:36; Job 2:12). Who is doing the crying, both here and in v. 14, is ambiguous. In this instance the last of the three f. pl. verbs in the chain ('they raised . . . they wept . . . they said') refer only to the daughters-in-law. The first verb in the chain ('she kissed') is set apart grammatically and refers only to Naomi. The structure as a whole indicates that Naomi does not cry along with her daughters-in-law. That the two daughters-in-law are the ones weeping receives further support from their actions: they cling to Naomi, but Naomi tries to send them away.

13. Hebr. *hălāhēn*, 'for them?', has an apparent f. pl. pr. as its last element, but the antecedent ('sons') is m. It is possible that the form is an Aram. particle meaning 'therefore', as in Dan. 2:6, 9, 4:24, but the connection is tenuous. Most commentators emend the text to *hălāhēn* ('to them?', m. pl.). See the discussions in Bush 1996: 29–30, 79 and Hubbard 1988a: 111, n.

tēʿāgēnâ, 'will you shut yourself off'; the verb occurs only here in the HB. Both the LXX and OL translate it in the sense of restraining or restricting, which may be supported by its use in the Mishnah.

15. The term translated 'sister-in-law' occurs elsewhere only in Deut. 25:7, 9, within the legislation on levirate marriage. There it designates the widow who is to be taken as a wife by her dead husband's brother. (The m. form also occurs and designates the brother-in-law.) Its use at the beginning of this story makes an allusion to the legislation and foreshadows its centrality in the climactic scene of the story (4:1–12).

ʾĕlōheyhā, 'her God' or 'her gods', can refer either to a single deity or multiple deities. If sg., it undoubtedly refers to Chemosh, the god of the Moabites (Judg. 11:24; 1 Kgs 11:33; 2 Kgs 23:13; Jer. 48:13). The Mesha Stela attributes the subjugation of Moab under the Omride dynasty to Chemosh's anger against his people, reports that the king's military campaigns were taken in obedience to Chemosh's commands and gives Chemosh praise for recovering Moabite territory from Israel (Mesha Stela 5–17). Ruth's use of the term in the next verse nudges the sense towards the sg.

17. Ruth's closing words take the form of a negative oath (1 Sam. 14:44; 20:13; 2 Sam. 3:9; 1 Kgs 2:23; 19:2).

'Death' receives emphasis in the Hebr. text. The construction can be translated either 'if even death separates me from you' (e.g. Hubbard 1988a; Campbell 1975) or 'if anything but death separates me from you' (e.g. Bush 1996; Nielsen 1997). If the former, Ruth's focus is on death; she is expanding on her declaration that she will be buried with Naomi. If the latter, Ruth's focus is on life; she will remain with Naomi until one of them dies. The importance attached to burial with the family tips the balance towards the former. By declaring that not even death will separate her from Naomi, Ruth implicitly claims Naomi as her family.

19. Many of the most reliable MSS of the LXX omit 'and when they came to Bethlehem', probably due to haplography.

21. The vocalization of *ʿnh* has generated significant discussion among commentators. The MT vocalizes the word as a qal pf. of a verb that, when followed by prep. *b*-, means 'to testify against' (1 Sam. 12:3; 2 Sam. 1:16; Isa. 3:9; Jer. 14:7; Job 15:6); thus Naomi declares that 'Yahweh has testified against me'. In the LXX and Peshitta, however, Naomi declares, 'the Lord has humbled me', indicating that the translators read the verb as the pi. pf. of a different verb that signifies suffering or abasement). This verb is nowhere else followed by prep. *b-*. It is, nonetheless, the better alternative. It is difficult to understand how Naomi might conceive her condition as Yahweh's 'testifying' against her. Vocalizing the verb as a referent to affliction renders the phrase synonymous with 'Yahweh has brought calamity to me' and so completes a poetic couplet. In the end we must entertain the possibility that the verb has been chosen because of its capacity to bring both senses into play (see Sasson 1989: 36 and M. Moore 1997: 237–238).

Form and structure

Ruth opens with a section of exposition (vv. 1–6), followed by two large sections of dialogue between Naomi and her daughters-in-law (vv. 7–18), and concludes with a shorter section of dialogue between Naomi and the women of Bethlehem (vv. 19–22). The first section between Naomi and the daughters-in-law centres on Naomi's commands that Ruth and Orpah leave her (vv. 7–14), while the second centres on Ruth's refusal to do so (vv. 15–18). The first section is further divided by the refusal of both daughters-in-law to leave (vv. 7–10), followed by opposing responses from Orpah and Ruth (vv. 11–14).

A pattern of departure and return unites the events of the first chapter. A short exposition (vv. 1–6) introduces Elimelech and his family and relates the circumstances that led them to depart from Bethlehem for the Field of Moab. The concluding episode relates Naomi's return to Bethlehem from Moab accompanied by Ruth (vv. 19–22). Situated between (both textually and geographically) are the two sections of dialogue (vv. 7–14, 15–18). Two narrative hinges, each comprising a repetition of information with variation, join the narrative to the sections of dialogue. The first hinge (vv. 6–7) closes off the opening exposition with a report that the women set out from Moab (v. 6) and initiates the motif of departure by reporting their journey to Judah (v. 7). The second (v. 19) closes off the dialogue by reporting the resumption of the women's journey to Bethlehem (v. 19a) and introduces the complementary theme of return by reporting the town's reaction at their arrival (v. 19b):

> So she *got up* and *turned her back* on the Field of Moab . . . *She set out* from the place where she had been, accompanied by her two daughters-in-law, and *travelled* on the road that would *bring her back* to the land of Judah. (Vv. 6, 7)

> (Dialogue between Naomi and her daughters-in-law, vv. 8–18.)

So the two of them *travelled* until they *arrived* at Bethlehem.
Their *arrival* in Bethlehem set the whole town buzzing. (V. 19a–b)

The hinges place the women's conversation (vv. 8–18) between Moab and
Bethlehem, old home and new home, and departure and return. References
to time ('when the judges held sway', v. 1, and 'at the beginning of the
barley harvest', v. 22) and place ('Bethlehem', vv. 1, 22) frame the entire
unit, alerting the reader to the symbolic journey the characters undertake
in the narrative – from emptiness to fullness – through references to
'famine' (v. 1) and 'harvest' (v. 22).

Interpreters have long admired the complex and carefully crafted symmetries that configure the chapter. Besides the structural symmetry noted
above, the narrator employs a matrix of *Leitwörter* (repeated, thematic
words) and wordplays. (For a synopsis of the discussion on structural
symmetry, see Korpel 2001: 1–29.) These devices work together to configure
and reconfigure the symbolic architecture of the narrative, facilitating
transformations of the story's symbolic system.

The repetition of thematic verbs configures the story along the
departure–return axis. The verb *šûb*, which denotes turning or returning,
occurs twelve times, with instances at the beginning and close of the
dialogue section. Three occurrences signify the departure of Naomi and
her daughters-in-law (vv. 6–7, 22a), and another refers to Ruth as 'the one
who returned' (v. 22b). The rest occur in the dialogue between the women
(vv. 8, 10–12, 15 [twice], 16) and in Naomi's response to the women of
Bethlehem (v. 21).

Within the HB *šûb* also signifies 'repentance'; thus a turning or returning
to God (Deut. 30:2–3, 10; 1 Kgs 8:33; Hos. 6:1; 7:10; Amos 4:6, 8–9) or
away from evil practices (1 Kgs 13:33; Jer. 18:8; Ezek. 13:22). Naomi's
'returning' and Ruth's 'turning' therefore carry deep symbolic resonances.
As Naomi returns to Bethlehem, she returns to the land Yahweh has given
to her people and to the place of his visitation (v. 6). Ruth's journey, on
the other hand, marks a turning towards a new life, a new community and
a new God.

The related verb *hālak*, which denotes 'walking' or 'going', occurs ten
times and carries similar associations. 'Walking' throughout the Bible
serves as a metaphor for life with God and obedience to the commandments (1 Kgs 2:4; 3:6; 2 Chr. 6:16). Enoch is commended for walking with
God (Gen. 5:22, 24), and Micah directs those who wish access to the Lord
'to walk humbly with your God' (Mic. 6:8). Walking comprises the main
activity of the Pentateuch, both in the case of the patriarchs and matriarchs
and in Israel's journey through the wilderness. The association continues
into the New Testament where, again, walking constitutes the narrative
thread that unites instruction and activity in the Gospels and Acts. The
ten references to walking in Ruth 1 (vv. 1, 7–8, 11–12, 16 [twice], 18–19,
21), therefore, suggest that the journey the two women undertake involves

much more than geography – and no more so than at those points where *hālak* and *šûb* occur together (vv. 7–8, 11–12, 16, 21).

Irony contributes to the transformation and redirection of themes and perspectives. 'Bethlehem' (Food House) enters the narrative as a place of famine but later becomes the space where the main characters find food and security. Words of divine blessing are directed towards Moabites (vv. 8–9), while the assertion that the Lord is an adversary issues from the mouth of an Israelite (v. 13b, 20b). Upon her arrival in Bethlehem, Naomi refers to Yahweh as a God who makes empty rather than a God who fulfils (v. 21).

The first unit (1:1–6) constitutes the exposition that introduces the main story. Commentators disagree on where the unit ends. The majority, followed by many translations, take their cue from the storyline, which shifts from the death of the sons (v. 5) to Naomi's decision to leave Moab (v. 6). The form of the narration, however, points to a unit that ends with v. 6. As noted above, v. 6 constitutes the first part of a narrative hinge that rounds off the exposition (v. 7 then repeating the information but redirecting from Moab to Judah). Vv. 1–6 thus form a unit that introduces the narrative's primary symbolic axes. Five references to Moab orient the reader to the issue of foreignness. Two occurrences of 'Moab' in v. 6 correspond to two occurrences in vv. 1 and 2, with the fifth reference to 'Moabite' situated at the centre (v. 4). Two references to 'Bethlehem of Judah' occur in the section as a counterpoint (vv. 1, 2) underscoring, through geographical reference, the opposing pole. A single ethnic referent, to Elimelech's family as 'Ephrathites' (v. 2b) matches a single reference to 'Moabite' (v. 4a).

References to 'famine' (v. 1) and 'food' (v. 6) enclose the ethnic and geographical oppositions in the exposition within the axis of emptiness and fullness. The male–female axis is also introduced by the change in the family that the journey brings: a predominantly male family goes to Moab but a female family departs from the land. Finally, the unit initiates the departing and returning axis by placing the thematic verbs *hālak* (going) at the beginning of the unit (v. 1) and *šûb* (returning) at the end (v. 6). V. 7 then transitions from exposition to dialogue by repeating both thematic verbs and shifting the geographical focus to Judah.

The Hebr. text of the exposition uses the repetition of sounds – kaph (k/ch) and ḥeth (guttural h), lamed (l) and to a lesser extent mem (m) – to connect the males with Bethlehem. The final three consonants of 'Elimelech' and 'Bethlehem' respectively are simply transpositions of the same three sounds. (The 'h' in English stands for ḥeth in Hebr., similar in sound though not identical to kaph.) 'Mahlon' represents a third variation, while 'Chilion' drops the mem but repeats the same order of ḥeth and lamed that configures his brother's name.

Brief reports enclose the dialogue between Naomi and her daughters-in-law and situate their conversation between Moab (v. 7) and Bethlehem

(v. 19a). The geographical 'in-betweenness' accentuates the 'in-betweenness' of Naomi and her daughters-in-law (Israelite travelling from Moab, Moabite travelling to Israel). Three speeches make up the bulk of the conversation that takes place in this in-between space, oscillating from the positive (Naomi, vv. 8–9), to the negative (Naomi, vv. 11–13) and back to the positive (Ruth, vv. 16–17).

The dialogue section as a whole (vv. 8–18) reconfigures the themes introduced in exposition. First, it becomes clear that men rather than food constitute the primary lack suffered by the characters. Naomi seeks security for her daughters-in-law within a patriarchal household (v. 9) and argues that she cannot provide such security because she has no hope of gaining either a husband or sons. Secondly, the referent of 'departing and returning' shifts from geography to family, people and deities. Naomi bids her daughters to depart to mothers and husbands (vv. 8–9), and then to people and gods (v. 15). The women, however, want to return with Naomi to her people (v. 10), and although Orpah departs, Ruth stays (vv. 14–15).

The conversation between the women also connects 'departing' to 'remaining'. Naomi leaves geographically and attempts to leave her daughters-in-law. Orpah leaves relationally but returns geographically. Ruth, on the other hand, remains relationally and leaves geographically. Kissing and weeping reinforce this relational axis. Naomi kisses her daughters-in-law after telling them to depart, whereupon the daughters-in-law weep (v. 9b). The daughters-in-law continue weeping even after Naomi tells them to leave. Orpah then kisses Naomi and departs, while Ruth remains and holds on (v. 14). Ruth's speech subsequently expresses departing and remaining in negative terms: she refuses to depart and separate (vv. 16–17).

As in the previous section, the concluding unit (vv. 19–22) frames dialogue with narration. Two references to Bethlehem in the opening report (v. 19) are answered by two references to Moab at the end (v. 22), bringing the geographical axis squarely back into focus. A symmetrical repetition of names configures the unit after the pattern of the exposition (vv. 1–6). 'Naomi' occurs four times, twice preceding and twice following the name 'Mara' (vv. 19c, 20a). The second and fourth references articulate a new set of oppositions ('sweet and bitter') through patterned repetition: 'Do not call me "sweet". Call me "bitter" . . . Why call me "sweet?"' (vv. 20a, 21b). The repetition of divine names also takes the form of a symmetry. Two references to 'Shaddai' enclose two references to Yahweh (v. 21).

Taken as a whole, the presence of repetitions, symmetry and dichotomies signals a sophisticated use of metaphor. Bethlehem as land and Ephrathite as ethnicity are opposed in the first chapter to Moab as land and Moabite as ethnicity. Likewise, the world of men is opposed to the world of women. Motifs of continuity (children vs. no children), well-being (food vs. famine, full vs. empty, sweet vs. bitter) and survival (life vs. death) interweave these dichotomies, forming an intricate pattern of associations. As the story begins, Elimelech takes his family on a journey outside his land and away from his kin to the land of Moab, which promises fullness and sustenance. The journey, however, results in death and endings for the men, who die without male heirs. Naomi then takes a journey back to Judah, spurred by the promise of food and accompanied by her Moabite daughters-in-law. On the way back the matriarch associates herself with not-marrying, no sons and 'the dead', while associating Orpah and Ruth's return to their land and kin with marrying, security ('in her husband's home') and divine blessing. The return of Moabite women to Moabite land, in other words, signifies well-being, whereas the journey of a Judahite woman to a Moabite land has brought, in Naomi's words, emptiness, bitterness and divine affliction. The narrator concludes by associating the return to Bethlehem with the promise of sustenance (v. 22). The inter-weaving of these associations and oppositions conveys a simple scheme: staying with one's own kin and within one's own land brings life and well-being; going outside brings death and emptiness.

Ruth, however, complicates the scheme by refusing to acknowledge it. By clinging to Naomi and leaving her home and family, Ruth implicitly challenges the logic that binds the oppositions and associations together. Naomi has gone outside and has lost everything. Ruth undertakes the same journey from the opposite direction. Will she too experience loss? Or will the scheme itself change?

Comment

1:1–6

The era of the judges evokes a time when ties to kin and the land configured identities and loyalties. The book of Judges depicts a fragmented nation defined by tribal loyalties and regional alliances. Tribes from the central highlands and Galilee unite to repel Midianite and Amalekite raiders in the Jezreel Valley (6:33–35), while Deborah's call to a larger group of tribes meets with mixed responses (5:12–18). Judahites are willing to deliver their Danite neighbour Samson to the Philistines to make matters easier for themselves (15:9–13), and Benjaminites doggedly defend their disgraced kinsmen, the men of Gibeah, when the rest of the tribes unite to punish them (20:1–17). As a whole, Israel in the period of the judges is constantly under threat from foreign oppressors and perpetually susceptible to the allure of foreign gods (2:1–23).

In contrast to Ruth the women in Judges are associated with violence, both as perpetrators and victims. Jael drives a tent peg through Sisera's head (4:17–22), and Deborah gloats in gory detail about his death (5:24–30). A woman crushes the skull of the would-be king Abimelech with a millstone (9:53), and Delilah renders Samson helpless before his enemies

(16:15–22). On the other hand, Jephthah's daughter becomes a sacrificial victim (10:34–40), Samson's bride is burned alive (15:6), a Levite's concubine is brutalized and cut into pieces (19:22–30) and the virgins of Jabesh-gilead and Shiloh are taken from their homes and forced into marriage (21:8–24).

Bethlehem of Judah is to be distinguished from another town of the same name, situated within the territory of Zebulun (Josh. 19:15). The former was located about 5 mi. (8 km) south-west of Jerusalem on the fringe of a well-watered and fertile area near the Judean wilderness. As the home town of David, it is associated with the monarchical society that replaced the kin-based society of the judges (1 Sam. 17:12–15; Mic. 5:2[1]). In Judges, however, Bethlehem carries less positive associations. It is the home town of a Levite-for-hire who left to become the priest of an Ephraimite's idolatrous shrine and then of the tribe of Dan (17:7–13; 18:14–26). Furthermore, it is the home of the concubine cast out to a lecherous crowd and butchered by another Levite (19:1–30).

The Moabite heartland was located on a high plateau east of the Jordan, bounded on the north and south by the rivers Arnon (Wadi el-Mujib) and Zered (Wadi el-Hesa) respectively, two watercourses surrounded by high and treacherous canyon walls. Although the habitable area comprised a narrow strip between the Dead Sea escarpment and the Arabian Desert, it was nevertheless well watered and provided good land for grazing, cereal crops and, in certain areas, orchards and vineyards. Moabite territorial claims extended north of the river Arnon, however, as far as Heshbon, an area also claimed by the Israelite tribe of Reuben. Biblical texts acknowledge that the region had once been part of Moab proper but assert that it was taken by the Amorites (Num. 21:25–31). Israel thus claimed the region by right of conquest, having destroyed the kingdom of Sihon, who reigned from Heshbon (Deut. 2:24–36; Josh. 13:15–21; Judg. 11:12–28).

The contested status of the area is borne out by reports of conflicts throughout Israel's occupation of the land. The Moabite king Eglon oppressed Israelites before he was assassinated by Ehud (Judg. 3:12–30), and Moabite raiders harassed Israel many times (2 Kgs 13:20; 24:2; 2 Chr. 20:1). Moab was subjugated by Saul (1 Sam. 14:47) and David (2 Sam. 8:12; 1 Chr. 18:2), and ruled by the Omride kings until King Mesha launched a successful rebellion (2 Kgs 3:4–27). The vicious nature of these conflicts points to an undercurrent of ethnic hatred. David is said to have arbitrarily slaughtered Moabite prisoners (2 Sam. 8:2). King Mesha of Moab, for his part, erected a stela to memorialize his recovery of territory from Israel, in which he claimed to have wiped out the Gadite population of Ataroth (Mesha Stela, 10–13).

A long history of enmity thus nuances Elimelech's journey to Moab, Mahlon and Chilion's decision to take Moabite wives, and Naomi's return to Bethlehem accompanied by a Moabite daughter-in-law. Apart from this history, each decision might seem reasonable and even necessary. Viewed with the history in mind, however, each exudes a sense of impropriety and danger. The impression is confirmed by early rabbinic speculation on why Elimelech would have left the Promised Land, even during a famine. An early tradition concluded that he was not a good person to begin with but left for Moab to avoid sharing his resources with the famished townspeople (*Ruth R.* 1.4).

Allusions to Israel's story, on the other hand, evoke positive associations. First, the pattern that configures Naomi's story – departure, sojourn in a foreign land and return – corresponds to the grand narratives that shape Israel's identity: (1) Jacob's/Israel's journey from Canaan to Egypt, a long (but tersely related) sojourn and the return to the land under Joshua; and (2) Judah's exile from the land under Nebuchadnezzar, a long (but briefly referenced) sojourn in Babylon and a return prompted by the decree of Cyrus. Secondly, biblical stories about childless women typically conclude with the birth of a significant individual, as is the case with Sarah and the birth of Isaac, Rachel and the birth of Joseph, and the wife of Manoah and the birth of Samson (Gen. 18:1–15; 21:1–2; 30:1–24; Judg. 13:1–25). The particulars of the introduction in Ruth, however, tie it most directly to the story of Elkanah and Hannah, the account that begins 1 Samuel (1:1–28). Both accounts introduce the stories of women by situating them within stories about men (Elimelech and Elkanah), both of whom are identified by their location and tribal affiliation. Elkanah takes his two wives to the sanctuary at Shiloh to celebrate a feast. Elimelech, on the other hand, takes his family out of the land to Moab to find food, and Naomi and her two daughters-in-law begin their return to the land with the same goal in mind. The most intriguing connection between the two stories, however, is the designation of both families as 'Ephrathites' (*'eprātîm*), denoting, in Ruth, a group living within the region of Bethlehem, and in 1 Samuel membership in the tribe of Ephraim (see 'Notes on the text' above).

The narrator introduces six characters within the span of the six verses. Three of the names are attested in the literature of the ANE. Cognates of Elimelech (My God Is King) occur in texts from Amarna and Ugarit (mid-second millennium). Cognates of Naomi (Sweetness) also occur at Ugarit and Mari (also second millennium), both in compound names and as epithets for deities and heroes, and variant forms are attested in the Old Testament as well (Gen. 4:22; 1 Kgs 14:21). A name corresponding to Chilion may occur in Ugaritic texts, where it perhaps means 'Perfect' or 'Complete'. Meanings and derivations for the other names, however, are elusive. Mahlon has been related to Arabic roots, but the linguistic connections are paper thin. Orpah sounds like the Hebr. word for 'neck', but the negative connotation this conveys has sent commentators on a hunt for possible derivations in Ugaritic, Akkadian and Arabic. Finally, Ruth sounds like the Hebr. word for 'companionship' or 'friendship', although the absence of the strong medial guttural sound signified by 'ayin makes the association problematic. Derivation from the Hebr. root *rwh* (to soak, to refresh) is an attractive alternative among many other proposals. For a full discussion of the names, with bibliographies, see Campbell 1975: 52–56 and Hubbard 1988a: 88–95.

Those who originally heard the book being read, however, may have been unfamiliar with the derivations of the names. More important is to discern the rhetorical effect of the names, that is, how they contribute to the ambience and meaning of the story. From this point of view the names convey the symbolic import picked up in many traditional readings. Elimelech (My God Is King) is a wonderfully ironic name for a character living in the period of the judges, when 'there was no king in Israel' and 'everyone did as they saw fit' (Judg. 17:6; 21:25) and when a man named Abimelech (My Father Is King) attempted to make himself king (Judg. 9:1–57). Mahlon and Chilion sound to the ear like derivatives of the Hebr. root *ḥlh*, which means to be 'weak', 'sickly' or 'finished'. We might call them 'Wasted' and 'Weakling'. The rhyming connection between the two names points to their incidental role in the story, a device attested in other contexts (cf. Gen. 22:21; 36:26; 46:21; Num. 11:26–27 [Campbell 1975: 54 and Sasson 1989: 18]). Orpah (Neck) turns away from Naomi to return to her people, while Ruth ('companion' or 'refreshing') accompanies Naomi and revives hope. Naomi (Sweetness) brings the symbolic character of names explicitly to the surface when she changes her name to reflect her situation ('Bitterness', v. 20).

On the level of the story, the reader encounters a family situated precariously between life and death. Survival drives decision-making. Separation, lack and grief configure life. We are drawn into a world fraught with uncertainty, insecurity and the sense that life can change for the worse in a heartbeat. Elimelech separates Naomi from her home and friends in Bethlehem. Death separates Naomi from her men. A pall of isolation and despair hangs over the women who are the subjects of the story. As we follow Naomi out of Moab, we accompany a woman who has relied on the decisions and security of her husband. Bereft of both husband and sons, she must make her own decisions in a world where, without a man, she has no place, little significance and scant hope of happiness. She does not 'belong' in Moab. Alone and destitute, Naomi makes the difficult decision to go home.

Yahweh enters the story at the conclusion of this section, the seventh character to appear, but does so off-stage and indirectly (v. 6). We are introduced to Yahweh from Naomi's perspective, through the words of unnamed others, from whom we learn that 'Yahweh had visited his people'. The verb *pāqad* often refers to Yahweh's intervention and involvement in human affairs, to bless (Gen. 50:24–25), deliver (Exod. 3:16, 19; Jer. 27:22), punish (Exod. 20:5; Jer. 21:14) or restore (Ps. 106:4; Jer. 27:22). It also appears in birth narratives to denote Yahweh's role in enabling a childless woman to bear children (Gen. 21:1; 1 Sam. 2:21).

For Naomi, 'Yahweh' means 'food', or, more accurately, the promise of food. Yahweh's action comes to Naomi only as a rumour that offers the prospect of survival. Yahweh has 'visited' his people. But Naomi is not among them. Her journey back to Bethlehem entails not just the possibility of eating again but also of belonging.

7–19a

7–9a. Naomi dismisses her daughters-in-law with a command and a blessing. The sequence recalls Yahweh's calling of Abram, who also left family in response to a command and a blessing (Gen. 12:1–3). The reference to the 'mother's home' (*bêt 'ēm*) is unusual. The phrase occurs elsewhere only in Gen. 24:28 and Song 8:2. The three texts present women as agents whose decisions affect others, and the mention in Ruth accentuates the focus on the world of women (Meyers 1993). The phrase, however, also makes a subtle separation between Naomi and the daughters-in-law. Now that all three have lost their men the daughters-in-law belong with their own mothers and not with Naomi.

Naomi attempts to send her daughters-in-law away with two blessings. The first blesses the women with Yahweh's devotion (*ḥesed*; see 'Introduction'). The motif thus appears first on the lips of Naomi, who has experienced devastation and is on her way back to Yahweh's land and people. Significantly, Naomi speaks of Yahweh's *ḥesed* as a response to human *ḥesed*. That is, she appeals to Yahweh to show her daughters-in-law the devotion they have shown her.

By all appearances, Naomi has not been the beneficiary of Yahweh's devotion but, as she will later announce to the women of Bethlehem, he has brought her low (v. 21). She now attempts to separate herself from her devoted daughters-in-law by sending them off to a good life with her blessing while associating herself with 'the dead' who have been the recipients of their kindness. Her words are tinged with irony. By commending Moabites for their devotion, Naomi blesses the very people who, according to Israel's memory, cursed Israelites as they migrated to the Promised Land (Deut. 23:4).

Naomi's second blessing (v. 9a) specifies how Yahweh will show devotion, that is, by providing refuge (*mĕnûḥâ*) in the 'house of her husband'. *Mĕnûḥâ* signifies a journey's end, or a place of rest and security. In Naomi's mind a place to settle down is associated with finding a man who will provide it. The 'husband's home' thus here complements the 'mother's home' (v. 8). The prospects of finding another husband, however, may not have been favourable. Whatever provision may have been made for widows in their society would surely have been complicated by the fact that both women had taken Israelite husbands. In any case Naomi associates 'security' with 'husband' and suggests that her daughters-in-law would fare better with their own people than with her.

9b–10. Naomi's benediction in v. 8 signals her intent to conclude the relationship (2 Sam. 15:20) and frees Orpah and Ruth from any further obligation to her (Sakenfeld 1999a: 24–25). Her kiss expresses both affection and separation. To 'raise one's voice and cry' is a common hendiadys, the joining of two equivalent nouns to express a concept (Gen. 21:16; 26:38; 29:11; Judg. 21:2; 1 Sam. 24:16; 30:4; 2 Sam. 3:32; 13:36; Job 2:12). It is not clear, however, who does the crying; the ambiguity is probably intentional. As discussed in the 'Notes on the text', the grammar of the sentence suggests that only the daughters-in-law cry aloud. They do not want to be separated from Naomi, even if it means they must be separated from their homes and kindred. Orpah and Ruth choose solidarity with Naomi ('your people') rather than ties to erstwhile or potential homes and families. In so doing they implicitly endorse the priority of marital bonds over the bonds of kinship that bind them to their people.

11–13. The unanticipated loyalty of her daughters-in-law does not please Naomi, and she takes a firmer stance. She does not acknowledge the courage and worthiness of their decision but redoubles her effort to convince them to leave her and return to their own people. Her retort focuses on men and the bonds of social contract that define women's place in the patriarchy. She thinks only of husbands and sons, neither of which she can provide. In her view of the world attachments to men trump attachments between women. Naomi cannot envision a future where she will have such attachments, nor can she see that a life with her alone might suffice. She has lost hope.

Naomi's hypothetical questions introduce the concept of levirate marriage. The practice obligated a man to marry the widow of a deceased brother (Deut. 25:5–9). Deuteronomy stipulates that the first son born through the marriage shall assume the name of the deceased, so that 'his name might not be blotted out in Israel'. In this way the line of the deceased brother continued, as the offspring were reckoned as his. The institution existed, then, for the sole purpose of perpetuating a patriarchal line and protecting a man from erasure within the patriarchal network. Genealogy defined a man's place within this network, and the levirate practice ensured that the place would not be lost.

The scenario Naomi envisions does not fit the particulars of the Deuteronomic legislation. Instead, it enters by way of allusion and as a foreshadowing of a later, more direct allusion that Boaz will make to legitimize his marriage to Ruth (4:5–10). Naomi refers to the practice generally to accentuate her hopelessness and persuade Orpah and Ruth to leave. Naomi's speech as a whole, then, identifies her with no hope, no husband, no sons, old age, death and bitterness, and associates 'turning around' with home, mother, husband and security. More implicitly, her words imply that leaving her will bring the bestowal of Yahweh's devotion (v. 8b), while staying with her will put the women on the wrong side of God (v. 13c).

With her final words Naomi reveals how she has explained the loss of husband and sons: Yahweh has turned against her. How she came to this conclusion is not hard to discern. She followed her husband and left Yahweh's land to live instead among the Moabites across the Jordan. Her husband then died. Could this be anything other than Yahweh's judgment? And was not the iniquity of the father visited on the sons as well (cf. Exod. 20:5)? Having left the people and land that define her, she now finds herself destitute in a foreign land, only to find that Yahweh has visited his people once again. What is there left to do but return home? In Bethlehem there are at least familiar faces and memories of happier days. Perhaps Yahweh may take pity and show mercy to her if she returns to the land.

Yet how will she be received if she returns with Moabite daughters-in-law? No matter how dearly she is attached to them, their presence represents suffering and reminds her of how much she has lost. And how will the people of Bethlehem receive her if she returns in the company of Moabite daughters-in-law? Will this not add to her humiliation and isolation? Will she not be the subject of gossip and reproach? And what of Yahweh? Can she really convince him of her intention to separate herself from Moab if she continues to take Moab with her in the persons of her daughters-in-law?

It is entirely possible, of course, that Naomi is motivated by a sincere desire to see that her daughters-in-law are properly cared for. And there is no reason to doubt her affection for them. Naomi's thoughts remain opaque, leaving the reader to glean her intentions and dispositions from the subtleties of her speech and action. What remains clear is that returning to Bethlehem with Moabites in tow will complicate her homecoming. It is better that her daughters-in-law return to their people and she to her own – and for all of them to put suffering as far behind as possible.

14–15. Orpah is convinced by Naomi's rhetoric, returns her kiss and leaves. Ruth, however, refuses the farewell kiss and clings to her mother-in-law. The report of weeping and kissing, now repeated but in reverse order (cf. v. 9b), draws a vivid contrast between Orpah's and Ruth's responses to Naomi's admonition. Orpah leaves her Israelite associations and leaves Naomi by returning to Moab. Ruth chooses an Israelite identity and remains with Naomi by leaving Moab. The nature of the contrast is captured nicely by the use of the verb *dābaq*, which can mean either 'to cling' or 'to cleave', to characterize Ruth's holding on to Naomi. The verb also signals the symbolic import of Ruth's decision, as it is used elsewhere in warnings that Israel not attach itself to the nations or their women (Josh. 23:12; 1 Kgs 11:2).

For the third time Naomi tells her daughter-in-law to turn around and go home (cf. vv. 8, 11). This last command, however, is conveyed somewhat differently, revealing Naomi's focus on Ruth's ethnic difference. In the first instance Naomi told the two women to return to their 'mother's home'. Now, however, she speaks of Orpah's return to 'her people and her god'.

Ethnic identity and religious identity are one and the same in Naomi's eyes. Ruth is a Moabite. She should therefore leave Israelite Naomi and go back to her own people and her god, presumably Chemosh, the national deity of the Moabites (see 'Notes on the text'). If we follow the logic of Naomi's words thus far, a return to her people and her god would benefit Ruth. Naomi has associated 'returning' with security (albeit through the blessing of Yahweh). Staying with Naomi's god, she has intimated, will subject Ruth to an adversarial deity who may make life even more difficult than it already is.

16–17. Ruth will have none of it. Once again she displays her devotion to Naomi by disobeying her command. The terse, symmetrical form of her words takes the form of a creed. The structure takes up Naomi's equation of ethnic and religious identity at the centre and turns it on its head:

> A   Declaration of devotion: 'Do not keep insisting that I leave . . .'
> > B   Declaration of companionship to a destination: 'Wherever you go, I will go'
> > > C   Declaration of solidarity: 'Wherever you lodge, I will lodge'
> > > > D   Declaration of identity: 'Your people are my people'
> > > > D' Declaration of identity: 'and your God is my God'
> > > C' Declaration of solidarity: 'Wherever you die, I will die'
> > B' Declaration of companionship to a destination: 'That is where I will be buried'
> A' Declaration of devotion: 'May Yahweh do to me, and even more . . .'

The chiastic structure of Ruth's speech is configured by both grammar and motifs. The verbs in the first and last elements (A and A') assume non-indicative modes (imperative and optative). Verbs in the indicative mode, then, configure the second, third, sixth and seventh elements (B, C, C', B'). Two nominal phrases occupy the centre (D, D'); no verbs occur in the Hebr. text. Motifs create a different set of associations. The first three elements are connected by verbs that express journeying and living ('leave', 'turn away' [A], 'go' [B] and 'lodge' [C]), while the last three are connected by the theme of death ('die' [C'], 'buried' [B']), 'death' [A']). As a whole, then, Ruth's speech opposes life to death and companionship to separation, while affirming Naomi's connection between a people's identity and a people's god.

Taken within the context of the story the speech is remarkable. It affirms Naomi's equation of group identity with religious identity but denies the implication, in Naomi's speech, that such identities are essential. By declaring 'your people are my people and your God is my God', Ruth counters Naomi's articulation of ethnic and religious identity. In her bold declaration for Naomi's people and Naomi's God Ruth affirms that these identities are intertwined but denies they are static. They may be changed. And if one is changed, the other will also be. In short, a decision to enter a new community will entail a change in religious identity, and a redirection of religious devotion will result in a change of ethnicity. Ruth's speech therefore has radical implications. If ethnic identity can be changed by a 'turning' of religious devotion, then Moabites – and all 'others' – may become members of the covenant community by such a turning. And if this is the case, membership in the covenant community cannot be defined by genealogies or kinship networks but rather by a decision to devote oneself to Yahweh and Yahweh's people.

It is fitting, then, that the entire section of dialogue begins and ends with complementary appeals to Yahweh, opening with a blessing through Naomi (vv. 8–9) and closing with an oath through Ruth (v. 17). Naomi invokes two blessings that, if Yahweh answers, will bring fulfilment through Yahweh and men. Ruth, however, utters an oath that if broken subjects her to death. The oath formula she employs, with the particle *kî* (here, 'if') in the protasis, occurs eleven times in the books of Samuel and Kings (e.g. 1 Sam. 14:44; 20:13; 2 Sam. 3:9; 1 Kgs 2:23; 19:2). Ruth's oath is distinctive in that it is only one of two instances in the Bible where the formula occurs with the name Yahweh rather than Elohim as the subject, the other being Jonathan's oath to David (1 Sam. 20:13). The two instances specifically invoke the name of the God of Israel rather than the generic term for deity. Many commentators have seen Ruth's invocation of Yahweh as an intentional expression of devotion to Israel's God. The similarity between the circumstances of her oath and that of Jonathan, however, raises the likelihood that it is a literary allusion. Both Ruth and Jonathan make their oaths to confirm loyalty to someone other than their own kin and to their own apparent disadvantage (Ziegler 2007: 79–80). Ruth thus seals her decision for Naomi, Naomi's people and Naomi's God by rejecting the promise of blessing that Naomi gave (vv. 8–9) and instead attaching her well-being to a destitute woman and a God whose hand is supposedly stretched out against her.

18–19a. Commentators diverge significantly on the intent of Naomi's response to Ruth. Those inclined towards a positive portrayal of Naomi view the report that Naomi stopped talking to Ruth as an indication of resignation and acceptance. The sense, then, is that Naomi stopped trying to convince Ruth to leave her when she realized that Ruth could not be dissuaded. On the other hand, the comment may be understood in the most direct sense, that is, that Naomi stopped talking to Ruth for the rest of their journey. Naomi's silence, on this reading, has been interpreted as a discrete response to Ruth's sacrifice (LaCocque 2004: 54, 56) or as an expression of Naomi's suffering. Yet the insights we gather from Naomi's interaction with her daughters-in-law, from her pessimistic words and from the complications Ruth's companionship entails suggest a different sense. Given Naomi's strident efforts to extricate herself from her daughters-in-law, and Ruth's refusal to be so extricated, we may well see vexation in the report. In other words, faced with Ruth's refusal to leave, Naomi stopped talking to her altogether. 'Ruth's choice', then, 'must be tempered by the thought that Ruth is offering an undesired "gift"' (Sakenfeld 1999a: 35). So the two women journeyed in silence to Bethlehem, Naomi perhaps hoping that Ruth might find the silence intolerable and leave, and Ruth enduring the silent treatment out of devotion to her mother-in-law.

19b–22

The unit opens in the Hebr. texts with *wayĕhî* (untranslated), signalling the beginning of a new narrative unit (see the 'Notes on the text' on v. 1), and is enclosed by references to the women's arrival (forms of Hebr. *bô*') in Bethlehem. As in the previous section, the narration creates the occasion for a dialogue among women, in this case between Naomi and the women of Bethlehem. The women respond to Naomi's return with a question that expresses their surprise and incredulity but that, on the story's thematic level, evokes the question of identity: *hăzō't nā'ŏmî*, lit. 'Is this Naomi?'

Naomi's response to the women brings the issue of identity directly to the surface (vv. 16–17). She separates herself from the women of Bethlehem by refusing the identity they give her ('Sweet') and claiming her own identity (Mara, 'Bitter'). She also separates herself from Yahweh, who has given his people food in this place (v. 6) but who has emptied Naomi. Her words express sorrow, suffering and anger through a barrage of four accusations levelled against Yahweh: 'Shaddai has made things very bitter . . . Yahweh brought me back empty . . . Yahweh has laid me low . . . Shaddai has brought calamity to me.' Naomi, the returnee from Moab, perceives herself outside the sphere of the gracious God who has visited his people. Her complaint puts her in the company of others whose suffering issues in protest to God (e.g. Jeremiah; see Campbell 1975: 83). Ignoring her daughter-in-law, whom she does not mention, refusing the welcome of the women of Bethlehem and characterizing Yahweh as a tormenter, she stands utterly alone. She has returned to her people and God but alienates herself from both.

The repetition of divine names assumes a chiastic pattern: Shaddai, Yahweh, Yahweh, Shaddai. The occurrence of the name Shaddai has generated considerable discussion. The name often occurs along with El, the name of the ancient Canaanite high god and of Israel's God as well. It sounds like the Hebr. words for 'destruction' (*šōd*) and 'breast' (*šād*), but its meaning and origins are obscure. It may reflect an element of the early history of the story. Whatever meaning and associations it originally had, however, were probably lost by the post-exilic era. Its occurrence in the narrative may be better explained along stylistic or thematic lines. First, the name is similar, in the consonantal text of the MT (*šdy*), to the variant form of 'Field of' (*śdy*) that occurs in other parts of the chapter (vv. 1–2, 6, 22; see notes on v. 1). The two unusual terms thus pun on each other, implicitly connecting God with what happens to Naomi in Moab. Secondly, Shaddai appears prominently in the book of Job, where it occurs thirty-one times. Its associations with Israel's traditions of protest against the divine render it a fitting epithet as Naomi expresses her own suffering. (For correspondences between Job and Ruth 1, see LaCocque 2004: 49 and Roop 2002: 40–41.) Finally, Shaddai may be employed because it was associated with the distant past in the minds of the post-exilic community (cf. Exod. 6:3) and may thus contribute to the nostalgic ambience.

The core of Naomi's accusation, that she left full but Yahweh has brought her back empty, articulates the basic polarity that configures the book. The 'emptiness' of which Naomi speaks is the absence of men, the plight that dominated her earlier speech (vv. 12–13). The absence of any reference to Ruth punctuates this sense of emptiness. Naomi has lost the companionship of men and isolates herself from women. She makes no reference to Ruth, who has also suffered the loss of men and must now make her way in a strange and forbidding land.

The narrator underscores the tension between Naomi's 'emptiness' and Ruth's devotion with an elaborate statement of Ruth's identity. In a list of descriptive terms that is unusual because of its length the Hebr. text identifies Ruth as 'Ruth the Moabite, her daughter-in-law, with her, the one who returned from the Field of Moab'. The names track the various levels of social relationship Ruth represents: ethnicity, marriage and 'returning'. Nestled in the midst of the sequence is the phrase 'with her' (*'immah*). The phrase refers back to the main clause (thus 'Naomi returned, and Ruth . . . with her') and follows proper syntax. But its location within the list of words that identify Ruth points to the crux of Naomi's situation. This woman, who represents 'otherness' in ethnicity, family and homeland, is 'with her'.

For Naomi, the arrival at Bethlehem is a return. Yet, as LaCocque has observed, Ruth's arrival is not truly a 'return', for she did not come from Bethlehem. Ruth, 'the one who returned', is more accurately 'the one who turned', that is, the one who has journeyed towards a new people and a new God (LaCocque 2004: 34–35). Her journey thus contrasts with the one that led Naomi to Moab in the first place. Famine drove Naomi to Moab. Devotion brought Ruth to Bethlehem.

Naomi, however, is not without faith. Even though she holds Yahweh responsible for her suffering, she does not abandon him. Rather, her suffering drives her back to the place of Yahweh's visitation. He shapes her people's identity and thus her own. She cannot abandon Yahweh, even when she believes he has turned against her. Both her return and her protest express her devotion to Yahweh. She clings to him even though she believes he has turned against her. Naomi thus joins those whose anguished complaints manifest an unshakable commitment to God, one that mirrors the devotion of a Creator who refuses to abandon those who turn away to other relationships (Pss 22:1–2; 60:1; 74:1; Jer. 15:15–18; 20:7–18; Lam. 3:1–44; cf. Mark 15:34).

The chapter concludes on a note of closure and anticipation (v. 22). The reference to the harvest complements the opening reference to a famine (v. 1), reversing the 'fullness to emptiness' trajectory of Naomi's speech and foreshadowing better things to come. The beginning of the barley harvest is also the time of the celebration of Passover and the Feast of Unleavened Bread, festivals that recall Yahweh's saving acts and Israel's journey to the Promised Land. In the course of the story the absence of food has been displaced by the absence of men, and the absence of men has been displaced by the absence of God. The chapter closes, however, with a glimmer of hope that Naomi's situation – and her relationship with God – may take a turn for the better.

Explanation

Naomi and Ruth embody two classes of people who occupied the periphery of Israel's communal life: resident aliens and widows. Both groups often faced a precarious existence that depended to a large degree on the goodwill and hospitality of the community. Their connection to the community was ambivalent. Foreigners were acknowledged as members of the Israelite community but were, at the same time, marked as outsiders. The identity of widows within the community could also be problematic, as the death of the husband severed a connection to the patriarchal network. The situation was particularly acute for widows who had no male children and thus no direct ties to the world of men that configured social relationships and property ownership. Resident aliens and widows therefore found themselves particularly vulnerable to the vicissitudes of life and to the attitudes and actions of those among whom they lived. For this reason both the narrative and legal literature of the Old Testament, following established ANE conventions, give special attention to their situation and how they should be treated.

The narrator alludes to Naomi's experience as a foreigner at the beginning of the story, through the report that she accompanied Elimelech when he departed from Bethlehem to sojourn in Moab (v. 1). The famine that drives the family to Moab evokes Israel's patriarchal traditions, specifically accounts of Abram and Isaac leaving the Promised Land, along with their families, in order to find food (Gen. 12:10–20; 26:1–11). The stories accentuate the patriarchs' apprehensiveness about entering a strange land, revealing the vulnerability foreigners faced in such situations.

Famine also brings Jacob and his family to Egypt, where they benefit from the protection of Joseph (Gen. 47:1–12). 'Foreigner' is a component of Abraham's identity, even within the Promised Land (Gen. 17:7–8; 23:4; 28:4), as it is for Isaac (37:1) and Jacob (28:4). The patriarchs' status as resident aliens linked them with their descendants, who would later go down to Egypt (Gen. 15:13; Exod. 6:4; cf. Exod. 23:9; Lev. 19:34; Deut. 10:19).

The memories of life as resident aliens had a profound impact on Israel's self-understanding. This is expressed, in its most succinct form, in a creedal statement that was to be recited when presenting the first fruits of the harvest to Yahweh: 'A nomadic Aramean was my father. He went down to Egypt and sojourned there, few in number. He became there a great, mighty and numerous nation' (Deut. 26:5). Memories of the Egyptian sojourn formed the foundation for commandments that mandated protection for resident aliens (Exod. 22:21[20]; Deut. 24:17–18):

Do not oppress a foreigner; you know the life of a foreigner, for you were foreigners in the land of Egypt. (Exod. 23:9)

In the case of the foreigner who sojourns among you in your land: do not afflict that person. Like a native, one of you, shall be to you the foreigner who sojourns among you. You shall love that person as you do yourself, because you were foreigners in the land of Egypt. I am Yahweh your God. (Lev. 19:33–34)

Resident aliens were members of the community that gathered to renew the covenant with Yahweh on the plains of Moab (Deut. 29:10–15) and joined those who took part in a similar ceremony between Mounts Ebal and Gerizim (Josh. 8:33, 35). Those who had been circumcised were permitted to celebrate Passover with the rest of the nation (Exod. 12:48–49; Num. 9:14) and were invited to take part in the other major festivals (Weeks [Deut. 16:10–11], Tabernacles [Deut. 16:13–14] and First Fruits [Deut. 26:1–11]). They were also bound by many of the same practices and restrictions that configured life in covenant with Yahweh. Resident aliens were forbidden to eat meat with the blood (Lev. 17:10–15) or to eat leaven during the Feast of Unleavened Bread (Exod. 12:19). They were eligible to make offerings to Yahweh (Num. 15:13–16) and could thereby receive the same benefits (Num. 15:26–29). Other laws protected foreigners from injustice and ensured that they would receive the same treatment as native Israelites (Lev. 24:22; Deut. 1:16–17; 24:17).

Legal protections were extended as well to widows who, along with orphans and resident aliens, symbolize the powerless in biblical literature. They were not to be oppressed, and resources were to be set aside to provide a measure of subsistence. Commandments that prohibit the powerful from depriving a resident alien of justice or taking a widow's garment in pledge immediately precede a command that requires harvesters to leave gleanings for them (Deut. 24:17–22). Aliens, orphans and widows, along with the Levites, also received the third-year tithe (Deut. 14:28–29; 26:12–13). These actions reflected the concerns of Yahweh, the God of justice, who was the advocate and protector of the powerless (Exod. 22:21–24[20–23]; Deut. 27:19). Yet, even with these provisions and protections in place, foreigners and aliens often found themselves in dire straits, particularly in times of economic hardship, prompting prophetic admonitions and denunciations throughout Israel's life in the land (Jer. 7:6; 22:3; Ezek. 22:7; Zech. 7:10; Mal. 3:5).

Ruth draws us into the world of the immigrant and the powerless and invites us to see the world through their eyes. The increasing numbers and visibility of immigrants in Western societies – and the tensions of identity and community their presence raises – make the biblical story especially relevant and pressing. In Elimelech and Naomi we see reflected the faces of contemporary immigrants who, like those in the biblical text, have left their homelands in search of a better life. In Ruth we meet a woman who has followed family into a foreign land and arrives without access to the resources and relationships enjoyed by members of her new community.

The plight of Naomi and Ruth also sets a theological tension before the reader. If Yahweh devotes special concern and attention to widows and aliens, why have these two women experienced such calamity? Where is God in the midst of their suffering? The narrator raises this tension by a straightforward style that offers no commentary or interpretation. No explanation is given for the famine that drives Elimelech and his family to Moab, for the deaths of Elimelech, Mahlon and Chilion, or for the child-lessness of Orpah and Ruth. The tragic events are presented matter-of-factly. God is indeed present in the story (vv. 8, 13, 16, 20–21), but only remotely, present only through the words of those whose lives have been affected by tragedy.

The tension between the unembellished narration and the characters' remarks about God draws attention to an experience of God's distance in times of suffering and the human need to find meaning in inexplicable experiences. This was what the early rabbis sought to do as they pondered why Elimelech and Naomi experienced catastrophe:

> Indeed, R. Simeon ben Yohai taught: Elimelech, Mahlon, and Chilion were the notables who led their generation. Why then were they punished [by untimely death]? Because they left the Land to go outside it, for it is written, 'All the city was astir concerning them, and the women said: "Is this Naomi?"' (Ruth 1:19). What did they mean by 'Is this Naomi?' They meant, said R. Isaac, 'Look at Naomi, who left the Land to go outside the Land – look what happened to her.' (*Gen. R.* 25.3 [quoted in Bialik and Ravnitzky 1992: 361])

The rabbis assumed that there must be a reason for Naomi's suffering and found one that made sense within the context of their beliefs: death and destitution came as a consequence of leaving her people and land. The explanation articulates a meaning implicit in Naomi's words to the women. Naomi does not believe her suffering is happenstance. Her cry of despair suggests that she interprets her suffering as punishment from God. Yahweh has turned against her. Consistent with the nuanced subtlety of the book, Naomi nowhere directly confronts or challenges her perceived tormentor. Rather, she expresses her accusations indirectly, by declaring that the hand of Yahweh is set against her and that he has made her life bitter.

Popular piety often accounts for the plight of the marginalized by holding that they are in some way responsible for their own condition. Likewise, it is common to attribute calamity or suffering to sin (Job 8:4; 11:13–20; 18:5–21; John 9:1–3) or lack of faith (Job 5:8–27). Although the view finds support in the Bible, many texts press the idea that calamity and suffering sometimes happen for reasons that are unknowable. Job, the quintessential sufferer, is never told what provokes the suffering he experiences, although the reader is made privy to the reason even before catastrophe befalls him: Job's righteousness has made him a target for Satan, who challenges God to a wager (Job 1:6 – 2:21).

Through characters such as Job and Naomi the Bible presents questioning and challenging God as a legitimate response to suffering, and even an expression of piety. Walter Brueggemann has pointed to the relational power and import of complaints directed at God. Laments transform biblical faith from monologue to dialogue and thus bring the believer into a relationship that is more than name only. They redress the redistribution of power between God and the petitioner, so that 'the petitioner is taken seriously and legitimately granted power in the relation' and therefore heard and valued. Failure to value the laments, he suggests, risks the loss of a genuine covenant interaction (by effectively silencing the human party or allowing only praise) and stifles the questions of theodicy through which issues of justice, and their implications for society, can be raised. He concludes:

> The lament makes an assertion about God: that this dangerous, available God matters in every dimension of life. Where God's dangerous availability is lost because we fail to carry out our part of the difficult conversation, where God's vulnerability and passion are removed from our speech, we are consigned to anxiety and despair and the world as we now have it becomes absolutized. Our understanding of faith is altered dramatically, depending on whether God is a dead cipher who cannot be addressed and is only the silent *guarantor* of the status quo, or whether God can be addressed in risky ways as the *transformer* of what has not yet appeared. (Brueggemann 1986: 64; italics his)

Naomi's complaints manifest a devotion to Yahweh and a determination to struggle through the relationship, even though it appears strained to the breaking point. She sees Yahweh as a tormentor rather than a protector, yet she has not turned instead to Chemosh or any other god. Rather, in the midst of her calamity, she turns around and returns to Bethlehem, the place where Yahweh can be found. Her complaints are not expressions of sinfulness or faithlessness but rather declarations of what she perceives to be the shattered state of the relationship. Her sense of estrangement from Yahweh was echoed by Christ who, in torment on the cross, quoted a lament and cried out, 'My God, my God, why have you abandoned me?' (Matt. 27:46; Mark 15:34). In so doing Christ sanctified Israel's traditions of protest and opened a way for seeing them as profound expressions of faith.

RUTH 2:1–23

Translation

²:¹Now Naomi had a relative on her husband's side, an eminent and powerful man, from the same clan as Elimelech. His name was Boaz. ²Ruth the Moabite said to Naomi, 'Let me go to the field and glean ears of grain behind someone who will look favourably on me.' She said to her, 'Go ahead, my daughter.' ³So she went, arrived at the field and gleaned after the harvesters. It just so happened that it was the parcel of the field that belonged to Boaz, who was from the same clan as Elimelech.

⁴Then Boaz arrived from Bethlehem. He said to the harvesters, 'Yahweh be with you!' They said, 'May Yahweh bless you!' ⁵Boaz said to the young man who supervised the harvesters, 'Whose young woman is that?' ⁶The young man who supervised the harvesters replied, 'She is the young Moabite woman who returned with Naomi from the Field of Moab. ⁷She said, "Please let me glean and gather grain among the sheaves after the harvesters." She has been on her feet since she came, from the morning until now. She has been staying in the shelter for a little while.'

⁸Boaz then said to Ruth, 'Will you not listen to me, my daughter? Do not go to glean in another field. Do not leave this one. Join my young women here, ⁹keeping your eyes on the field where they are harvesting. Follow them. I hereby order the young men not to harass you! If you get thirsty, go over to the water jars and drink from what the young men have drawn.' ¹⁰Ruth then fell face down and bowed to the ground. She said to him, 'Why have I found favour in your sight, that you would notice me, since I am a foreigner?' ¹¹Boaz replied, 'I have been fully informed of everything you have done for your mother-in-law since the death of your husband. You left your father, mother and native land behind and came to a people you had never known. ¹²May Yahweh repay you for what you have done, and may you receive payment in full from Yahweh, the God of Israel, under whose wings

you have come for refuge.' [13]She said, 'May I continue to find favour in your sight, my lord. You have encouraged me and spoken very tenderly to your maidservant, though I am not even one of your maidservants.'

[14]Boaz said to her at mealtime, 'Come over here and have some bread. Dip your piece in the vinegar.' So she sat down alongside the harvesters. Then he handed her some roasted grain. She ate and was satisfied, and she had some left over. [15]When she got up to continue gleaning, Boaz issued a command to his young men: 'Let her glean even among the cut stalks. Do nothing to humiliate her! [16]What is more, be sure to pull out some handfuls for her and leave them for her to glean. And do not rebuke her!'

[17]So Ruth gleaned in the field until evening and beat out what she had gleaned. It came to about an ephah of barley. [18]Then she carried it back to the village. She showed her mother-in-law what she had gleaned. Then she took out and gave her what was left over after she had eaten her fill. [19]Her mother-in-law said to her, 'Where did you glean today? Where did you work? May whoever noticed you be blessed!' She told her mother-in-law about the man with whom she had worked. She said, 'The name of the man with whom I worked today is Boaz.' [20]Naomi said to her daughter-in-law, 'Blessed is he by Yahweh, who has not given up his devotion to the living and the dead!' Naomi said to her, 'The man is a close relative of ours. He is one of our family redeemers.' [21]Ruth the Moabite replied, 'He also said to me, "Join my young men until they have finished my part of the harvest."' [22]Naomi said to Ruth her daughter-in-law, 'It is a good thing, my daughter, for you to accompany his young women so you will not be harmed in another field.' [23]So Ruth joined the young women of Boaz, gleaning until the end of the barley harvest and the wheat harvest. She stayed with her mother-in-law.

Notes on the text

2:1. 'relative' follows the Q *môdāʿ*, which is attested in a number of Hebr. MSS and the LXX. The K *mĕyuddaʿ* (associate, friend) occurs elsewhere in 2 Kgs 10:11; Pss 31:11[12]; 55:13[14]; 88:8, 18[9, 19]; Job 19:14, while *môdāʿ* occurs only in Prov. 7:14 and, in the f. form, in Ruth 3:2. Campbell (1975: 88–90) argues for retaining the K and sees a connection with covenant practices based on a putative use of the verb *yādaʿ* in those contexts. He proposes that it is an archaic term referring to obligations within the larger social system and translates it 'covenant-brother'. Hubbard (1988a: 132–133) also adopts the K, arguing that the Q is redundant and unnecessary; the kinship association between Boaz and Elimelech is made later in the sentence by identifying the two as members of the same clan. Redundancy, however, is not a strong argument against the Q. The narrator sometimes employs the device to signal connections, as is the case with a twofold occurrence of 'Ruth the Moabite' in 1:22 and 2:2. As Bush (1996: 100) has observed, the fact that Boaz is a relative through Elimelech is an important distinction to make at this point, as it introduces the former's role in the story. Naomi will later refer to Boaz as a 'relative' (*môdaʿat*) as she sends Ruth to meet him at the threshing floor (3:2).

2. *ēlĕkâ-nā' haśśādeh*, 'let me go to the field': the cohort. with *nā'* signifies a request for permission. Some commentators take the phrase to be a declaration or expression of resolve (Campbell 1975: 91–92; Hubbard 1988a: 136–137); thus 'I am going.' Bush (1996: 102–103), however, regards the phrase as an idiom that 'functions as a polite request, frequently addressed to someone in a position of authority or respect'. The context favours the latter. Within the context of a stratified society we may regard *nā'* as a verbal acknowledgment of the hearer's higher status. The construction appears in requests made by a person of lower social class to a person of higher social class (Exod. 3:18; 4:18; 1 Sam. 20:29; 2 Sam. 14:15; 15:7; 2 Kgs 6:2).

haśśādeh, 'the field', refers generally to the area of cultivated land outside the village, as opposed to a particular piece of property. As the next verse indicates, this land is divided into plots parcelled out to individual owners.

7. The supervisor's report presents the translator with a number of challenges. The first has to do with what Ruth requests: *'ălaqŏṭâ-nā' wĕ'āsaptî bōʿŏmārîm 'aḥărê haqqôṣĕrîm*. Reading this as a request – 'May I glean and gather among the sheaves after the harvesters?' – suggests that Ruth is asking to glean among sheaves already harvested. If this is the sense, it would be an extraordinary request. Hubbard (1988a: 148–150) and Sasson (1989: 44–48) view it as such, Sasson proposing that Ruth intentionally confronts the supervisor with a request that he has no authority to grant, and Hubbard viewing the request as a calculated risk. Both understand the supervisor's following statement (*wattaʿămōd mē'āz habbōqer wĕʿād-ʿattâ*, 'and she has stood from then, the morning until now') at face value, that is, Ruth has been 'standing' (waiting) all day for an affirmative response to her request. Bush (1996: 113–118), on the other hand, argues that such a request would constitute too great a breach of social protocol and does not accord with our understanding of harvesting practices in ancient Israel. He is unconvinced that Ruth has indeed been standing all day and, taking a cue from an Aram. translation of Ruth, sees *bōʿŏmārîm* as an adverbial phrase yielding, 'May I glean stalks of grain and gather them in bundles behind the harvesters?' The phrase, in short, resists definitive translation. Against Sasson and Hubbard, there is little to suggest that either the narrator or anyone in the story regards Ruth's request as overstepping or offensive. The fact that we have already been informed that Ruth went to the field and gleaned after the reapers (v. 3) weighs against a view that sees her waiting all day for permission, even if v. 3 is taken as a summary statement and vv. 4–16 comprise a flashback.

The second problem involves the supervisor's final comment, *zeh šibtāh habbayit mĕʿāt*, lit. 'this her sitting the house a little'; the construction may reflect an error in transmission, but if so it must have occurred at an early stage, as it also stands behind the LXX (which, however, reads 'field' for MT 'house'). Beattie (1977a: 122–124) provides a concise summary of proposals to that date, while Bush (1996: 118–119) evaluates subsequent readings. A number of proposals have been advanced that explain the phrase in terms of its literary impact. Hurvitz (1983: 122–123) sees the construction as a befuddled response arising from the supervisor's uncertainty about how Boaz will respond to his decision to allow Ruth to stay in a hut reserved for workers, supporting this view by analogy to the women's garbled response to Saul's question about the seer in 1 Sam. 9:12–13. The view is followed by Carasik (1995: 492–494), who suggests that the confused speech indicates that the supervisor has witnessed Ruth being harassed. M. Moore (1997: 238–242), however, offers the best explanation. He argues that the verb *šibtāh*, 'her sitting', is chosen intentionally because of its polysemantic and polymorphic qualities. That is, it precipitates a complex wordplay, evoking associations with 'the one who returned' (*haššābâ*, v. 6), staying or dwelling (*yašab*, v. 23) and stopping (*šābat*). The proposal fits well with the book's overall play with words and metaphors and has the virtue of allowing the simplest explanation of the construction, that is, it refers in some way to Ruth's brief respite in a shelter.

9. Many translations of *nogʿēk*, 'touching you', give the impression of unwelcome but innocuous or unspecified contact; thus, for example, 'touch' (NASB, ESV), 'bother' (NRSV) and 'lay a hand on' (TNIV). Shepherd (2001: 444–463), however, has convincingly argued that the verb in this case refers to malicious or violent action, adducing relevant parallels in Gen. 20:6; Josh. 9:19; and Prov. 6:29; cf. 'molest' (NJB), 'treat roughly' (NLT).

10. Campbell (1975: 98–99) has identified wordplay and assonance in Ruth's response: *lĕhakkirēnî wĕʾānōkî nokrîyyâ*, 'to notice me since I am a foreigner'; the verb *nākar* (notice) puns on Ruth's status as a 'foreigner'.

15. The verb *kālam* signifies humiliation, usually in a public setting (1 Sam. 20:34; Prov. 25:8) and sometimes as the result of physical abuse (Judg. 18:7; 1 Sam. 25:7, 15; 2 Sam. 10:5; 19:4). It is frequently paired with *bôš* ('to be ashamed'; e.g. Ps. 35:4; Isa. 41:11; 45:16; Jer. 6:15; 14:3). Most modern translations and recent interpreters hold that Boaz is forbidding the young men to rebuke Ruth. The context, however, suggests that he is warning them not to debase her. While the verb can sometimes signify a rebuke (Job 11:3; 19:3), the basic sense of humiliation is present even in these instances. The argument that it is roughly synonymous with *gāʿar*, 'rebuke', in v. 16 is tenuous. The prominence of dishonour and honour in the culture and the text (see comment below), along with the hostile ethnic sentiments Ruth evokes, indicates that Boaz is forbidding the men from doing anything that humiliates the Moabite woman. The sense is confirmed by the LXX. Boaz's command thus accentuates Ruth's vulnerability as a young, foreign woman and casts him as her protector,

the human expression of the wings of Yahweh to whom she has come for refuge.

16. The meaning of the phrase *šōl tāšōllû lāh min haṣṣĕbātîm*, lit. 'you shall surely plunder for her from the bundles', is difficult to ascertain. The verb *šālal* constitutes either an idiomatic use of a verb that otherwise signifies plundering or destruction, or a sg. use of a different verb. The noun *ṣĕbātîm* (handfuls or bundles of grain) occurs only here. The exact referent cannot be determined. Commentators are agreed, however, that the command stipulates deliberately pulling out what has already been harvested so that Ruth may take even more (e.g. Eskenazi and Frymer-Kensky 2011: 41–42; Hubbard 1988a: 177–178; Campbell 1975: 103–104; Bush 1996: 126–127).

Form and structure

The second act of the drama follows the pattern that configures the first. The narrator begins with a reference to a male, thus situating the stories of the women within the world of men (Boaz; v. 1; cf. Elimelech; 1:1). There follows a series of conversations connected by sparse narration. Ruth asks Naomi for permission to glean for grain, and Naomi gives it (v. 2), whereupon Ruth departs and gleans in the field of Boaz (v. 3). As she gleans, Boaz arrives and enquires about her (vv. 4–7). This sets the stage for a conversation between Boaz and Ruth, during which Boaz commends Ruth and she in turn acknowledges his kindness (vv. 8–13). At mealtime Boaz singles her out for special attention by inviting her to eat with the harvesters and instructing them to leave bundles for her to glean (vv. 14–16). Her return home, after a day of gleaning, leads to a scene of recognition during which Naomi realizes that Ruth has gleaned in the field of a kinsman (vv. 17–22). The narrator then concludes with a reference to harvests (v. 23).

Parallel motifs bracket Ruth 1 and 2. First, references to a *field* (*śādeh*) draw attention to land and raise the motif of departure and return – from home to an outside space and back again. The Field of Moab constitutes the spatial focus of Ruth 1, which begins with two references to the departure of Elimelech's family to 'the Field of Moab' (*śĕdê mô'āb*, vv. 1–2) and another two references that report Naomi's decision to return to Judah (v. 6). That chapter ends with the narrator's description of Ruth as 'the one who returned from the Field of Moab' (v. 22). The spatial focus of Ruth 2, on the other hand, is a field outside Bethlehem. The events of this chapter begin with Ruth's request to leave the house and glean in a field (*śādeh*, v. 2) and a report that she did so (v. 3a). Subsequent references situate Ruth within the field that belongs to Boaz (vv. 3b, 8–9, 22) and report her return to Naomi (v. 17). A single designation of Ruth as 'the one who returned with Naomi from the Field of Moab' ties the two chapters together (v. 6).

The use of relational terms draws attention to the social bonds that configure the community and organize its life in the land. As noted above, each chapter begins with an allusion to the patriarchal network through the introduction of an Israelite man: Elimelech, the husband of Naomi (1:1–2), and Boaz, a relative of Naomi on her husband's side (2:1). Each ends by evoking the 'in-law' relationships that link kinship groups to a larger network of relationships. Ruth 1 concludes by marking Ruth's outsider status and the bond that unites her to Naomi: 'Ruth the Moabite, her daughter-in-law, who returned with her from the Field of Moab' (1:22). Ruth 2 concludes by marking both the kinship bond that ties the women to Boaz ('a close relative of ours . . . one of our family redeemers'; v. 20) and the out-group bonds that define Ruth and Naomi's relationship to each other ('mother-in-law' [vv. 18–19, 23 (twice)] and 'daughter-in-law' [vv. 20, 22]).

The narrator thus renders land and relationships as arenas of trans-formations for Naomi and Ruth. Ruth 1 and 2 both begin with a lack of food (explicit with a report of famine in 1:1 and implicit in Ruth's decision to glean in 2:2). Both end with references to a harvest (1:22; 2:23). The harvest references contrast the situations the two women find themselves in as a result of the events.

The plotline of Ruth 1 moves from emptiness to fullness and back to emptiness again. Naomi leaves Bethlehem because there is no food and travels to the Field of Moab, where she evidently enjoys sufficient means to raise a family. While in the Field, however, she loses her men (her husband and two sons) and acquires two women (her daughters-in-law). The thread of the plot brings to the surface a tension between competing loyalties: on the one hand, the bonds of kinship that configure the in-group, and, on the other, the bonds forged by marriage, which connect the family to the larger society. By insisting that her daughters-in-law return to their own land and people, Naomi signals the priority of in-group relationships. Orpah complies with the request. Ruth, however, holds on to her mother-in-law. Naomi thus departs from her home with a Judahite husband but returns with a Moabite daughter-in-law. She returns empty. The reference to the harvest, which concludes the chapter, thus signals what Naomi does not have while at the same time portending the change in fortune that will take place in the events of the next chapter.

The plot of Ruth 2 moves in the opposite direction. The redirection takes place by merging references to the in-group by introducing Boaz as a relative and redeemer (v. 1) and the out-group by marking Ruth as 'the Moabite' (v. 2). The focus of the story shifts from Naomi to Ruth, who leaves home with no food, goes to a field and returns with plenty to eat. Ruth enters Judahite space as an outsider but is gradually drawn into the community, so that her return to Naomi not only promises provision but reintegration into the village society. The women of Bethlehem ask a question about Naomi's identity that expresses incredulity (1:19b). Boaz asks a question about Ruth's identity (2:5) that subsequently leads to recognition (2:10b) and ultimately to welcome.

The decision about joining and separating in this field is Boaz's to make. Shall 'the young Moabite woman' (2:6) who has entered the field live outside the community or within it? Echoing Naomi's speech to her daughters-in-law, Boaz speaks of 'holding on' (*dābaq*). He uses the term as an invitation, in contrast to the use of the verb in the previous chapter to signify Ruth's refusal to obey Naomi's command to leave (2:8; 1:14). Holding on to Naomi also marks a refusal, within the symbolic matrix of the narrative, to endorse the 'stay with your own kind' view expressed by Naomi's directions. Now the narrator drops 'the Moabite' from Ruth's name to relate Boaz's invitation to the foreigner who has entered his space. In so doing Boaz's speech overturns Naomi's by endorsing the bond of loyalty over that of kinship (2:11–12). Two more references to joining confirm the redirection of relational priority (vv. 21, 23) and associate the joining of outsider to insiders with plenty to eat and connection to the community (v. 23).

Boaz is the key to the transformations that occur in the field outside Bethlehem. While Ruth enters the field as the archetypal outsider, Boaz arrives as the quintessential insider. He is an eminent and powerful man. She is a poor Moabite woman. The geographical and social space between the two diminishes as Boaz draws Ruth from the outside of the group gathered in the field – a microcosm of the village community – to a place of favour within it. This is accomplished by a series of commands that associate Ruth first with the young women (v. 8), then with the young men (vv. 9, 14) and finally to a place of privilege that sets her apart from the rest (vv. 15–16). As the chapter begins, Ruth is an impoverished outsider. When it ends, Ruth has a place within the field society. The intervening directives issued by Boaz facilitate a symbolic traversal of the community's social hierarchy that results in Ruth's repositioning near the centre of the community.

The narrator reiterates the hierarchy and punctuates the transformation in Ruth's status through the concluding exchange between Ruth and Naomi. Ruth reports that Boaz instructed her to join his young men (v. 21), Naomi affirms that she should accompany his young women (v. 22) and the narrator reports that Ruth did so (v. 23). Ruth has been incorporated into the community. Yet she is still 'Ruth the Moabite' (v. 21). She now bears a hybrid identity. When she entered the field, her Moabite ethnicity marked her as an outsider connected to a different field, the Field of Moab (v. 6). At the conclusion of the chapter it signals that she is still an outsider, even though she has been incorporated into the village society. Her journey is not yet complete.

The narrator reinforces the symbolic reconfiguration of relationships by turning a common storytelling convention on its head. Robert Alter (1981: 51–60) was the first to observe the narrator's skilful use of the 'betrothal type-scene', that is, the common pattern by which biblical narratives tell the story of the betrothal. Although differing in details, betrothal stories follow a common structure and include common elements (Gen. 24:10–61; 29:1–20; Exod. 2:15b–21). The future bridegroom or his surrogate journeys to a foreign land, where he encounters a *na'ărâ* (a young woman) at a well. One of the characters (usually the woman) draws water and, at a later point, the girl leaves to inform her family of the stranger's arrival. The story ends with a formal agreement of betrothal after the stranger has been invited to share a meal with the young woman's family.

With the exception of the well, each of these elements appears in Ruth 2. In this instance, however, the type-scene unfolds in unconventional ways. The protagonist is not an Israelite patriarch but a Moabite woman (and eventual matriarch; cf. 4:11–12). The 'foreign land' to which she has travelled is Israel's homeland. Yet she is also the 'young woman' (*na'ărâ*) whom the bridegroom meets (v. 6). Within the context of the type-scene the character of Ruth thus conflates both the 'foreign' and the 'ancestral' in her own person. More reversals follow. Water is drawn for the protagonist, but young men rather than young women do it. Finally, the patriarch himself invites the stranger to a feast that bestows recognition and honour.

The narrator of Ruth thus rotates the betrothal type-scene '180 degrees on the axes of gender and geography' (Alter 1981: 58) and, we may add, ethnicity. The pivotal point in the story as Alter views it is Boaz's commendation of Ruth for leaving her parents and native land to journey to an unknown people (v. 11). The statement echoes Yahweh's command to Abram to leave his native land, kindred and family and journey to an unknown land (Gen. 12:1). The allusion prompts the reader to view Ruth as 'a kind of matriarch by adoption', a key figure in Israel's story whose descendant David will establish an everlasting dynasty in Jerusalem.

The skilful use of the betrothal type-scene brings about a reconfiguration of identities within the deep structure of the narrative. The conventional type-scene relates the hero's emergence from his immediate family (symbolizing the in-group) and journey to the outside world (the out-group) to find a mate who will bridge the two groups. The story narrated in Ruth 2 mixes up the type's roles and conventions. Ruth the Moabite is both bride and ancestor. Boaz the eminent and powerful man is both bridegroom and host on foreign soil who welcomes the stranger. The pair will have to navigate complicated interpersonal and social spaces in order to create the new unit that will later give rise, in the person of David, to a new reconfiguration of Israel's social, political and theological make-up.

The catalyst for the transformation is the extraordinary initiative that, on the one hand, Ruth undertakes to provide for herself and Naomi and, on the other, the hospitality Boaz extends to Ruth the Moabite. As Boaz draws Ruth progressively into the social network that configures the village community, he exemplifies an unconventional hospitality that welcomes the foreigner who, like Abram, chooses Israel's God and journeys to a new people and a new land. Boaz becomes Ruth's advocate, her pathway into the community and, by extension, Naomi's path to reintegration and well-being. What takes place in the field of Boaz constitutes the first stage of the foreigner's inclusion within the people of Yahweh. In the next chapter Ruth will be joined to Boaz, the central figure in the field, and at the same time will open the way for Naomi, the one-who-returned, to be reintegrated into the community of those who never left.

Comment

1–3

As noted above, the narrator sets the story of the two women within the world of men by evoking the patriarchal network through the introduction of a male character (v. 1). In this case, however, the act begins with one-who-stayed (Boaz), rather than one-who-left (Elimelech). The narrator introduces Boaz with identifiers that parallel the description of Ruth, which concludes the previous act (1:22; see the diagram below).

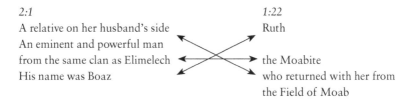

The elements that define Ruth and Boaz accentuate the opposite identities of Ruth and Boaz, with Naomi as the point of reference. Naomi is connected to Boaz through her husband ('a relative on her husband's side') and to Ruth through her son ('her daughter-in-law'). Boaz is from the same clan as Elimelech; Ruth is a Moabite. At the symbolic level the descriptions articulate inside (relative, clan), outside (Moabite, one who returns) and mediating relationships (daughter-in-law, husband). The additional element with reference to Boaz, that he is 'an eminent and powerful man', contrasts with the women's indigent status but, by virtue of its singularity, signals a shift in the story and in the women's fortunes.

Ruth and Naomi live on the periphery of the village's society; they are returnees who apparently do not have access to land or livelihood. Boaz, on the other hand, occupies an influential position at the centre of village life; he is 'an eminent and powerful man' (*gibbôr ḥayil*). The Hebr. phrase commonly signifies a warrior (Judg. 11:1; 2 Kgs 5:1; 2 Chr. 13:3; 25:6; 32:3) but is used generally to denote someone of status, ability or influence. The phrase, for example, identifies Jeroboam, whom Solomon recognizes as the type of 'can do' individual who can oversee forced labour (1 Kgs 11:28).

The f. form denotes the industrious wife of Proverbs who excels all others (31:10). With reference to Gideon (Judg. 6:12) and Saul (1 Sam. 9:1) the phrase highlights the character's status and influence over against the insignificance of their tribes. In short, *gibbôr ḥayil* signifies a powerful person, whether that power is extended through status, ability, wealth or military prowess. The name 'Boaz', which means 'strength is in him' (Campbell 1975: 90–91) is thus particularly apt.

The narrator makes a point of mentioning that Boaz is 'from the same clan as Elimelech'. The social unit signified by *mišpāḥâ* (here translated 'clan') cannot be determined with certainty, as its use in biblical texts and the character of the social unit it denotes are both fluid. Readers are directed to McNutt 1999: 88–94 for a discussion of the complexities involved in describing Israel's social structures and defining what a *mišpāḥâ* signified within them. For our purposes it is sufficient to note that the term signifies a tribal subdivision whose members traced descent to a common ancestor, usually a grandson of Jacob within Israelite society. Clans were also often associated with geographical areas and ownership of territory, a connection underscored by a threefold repetition of the word 'field' (*śādeh*, vv. 2, 3 [twice]) immediately following. The kinship relationship shared by Boaz and Elimelech in short was probably configured by relational and territorial bonds, although the men might not have been close or familiar with each other.

Ruth intends to locate a field where someone will allow her to glean after the harvesters (v. 2). Gleaning entailed gathering what was left over in the fields after they had been reaped. Reapers grabbed a bundle of sheaves with one hand and cut them with a scythe held in the other. The stalks that fell during the process belonged to the poor. Landowners were prohibited from doubling back to pick up the stalks and from harvesting the corners of their fields (Lev. 19:9–10; 23:22; Deut. 24:21). The legislation provided a means for the poor and resident aliens to participate in the harvests and get enough to eat; those in other words who had no access to the produce of the land. Ruth's request thus confirms that she and her mother-in-law are destitute.

While Ruth may be thinking of anyone 'who will look favourably on me', her words anticipate what she will later say to Boaz in response to the kindness he has shown her (v. 10). The phrase commonly occurs on the lips of someone subordinate to the object of address and often communicates the speaker's dependence on the superior (Hubbard 1988a: 138–139). The referent for the pr. is vague. Ruth could be thinking of the owner of the field or simply a reaper who would allow her to follow without bothering her. A Bethlehemite gleaner would be one thing, but a Moabite gleaner would be another altogether. Ruth's intention to glean requires courage. Entering foreign space with no protector is perilous, a fact that the words of Boaz and Naomi will accentuate (vv. 9, 15, 22).

Naomi's response is terse and clipped: 'Go ahead, my daughter' (v. 2). While the phrase 'my daughter' may express a measure of affection, it may just as well constitute a socially coded term that reciprocates Ruth's deferential language. That is, 'my daughter' acknowledges the nature of the social relationship that binds the two women and signifies Naomi's higher status in that relationship. Boaz will later address Ruth with the same term, from a position of power (2:8; 3:10–11). We continue to be left in the dark about Naomi's disposition towards Ruth. Is she happy or unhappy that Ruth is with her? Whatever the case, Naomi expresses no reservation about allowing her foreign daughter-in-law to enter a strange field alone, despite the fact that in so doing Ruth will expose herself to the possibility of assault. The Hebr. text conveys Ruth's resolve through a chain of three verbs ('so she went and arrived and gleaned'; v. 3).

Before the action continues, however, the narrator intrudes with a brief comment, noteworthy not only because the narrator rarely does so in this story but also because of what the narrator says: 'It just so happened that it was the parcel of the field that belonged to Boaz, who was from the same clan as Elimelech' (v. 3b). By making reference to Boaz's kinship to Elimelech after Ruth's declaration to find a welcome space to glean, the narrator invites the reader to make the connections that will play out in the ensuing story. The language of the report intimates that her arrival at the field is a matter of happenstance. This has led many commentators (e.g. Nielsen 1997: 55) to propose that the narrator is sending a subliminal message; specifically, that Yahweh is guiding Ruth without her awareness. When taken at face value, however, the narrator's report prompts the reader to see Ruth's arrival in the field as sheer coincidence. The phrase *wayyiqer miqrehā* (her happening happened) corresponds to a similar phrase in Eccl. 2:14 that refers to the wise and foolish suffering the same fate. The noun *miqrê* stands over against the notion of divine guidance in 1 Sam. 6:9, when the Philistine priests and diviners place the ark of Yahweh on a cart pulled by oxen and declare that the direction the oxen take will reveal whether the calamity they have suffered has come from Yahweh or has been a random act. In short the narrator presents Ruth's arrival at the field of Boaz as a coincidence and leaves it to the reader to impute divine involvement.

4–13

The narrator tracks Ruth's journey from the outside to the inside through a series of dialogues. The first, which takes place between Boaz and the supervisor of the work party, begins the process by reiterating Ruth's status as an outsider, on one hand, and, on the other, with a greeting that aligns Yahweh with Boaz and the Bethlehemite workers (vv. 4–7). Boaz enters the field with a greeting that affirms Yahweh's presence with the people: 'Yahweh be with you!' The harvesters in return invoke Yahweh's beneficent activity: 'May Yahweh bless you!' The declarations of Yahweh's presence and blessing among the people of Bethlehem stand in counterpoint to Naomi's earlier declaration that Yahweh has afflicted her and brought her back empty (1:21). Yahweh is with his people and blesses them. Naomi and Ruth, however, presently stand outside the sphere of Yahweh's blessing and community belonging.

Boaz then asks a question with symbolic import: 'Whose young woman is that?' The question signals Ruth's disconnection from the patriarchal network that binds the community together. She does not belong to any man. On its face Boaz is simply enquiring about Ruth's status within the community. With what man is she connected? His words may express detached and noble kindness to a foreigner, or they may signal more than a casual interest in this young woman who has appeared among his workers. Ruth has clearly caught Boaz's eye. As marriages in this culture are negotiated by men, and in the light of how events will unfold, Boaz's words take on a romantic suggestiveness. Is Boaz subtly enquiring about the man to whom he will speak if he is interested in Ruth?

At a deeper level Boaz's question brings the question of Ruth's identity to the surface. This gives the narrator the opportunity, now within the context of communal interactions, to reiterate those characteristics that mark Ruth as the quintessential outsider. The supervisor's response (v. 6) sets Ruth apart – sexually, socially and spatially – from those with the harvesting community that Yahweh blesses. She is a 'young woman' (na'ărâ) in opposition to the 'young man' (na'ar) who identifies her, and thus of opposite gender. She is a Moabite, in opposition to the people of Bethlehem and thus of opposite ethnicity. She is from the 'Field of Moab' rather than the field where the community gathers, and thus of opposite geographical attachment. Furthermore, she is one who 'returned' with Naomi, as opposed to those who stayed. She does not belong with the group that harvests in this field but rather picks up after them (v. 7a). This last dichotomy is reinforced with a wordplay on 'returning' and 'staying'. The supervisor characterizes Ruth as the woman who 'returned' (haššābâ) with Naomi (v. 6) and later informs Boaz that she has been 'staying' (šibtāh) in the shelter for a little while (v. 7).

The supervisor's garbled speech (in the Hebr. text) requires an explanation. Hurvitz (1983: 121–123) views the response as a confused attempt to explain why Ruth has been allowed to stay so long in a hut reserved for workers. It is also possible that the supervisor is flustered because he is unsure of Boaz's response to a Moabite woman gleaning in his field. Grossman (2007: 703–716) offers an intriguing proposal: that the supervisor has reworded Ruth's request in order to cast the Moabite woman in a negative light. He notes that, when compared with Ruth's stated intention (v. 2), the supervisor's report to Boaz makes minor but significant changes. Ruth declares that she intends to gather among the ears of grain. The supervisor, however, reports that she asked to glean and gather among the sheaves, giving the impression that Ruth is a presumptuous woman. He does this, Grossman suggests, in order to cast her in a negative light and so restrict her activity.

Following this line of interpretation links 'the young man who supervised the harvesters' to the other young men rather than Boaz. This conforms to the narrator's strategy to depict Boaz as beneficent and gracious, in contrast to the young men in the field, who may threaten Ruth without Boaz's intervention. Consequently, the dialogue between Boaz and the supervisor expresses different views on the issue of a foreigner in the community, the supervisor and young men representing an exclusive sentiment as opposed to the welcoming stance of Boaz.

Boaz's address to Ruth takes the form of invitation and blessing. He begins by invoking the language of kinship and belonging: 'Listen, my daughter.' The form of address forges an implicit but strong association with Naomi, who has also addressed Ruth in this way (2:2). In contrast to the supervisor's comments, which identify her as 'the young Moabite woman', Boaz thus implicitly identifies Ruth as family and so by extension a part of the community. He follows with an invitation, in the form of two negative imperatives, which attach her to the space the community calls its own: 'Do not go to glean in another field' and 'Do not leave this one.' Boaz declares, in as many words, that Ruth belongs in *this* field rather than the field of her origin; she belongs in Israelite space. He follows with a second invitation, now in the form of two positive commands, which draws her directly into the social network: 'Join my young women . . . Follow them.' The two complementary pairs of imperatives thus bring Ruth into Bethlehem's geographical space and into the outer rung of the social universe that orbits around this eminent and powerful man.

Boaz concludes with a third invitation comprising two commands – one negative, one positive – that indirectly associates Ruth with the young men (v. 9b). First, he declares that the young men are not to harass Ruth. He then invites her to drink from the water drawn by the young men, making her the beneficiary of their labour and giving her access to resources available to all the workers. The third set of commands thus confirms her incorporation into the community through the bestowal of protection and provision.

Ruth responds by falling to her feet and bowing to the ground, an action that expresses both gratitude and an acknowledgment that Boaz possesses greater status and power (cf. 1 Sam. 20:41; 25:23; 2 Sam. 14:4, 22). She then asks a question that brings the narrative's primary tension to the surface: 'Why have I found favour in your sight, that you would notice me, since I am a foreigner?' (v. 10). Why has this foreigner received favour? Why has she been included in the community and been invited to share its life and resources? On the surface the question confirms that Ruth has accomplished what she set out to do (v. 2). The deeper import of her question, however, strikes at the core of Israelite identity. If foreigners may become part of the covenant community, on what basis and by what criteria? Ruth highlights the question by identifying herself as a 'foreigner' rather than as a Moabite, as one might expect. Her choice of words creates a striking wordplay between recognition (*lĕhakkîrēni*, 'to notice me') and foreignness (*nokrîyyâ*, 'foreigner').

Boaz's response answers both the surface and deeper questions (v. 11). He draws attention to two actions that have come to his attention. First, he knows that Ruth has remained loyal to Naomi, even though she could have gone back to her own people after the death of her husband. Secondly, he knows that she has left her own people and native land in order to settle with a new people in a new place. Ruth's journey has paralleled Naomi's. She left a place of need to settle in a place of plenty. Yet unlike Naomi, whom we may assume had no choice in the matter, Ruth has made a free decision to accompany the family member. Naomi departed and returned; Ruth enters from a completely different place and people. Boaz's response therefore not only commends Ruth but also implicitly endorses the inclusion of those outsiders who freely and intentionally join the Judahite community. Ruth's loyalty to a community member and her decision to sever attachments to her own people and land are the grounds by which she, as the epitome of all foreigners, may join Yahweh's people and find her way into the heart of the nation's life.

Boaz, who has been the recipient of Yahweh's blessing (v. 4), now signals Yahweh's acceptance of Ruth into the covenant community by conferring a blessing through 'Yahweh, the God of Israel' (v. 12). The invocation draws attention to Yahweh's commitment to equity and restorative justice. First, Boaz declares that Yahweh will reward Ruth for what she has done. The verb here translated 'reward' (*yĕšallēm*) refers to compensating someone or restoring something to a state of harmony and well-being. When Yahweh is the subject, it often signifies his practice of fully repaying or recompensing individuals or groups for their actions, that is, giving them their just deserts (2 Sam. 3:39; Job 34:11; Isa. 59:18; Joel 2:25). The second phrase approximates the first but in specifically material terms: 'may you receive payment in full'. The concept is payment for services rendered (wages) and here expresses comfort and encouragement for the distressed (Novick 2011: 708–722). Within the context of the story the implications are hard to miss. Boaz, who pays wages to the workers in the field, implies that this foreign woman is, in Yahweh's eyes, also deserving of equitable wages.

Boaz pointedly refers to Yahweh, the God of Israel, as the protector of refugees. References to the wings of Yahweh occur primarily in the Psalms (Pss 17:8; 36:8[7]; 57:1; 61:5[4]; 63:8[7]; 91:4; cf. Mal. 3:20). The metaphor evokes an image well known in Syro-Palestinian iconography (LeMon 2010: 27–58). The closest biblical parallel is Ps. 91:4, where the wings of Yahweh signify a place of refuge with Yahweh. The psalm portrays Yahweh as a warrior who protects the refugee (in this case, probably the king) against the threatening powers of evil and destruction. The wings of

Yahweh evoke an ANE motif that depicts winged deities in combat with and prevailing over evil entities (often portrayed as lions or serpents [LeMon 2010: 169–185]). Boaz's speech thus presents Yahweh as a mighty warrior and defender and identifies Ruth as a refugee. The implied message would probably not be lost on the young men who have been working the field in Boaz's employ. As a foreign woman and outsider, Ruth has no defender in the community and is therefore vulnerable to maltreatment and violence. Given the ethnic antagonisms between Judahites and Moabites attested throughout the HB, her situation is all the more perilous. Should any of the men decide to abuse her, there would probably be no hand raised in her defence. The reality of the danger she faces is confirmed by Boaz's command to his young men not to harass her (v. 9) and Naomi's later comment that Ruth may be subject to abuse if she gleans in another field (v. 22). Boaz and Yahweh welcome this refugee who has come to their community and land. Boaz demonstrates his determination to defend Ruth by pre-empting any violence against her and comforts her with the knowledge that Yahweh also will come to her defence.

Ruth's request that she continue to find favour in Boaz's eyes is therefore more than a polite pleasantry (v. 13). She and Naomi need access to the fields in order to survive. She stands outside the social network that binds the community together. She is a Moabite woman living in constant peril of abuse. Boaz, however, has shown her kindness. He has offered himself as a provider, advocate and defender. Because of Boaz, Ruth and Naomi will have enough to eat. Boaz, in sum, has become the bridge by which the women can enter the community and participate in its life. Boaz, like Yahweh, offers shelter and protection. At this point it is worth noting that Ruth does not know what the reader (and perhaps Boaz) knows: Boaz and Naomi's late husband are related. All Ruth knows is that this powerful man has noticed her and come to her aid. His continued attention will be essential for her well-being. Ruth's reference to herself as both 'your maidservant' and 'not even one of your maidservants' directly articulates her transitional status within the community. She is an outsider who has been invited in.

What would prompt this village elder to show such kindness to a Moabite woman? Does his kindness emanate from compassion and generosity? Could there be a spark of romantic interest? Ruth does not know. It will be crucial, in any case, to take the opportunity of his kindness to forge a strong relationship. Ruth therefore responds by expressing the personal and emotional effect of Boaz's kindness: Boaz has encouraged and spoken tenderly to her. The latter phrase (lit. 'speaking to the heart') conveys intimacy. The phrase is utilized to describe the affection that motivates Joseph to reassure his brothers that he has forgiven them (Gen. 50:21, also as here, in tandem with Hebr. *nāḥam*, 'encourage', 'comfort'). More commonly the expression signifies a man wooing a woman (Shechem to Dinah [Gen. 34:3] and a Levite his concubine [Judg. 19:3]; metaphorically of Yahweh to Israel [Hos. 2:16] and Jerusalem [Isa. 40:2]).

Ruth's response therefore skilfully observes social protocols while at the same time inviting personal intimacy. Her use of 'lord' with reference to Boaz and 'maidservant' with reference to herself acknowledges the social distance between her and her benefactor. At the same time she signals that she understands his words as an expression of personal caring and, perhaps, an invitation to a relationship that would dissolve the ethnic boundary between them.

14–16

The previous scene relates Ruth's entry into the outer rings of the village community, as Boaz invites her to join his young women and then to the water his young men have drawn. In this scene Boaz draws Ruth closer to the centre by singling her out for special treatment. The waw-conversive verb that opens the scene in the Hebr. text (*wayyō'mer*, 'and he said') gives the impression that the conversation between Boaz and Ruth continues unbroken, as the main plot line in biblical narrative is commonly carried by this verbal form. 'At mealtime' follows, however, to signify that the conversation later picked up where it left off. Once again Boaz invites Ruth into the community circle. Whereas in the previous scene he offered her water, he now offers her food: bread and roasted grain (v. 14). The narrator's report that she sat down alongside the harvesters confirms that she is now part of the group, although the choice of the prep. *miṣṣad* (alongside) rather than 'among' conveys her still-transitional status as both insider and outsider. Boaz's gift of food is lavish. Presumably Ruth has not brought any food: she has come to the field because she has none. Now Boaz gives her more than she can eat.

After Ruth resumes gleaning, Boaz directs his workers to make sure that she leaves with an ample supply of grain. Taking a line from the supervisor's report of Ruth's original request, Boaz now directs his workers to allow her to glean among the cut stalks (v. 15; cf. v. 7). He follows this with another command that goes even beyond this extraordinary privilege: the workers must pull out some handfuls from the harvested grain and leave them for her (v. 16). A prohibition follows each command. He next issues a command that is generally softened in modern translations (v. 15): 'do not reproach her' (ESV, NRSV), 'do not reprimand her' (TNIV), 'without interference' (JPS). The hiph. form of the verb occurring here (*kālam*) refers to actions that bring shame and humiliation, whether by a slight (1 Sam. 20:34) or insult (1 Sam. 25:7; Job 19:3), or that bring disgrace (Prov. 28:7). The corresponding noun *kĕlimmâ* carries the same sense. Many translators view the verb in this instance as a synonym of the verb 'rebuke' (*gā'ar*) that appears in the second prohibition (v. 16). Ruth's vulnerability in the field, however, indicates that it conveys the sense of humiliation here that it does in other cases.

As he does in the previous scene, Boaz acts as Ruth's defender and issues a total of three prohibitions to his workers regarding Ruth: they are not to harass (v. 9), humiliate (v. 15) or rebuke her (v. 16). The fact that Boaz must reiterate essentially the same command in three different forms draws attention to the mistreatment Ruth would probably endure from their hands apart from his intervention. Acting also as her provider, Boaz ensures she will be able to complete her task and return home with more than enough to eat. Ruth's carefully worded response seems to have hit home.

17–23

Ruth takes full advantage of the opportunity Boaz makes for her, as she gathers barley until the evening and then threshes it. Threshing involved bringing bundled sheaves to a flat, open area where the grain was separated from the stalks, often through the use of a threshing sledge drawn by oxen or donkeys (King and Stager 2001: 90). The amount of grain she brings back to Naomi, an ephah, is well beyond what anyone could expect to glean in a day. Estimates of the volume of an ephah range from 4 gal (21 l; Hubbard 1988a: 179) to 9 gal (42 l; LaCocque 2004: 76) – approximately 1.6 to 1.2 bushels – enough to feed two individuals for five to seven days (Sakenfeld 1999a: 46).

Ruth left Naomi in a destitute state. Now she returns with an astounding amount of grain. When she shows her mother-in-law how much she has gleaned, and 'what was left over after she had eaten her fill' (the roasted grain Boaz had given her), Naomi is astonished. The plentiful amount of grain is one matter, but the surplus of roasted grain is quite another. Naomi might reasonably have expected that her Moabite daughter-in-law would return with very little to show for her efforts. The abundant yield and roasted grain, however, reveal that Ruth has been the beneficiary of unexpected generosity. Who would be so generous to a Moabite woman, and why? Naomi immediately enquires about the field, punctuating her questions with a blessing on the one who has noticed Ruth (v. 19a). In the Hebr. text her first question utilizes wordplay to associate the hospitable space Ruth has entered with the sustenance it promises: 'where' (*'êpōh*) and 'ephah' (*'êpâ*).

The conversation between the women reinforces the symbolic transformation of status that has taken place in the field by echoing the pattern of Ruth's conversation with Boaz in the field:

1. Blessing
Boaz: 'May Yahweh bless you!' (v. 4)
Naomi: 'Blessed is he by Yahweh, who has not given up his devotion to the living and the dead!' (20a)

2. Question
Boaz: 'Whose young woman is that?' (v. 5)
Naomi: 'Where did you glean today? Where did you work?' (v. 19)

3. Identification
Overseer: 'She is the young Moabite woman who returned
with Naomi' (v. 6)
Naomi: 'The man is a close relative of ours' (v. 20b)

4. Invitation
Boaz: 'Join my young women here' (v. 8)
Ruth: 'Join my young men until they have finished my part of
the harvest' (v. 21)

5. Protection
Boaz: 'keeping your eyes on the field where they are harvesting
. . . I hereby order the young men not to harass you!' (v. 9)
Naomi: 'It is a good thing, my daughter, for you to accompany
his young women so you won't be harmed in another field' (v. 22)

The naming of characters complements the structural scheme. The chapter begins with references to the kinship bonds that unite the community ('a relative on her husband's side', v. 1; 'my daughter', v. 2). The final scene now repeats the designations through Naomi's speech ('a close relative of ours', v. 20b; 'my daughter', v. 22). 'My daughter' in particular names Ruth as family. Naomi's second reiteration of the address (corresponding to two by Boaz, v. 8) here signals a change in Naomi's perception of Ruth and of their circumstances. The first instance caps a brusque response to Ruth's request to glean (v. 2). Now it signals concern and hope. In fact, Naomi's speech dominates the dialogue.

The narrator pointedly shifts to in-law language to name the women, signalling an intermingling of in-group and out-group relationships: 'mother-in-law' for Naomi (vv. 18, 19 [twice], 23) and 'daughter-in-law' for Ruth (vv. 20, 22). The merging of kin and in-law language in the concluding speech accentuates Ruth's new status as insider-yet-outsider. Punctuating her status, the narrator again identifies the young woman as 'Ruth the Moabite' immediately after Naomi discloses that Boaz is a 'close relative of ours', echoing the narrator's introduction of Boaz by the same title, also following a disclosure of Boaz's family connection (vv. 1–2, 20–21). She then extends the kinship tie to introduce the trajectory that will carry the story forward in the next chapter: Boaz is 'one of our family redeemers' (v. 20). With this declaration Naomi confirms that Ruth has been woven into the social fabric that binds the community and therefore may benefit from the kinship relationships that configure it.

To underscore Ruth's inclusion the narrator repeats the thematic verb 'join' (*dābaq*), first in Naomi's speech and then in a concluding report (vv. 21–23). The first utterance alludes to Naomi's directions to Orpah and Ruth, when the former left to return to her people and the latter 'held on' to her mother-in-law (1:14). It also follows an earlier instance in this chapter, when Boaz brought Ruth into the outer rung of the village society ('Join my young women' [2:8]). The second and third instances of *dābaq* complement Boaz's invitation to join the covenant community, on the part of Naomi and the narrator, respectively. On the journey from the Field of Moab Ruth held only to Naomi. Having entered a field in Bethlehem, she now holds to the young women who work for Boaz. For her part, Ruth seems to recognize that she now occupies a significant place of belonging because of Boaz's kindness. When she reports Boaz's invitation to join his young women, she subtly replaces 'young women' with 'young men' and thus associates herself with the village community as a whole (v. 21; cf. v. 8).

Naomi's blessing of Boaz (v. 20) forges an additional connection to the words she spoke to her daughters-in-law upon leaving Moab. On that occasion Naomi dismissed Orpah and Ruth by saying, 'May Yahweh show you the same devotion that you have shown to the dead and to me. May Yahweh grant that each of you find a place to settle down in her husband's home' (1:8). Her words associated her with 'the dead'. Now, upon learning that Ruth's benefactor is Boaz, Naomi echoes those words by declaring, 'Blessed is he by Yahweh, who has not given up his devotion to the living and the dead!' (v. 20a). The exclamation signals a change in Naomi's outlook. The difference is that in this case Naomi associates herself with 'the living' as opposed to 'the dead'. The gift of grain signals to her that she has become the recipient, along with the living, of unexpected kindness. Now seeing herself among the living, Naomi moves from despair to hope. She does not identify the one 'who has not given up his devotion'. The antecedent could be either Boaz or Yahweh. The ambiguity has prompted a number of attempts to clarify the phrase (see Bush 1996: 134–136). The ambiguity, however, is probably intentional, suggesting that Naomi sees Boaz and Yahweh acting in concert as agents of blessing.

Naomi no longer speaks of Yahweh as a threatening deity or of bitter circumstances. Instead, she now sees him as a provider whose faithfulness has been conveyed through this Moabite woman. The blessing she speaks over Boaz thus complements his invocation over Ruth. Boaz speaks of Yahweh as a protector of the refugee; Naomi speaks of Yahweh's devotion to the living and the dead. Bush sums up well (1996: 142): 'Naomi has indeed come back to life . . . but at this stage of the story it is a rebirth of hope. "Yahweh has seen to the needs of his people by giving them food" (1:6c), and now Boaz's *ḥesed* has given them a share in that provision.'

Naomi's disclosure that Boaz is 'one of our family redeemers' confirms the vehicle by which the two women will be integrated into the village community. The decision to disclose this key bit of information now, rather than when introducing Boaz (v. 1), allows the narrator to emphasize largesse and hospitality towards the outsider. The family redeemer (gō'ēl) had the responsibility of maintaining and restoring the bonds that united the family to each other and to their land (Hubbard 1988a: 188–189; Bush 1996: 136–137). He bought back family land that had been sold out of economic necessity and family members who had sold themselves into slavery (Lev. 25:23–35, 47– 55). As the representative of the family, he received compensation paid as restitution for wrongdoing against the family (Num. 5:8). Assuming that Yahweh's role as redeemer is based on this social function, the redeemer may also have served as an advocate for family members involved in lawsuits (Ps. 119:154; Prov. 23:11; Jer. 50:34). If he was the same individual as the 'redeemer of blood' (gō'ēl haddām), the family redeemer would also have had the responsibility for avenging the death of a family member (Num. 35:12, 19–27; Deut. 19:6, 12; Josh. 20:2–3, 5, 9).

Naomi now perceives Ruth differently. No longer a burden or embarrassment, Ruth is Naomi's pathway to restoration. Through her Yahweh has displayed his devotion to her ('the living') and her late husband and sons ('the dead'). Whereas Naomi spoke tersely in response to Ruth at the beginning of the chapter, she is now energetically talkative. She does not know why Boaz has noticed Ruth. Yet the fact that her daughter-in-law has gained the attention of an influential village elder, who happens also to be a family redeemer, reveals to her the presence of Yahweh. The promise of a bright future begins to dawn. It is not hard to connect the dots. Boaz has noticed Ruth. Boaz is a family redeemer. If Ruth's encounter with Boaz is due to Yahweh's working, then security for both women may be in the offing. Although undoubtedly aware of the danger Ruth faced when she left for the fields that morning, Naomi gave Ruth no warning or advice at that time. Now, however, she displays a pronounced concern for the well-being of her daughter-in-law, advising Ruth that she must continue to glean only in Boaz's field so she will not risk being assaulted.

What of Boaz's motives? Has he shown such kindness to Ruth simply in response to the kindness Ruth has shown to Naomi, the wife of his deceased kinsman? Or is there something about her that he finds attractive? The conversation between Ruth and Boaz is proper and polite. Yet there is enough in what each says to suggest a careful sounding out of the other's intentions and disposition. Ruth may well wonder why a prominent elder would be drawn to a foreign woman, and a Moabite at that. Boaz, as will be revealed later, perhaps wonders why Ruth would be drawn to him rather than to the young men of the town (3:10). In their conversation in the field we may detect a delicate dance of reserve and disclosure as each seeks to discern the interest of the other. Naomi, as the next chapter reveals, seems already to have drawn her own conclusion.

Explanation

With the introduction of Boaz the focus of the story shifts dramatically from emptiness to fullness, despair to hope, and separation to inclusion. As in the prior chapter, Ruth continues as a character whose identity is defined and redefined with reference to another. Faced with Naomi's declaration that she should leave and go back to Moab with her sister-in-law, Ruth decides to embrace a new identity in order to stay with her mother-in-law (1:14–17) and so enters Bethlehem as a newcomer and foreigner. Boaz proves to be the door through which she enters this new community and consequently Ruth becomes a bridge of blessing for Naomi. Boaz facilitates the process of drawing Ruth into the community through unconventional and surprising acts of hospitality towards a foreigner.

At the frames of the story the narrator sets the community's periphery, in the person of 'Ruth the Moabite', the quintessential outsider (2:2, 21), over against its centre – the person of Boaz, 'an eminent and powerful man' (v. 1). Within the confines of the field outside Bethlehem one of Boaz's workers identifies Ruth by her Moabite ethnicity (v. 6), but Ruth identifies herself to Boaz as a 'foreigner' (*nokrîyyâ*, v. 10). The latter term denotes anyone who stands completely apart from the Israelite community in ethnicity, practices and commitments. Solomon, for example, refers to foreigners as those who are 'not one of your Israelite people' (1 Kgs 8:41; cf. 2 Sam. 15:19). In many biblical contexts the foreigner is distinguished from the sojourner (*gēr*; see Milgrom 2000: 1493–1501). In these instances sojourners differ from foreigners in that the former share in Israel's covenantal life and commitments. Thus sojourners (but not foreigners) are numbered among those who renew the covenant on the plains of Moab (Deut. 29:1[10]) and at Mounts Ebal and Gerizim (Josh. 8:35; cf. Deut. 31:12). A foreigner, in short, signifies someone who is wholly 'other'. In the ascription of Israelite identity the foreigner – and particularly the foreign *woman* – stands as the symbol of everything Israel is *not* and must *not become*. This is most apparent in the book of Proverbs, where the speech of the 'foreign woman' stands in direct and threatening opposition to the speech of the wise father. Here she is a seductive entity who uses her smooth speech to lure the young man onto an opposing and destructive path (Prov. 2:16; 5:20; 6:24; 7:5; 23:27; 27:13; see Newsom 1989: 142–160).

The motif of the 'foreign woman' (*nokrîyyâ*), then, radiates a sense of danger and apostasy. The point is made vividly in Israel's memory by the account of Solomon's foreign wives, who turned the king's heart away from following Yahweh and provoked Yahweh's anger (1 Kgs 11:1–13). It is clearly the image that Ezra and those who returned with him had in their minds as they contemplated the cause of the exile and the restoration of their nation. In his public prayer of confession Ezra casts intermarriage with the women of the land as Israel's archetypal sin (Ezra 9:10–15). He declares that the people have broken what was 'commanded through your servants the prophets' and characterizes the whole of Israel's life prior to the exile as a continual display of disobedience. He then singles out the Mosaic commandments against intermarriage as the quintessential manifestation of Israel's rebellion and the direct cause of the divine punishment suffered by the nation (v. 13). Although even a cursory reading of the prophets reveals multiple indictments against the nation (and a corresponding omission of references to foreign women), Ezra's prayer suggests that the exile is the result of intermarriage. His hermeneutical strategy provides the warrant for cleansing Israel of every foreign element. By evoking the image of foreign women as the quintessential *femmes fatales*, Ezra legitimizes the ensuing divorce of foreign wives and the disowning of their children. If marriage to foreign women is the parade example of Israelite disobedience, divorcing such women is necessary to demonstrate repentance and prevent another outpouring of divine wrath (9:14).

When Ruth identifies herself to Boaz as a foreigner, she therefore strikes a chord of threat and revulsion. A good Israelite man, especially a member of the post-exilic community, knows what to do when confronted by a foreign woman. Boaz, however, does something both shocking and subversive. Instead of expelling her or taking measures to protect the community from her contaminating influence, he does exactly the opposite. He welcomes her into his space, acknowledges and commends her, and becomes her advocate.

As noted in the 'Comment' section, the narrator constructs the story to draw our attention to the unexpectedly gracious character of Boaz's decision to help this foreign widow; unexpectedly gracious because other decisions are possible and perhaps more to be expected. The three references to potential harassment and abuse by the young men in Boaz's employ (vv. 9, 16, 22) underscore the attitudes and treatment Ruth faces as she enters their space, attitudes that resonate with the exclusivist vision of the Ezra party. A foreign woman has no connection or worth within the community and represents a threatening presence. She is therefore fair game for mistreatment. Boaz, however, chooses differently. In his capacity as an individual of eminence and influence, he not only meets the needs of the young refugee but stretches communal boundaries to include her.

Boaz's response to Ruth epitomizes the biblical practice of extending hospitality to the stranger. Although a fundamental aspect of Christian thought and practice throughout the centuries, hospitality as an organizing vision and expression of the gospel has virtually disappeared in the modern Western church. Christine Pohl (1999) has written about the recovery of this practice in ways that illumine both the biblical text and the vision it sets before the modern Christian reader. Especially germane is her discussion of the essential connection between hospitality and recognition in the Christian tradition (61–103). 'Recognition', she writes, 'involves respecting the dignity and equal worth of every person and valuing their contributions, or at least their potential contributions, to the larger community' (61). Welcoming the foreigner recognizes the humanity of those who have been excluded, devalued or rendered invisible by a larger society that defines human worth by constructing social differences and boundaries. Hospitality is therefore profoundly countercultural and subversive. It witnesses to a vision of humanity that views even 'the least of these' as those who bear the image of God. The practice, in so doing, witnesses to the larger community, challenging it to reassess the ways it determines human value.

Hospitality must be lived out in concrete actions and relationships. It entails universalizing the 'neighbour' as anyone in need, and caring for the neighbour as the Samaritan cared for the man who had fallen into the hands of robbers (Luke 10:29–37). Beyond caring for the material needs of the poor, refugees, widows, orphans, resident aliens and others on the social periphery, hospitality can initiate a journey towards social visibility for those who are devalued or ignored by the community. The practice requires a community that fosters a sense of respect and an appreciation of the gifts that outsiders have to offer. It is expressed, above all, in sharing meals together, the fundamental social expression of mutuality, belonging and respect. In Pohl's words:

> Hospitality resists boundaries that endanger persons by denying their humanness. It saves others from the invisibility that comes from social abandonment. Sometimes, by the very acting out of welcome, a vision for a whole society is offered, a small evidence that transformed relations are possible. (Pohl 1999: 64)

Ruth's situation has the ring of the familiar for contemporary readers in an age of global migration and dislocation. The young immigrant enters Israel's space driven by loyalty to her family and the desire to make a better life. She arrives with little in the way of economic resources, hoping only to glean what is left over from the labour of those in the field. She seeks refuge among a people who mark her as an outsider. She embodies, in the eyes of the community, the quintessence of what threatens the nation, and as a consequence she works under a sense of threat.

Boaz, however, welcomes Ruth with tangible expressions of caring and belonging. He not only meets her need for food but does so abundantly. He sees to her well-being and ensures she has a safe place to work. He welcomes her into the community and invites her to eat with him and his workers. He makes it easier for her to work. Although a field hand refers to her only as 'the young Moabite woman', and she refers to herself as a foreigner and a maidservant, Boaz speaks to her as a daughter and so confers dignity and offers encouragement (v. 13). Everyone else in the field sees a foreigner. Boaz sees a woman of commendable character and devotion, a person worthy of the blessing bestowed on the community. He does not keep his distance. Instead, he utilizes his influence and social standing to bring the immigrant from the outside into full participation in the community's life and to be able to access its resources.

Boaz personifies the hospitality of a welcoming community. He is, furthermore, the agent of Yahweh's *ḥesed* towards the destitute and excluded. The two references to Yahweh in this chapter point to him as a deity who deals equitably with human beings. Yahweh welcomes and protects refugees (v. 12). He displays unwavering devotion, giving hope to the despairing and fullness to the needy (v. 20). The many facets of hospitality depicted in this story are tangible expressions of Yahweh's *ḥesed* and an instance in which 'persons act as God to one another in our story' (Campbell 1975: 113).

The events that unfold in the field of Boaz render a vision of the hospitality that reflects Yahweh's welcome of the outsider, the immigrant and the marginalized. Readers are left to ponder how this calling can be lived out in their own fields and faith communities. What adjustments in attitudes and practices shape a welcoming community? What practices of hospitality must challenge the perspectives and actions that devalue and exclude those consigned to the margins? How does the generosity of Boaz shape Christian dispositions and commitments to the refugee, the immigrant, the indigent and the homeless? How, in short, do faithful communities become embodiments of Yahweh's *ḥesed* in a divided and contentious world?

RUTH 3:1–18

Translation

[3:1]Naomi her mother-in-law said to her, 'My daughter, should I not try to find a place for you to settle down, so that it may go well with you? [2]Now is not Boaz our kin – the man whose young women you have been associating with? Look, he is winnowing barley at the threshing floor tonight. [3]So wash, anoint yourself, dress up and go down to the threshing floor. Do not make yourself known to the man until he has finished eating and drinking. [4]When he lies down, take note of where he is lying. Then go over, uncover his feet and lie down. He will tell you what to do.' [5]She said to her, 'Everything you have said to me, I will do.' [6]So she went down to the threshing floor and did everything her mother-in-law directed her to do.

[7]Boaz ate and drank and was in a good mood. He went over to lie down at the edge of the pile of grain. Then Ruth crept over, uncovered his feet and lay down. [8]In the middle of the night he started, rolled over, and look – a woman, lying at his feet! [9]'Who are you?' he exclaimed. She said, 'I am Ruth, your humble servant. You should spread your wing over your humble servant, for you are a family redeemer.' [10]He said, 'Blessed are you by Yahweh, my daughter! This, your latest act of devotion, is better than the first one, for you have not gone after the young

men, whether poor or rich! ¹¹Now, my daughter, do not worry. Everything you have said, I will do for you. Indeed, the entire town council knows you to be an admirable woman. ¹²Now it is indeed true that I am a family redeemer. But there is a family redeemer closer related than I am. ¹³Stay here for the night. If he wants to redeem you when morning comes, fine. Let him redeem you. But if he is not interested in redeeming you, then I will redeem you, as Yahweh lives. Lie here until morning.' ¹⁴So Ruth lay at his feet until the morning.

She got up before one person could recognize another. Boaz said to himself, 'No one must know that the woman has come to the threshing floor.' ¹⁵He also said, 'Give me the cloak you are wearing but keep hold of it.' So she kept hold of it. He measured out six portions of barley and put it on her. Then he went back to the town.¹⁶She went back to her mother-in-law, who said, 'Who are you, my daughter?' She told her everything the man did for her. ¹⁷She said, 'He gave me these six portions of barley and said to me, "You must not go back to your mother-in-law empty."' ¹⁸Naomi said, 'Sit tight, my daughter until you know how things play out. That man will not rest until he resolves the matter today.'

Notes on the text

3:1. Most translators view *'ăšer yîṭab lāk* as a result or purpose clause: 'so that it may be well with you' (NRSV). A parallel phrase in Deut. 4:40 conveys this sense (*'ăšer yîṭab lĕkā*, 'that it may go well with you'). The phrase can also be taken as a relative clause (cf. JPS, 'where you may be happy'). Holmstedt (2010: 148) sees an implicit comparative sense: 'a place of rest that is better for you (than here)'. On the basis of its parallel in Deut. 4:40, my translation views the phrase as a purpose clause.

môda'tānû, 'our kin'; the noun occurs only here in the HB.

3. The K *śmltk*, 'cloak, robe', indicates a single garment, but the Q is pl., *śimlōtayik*, 'clothing'. Those commentators who follow the Q generally understand the text to refer to nice clothing or an extra set of clothes, while those who adopt the K view it as a reference to normal apparel. On the basis of the parallel verb sequence in 2 Sam. 14:2, Bush (1996: 150–152) proposes that 'putting on the robe' refers to the end of the period of mourning, meaning that Naomi is instructing Ruth to don normal clothing to signal that she is available for marriage. The motif of changing clothes, moreover, can symbolize a change in identity or status (see 'Commentary'). Since Naomi's plan depends on Ruth's making a good impression, the Q fits better.

A second K (*wyrdty*) appears to mean 'I will go down', which makes no sense and has been corrected in the Q to read '(you shall) go down', *yāradt*. The LXX corroborates the Q. The K here and in a second occurrence in v. 3 may be an old form of the 2 f. sg.; it is of interest as a possible instance of archaizing language (Bush 1996: 145, n. 3). Alternatively, the form may be a variant of the 2 imp. that displays the influence of Aram. (LaCocque 2004: 90).

5. The Q inserts vowels that indicate that *'ēlay*, 'to me', is to follow *tō'mĕrî*, 'you say'. The omission in the K is generally explained as an instance of parablepsis: the scribe skipped from the aleph that begins *'ēlay* to the aleph that begins the next word *'e'ĕśeh*, 'I will do'. This explanation argues strongly in favour of the Q.

9. The Hebr. text is pointed to read 'your wings' (defectively written), corresponding to the pl. form in Boaz's blessing of Ruth in 2:12. If we follow the Q on this basis, 'wings' refers to the blessing and protection Boaz has spoken of in the field. The sg. form indicated by the K, however, fits the immediate context better; it refers to the hem or corner of Boaz's robe. *kānāp* (wing) evokes a variety of associations. It can refer to the extremities of an object, e.g. the 'ends' of the earth (Job 37:3; 38:13; Isa. 11:12; 24:16; Ezek. 7:2), or the hem (1 Sam. 15:27; 24:5; Ezek. 5:3), or corners (Num. 15:38; Deut. 22:12) of a robe. It may also denote an entire garment (Jer. 2:34; Zech. 8:23). The closest relevant parallel occurs in Ezekiel's allegory of Jerusalem as a profligate ingrate, where Yahweh speaks of spreading his wing over the abandoned child, covering her nakedness, making a covenant with her and taking her to himself (16:8). Many interpreters see a reference to a betrothal custom here and by analogy understand Ruth's request as a proposal of marriage, although the text does not necessarily lead in that direction (see Beattie 1978: 43; Fewell and Gunn 1990: 128–129). Finally, the term occurs in Deuteronomic legislation that forbids a man from sexual intercourse with his father's wife, an act described as uncovering his father's wing (Deut. 23:1; 27:20). It is worth noting that the commandment in 23:1 is set within a collection of laws that pivots from the topic of illicit sexuality to that of people who must be excluded from the Israelite assembly. The constellation of associations evoked by the term, therefore, makes it impossible to determine with certainty what Ruth is asking. The K is therefore preferable, as it conveys the ambiguous ambience of Ruth's request.

'ămātekā/'ămātkā, 'your humble servant', occurs often in petitions and may communicate a greater sense of dignity than the synonymous term *šipḥâ*, 'maidservant'; cf. 2:13. The English idiom expresses a corresponding connotation.

12. *kî 'omnām kî 'm* does not make sense as written. The final word (*'m*) is not vocalized, one of eight examples in the HB of a word 'written but not read'. The vocalized form, *kî 'm*, signifies a strong disjunction, but that cannot be the case here. Boaz is not denying that he is a redeemer but agreeing that he is. *'m* is therefore to be explained as an instance of dittography (*ky'm*) and is not translated. The remaining phrase, *kî 'omnām*, is either an emphatic or concessive construction, 'it is indeed true' or 'although it is true'. Since it occurs in coordination with *wĕgām*, 'and also', which is to be taken in a concessive sense, the former is preferable.

16. *mî-'at*, 'Who are you?' The plain sense of Naomi's greeting does not appear to fit the context. Presumably, Naomi has been expecting Ruth,

and the following 'my daughter' suggests that she recognizes her. For these reasons most interpreters (e.g. Sasson 1989: 100–101; Linafelt 1999: 60; Block 1999: 699) regard the phrase as an enquiry about Ruth's status and identity. Is she still her son's widow or now the intended wife of Boaz? Is she well? How did things go with Boaz? Thematic and grammatical allusions to the story of Isaac's deception by Jacob (Gen. 37:1–40), however, make a strong case that the question should be taken at face value (Jones 2014: 653–664). Isaac asks a corresponding question to Jacob in a context that suggests surprise, uncertainty and obscured vision. The question may therefore be a stylistic device to evoke the sense of risk and trickery that infuses the Genesis account. We note as well that it repeats Boaz's question to Ruth in 3:9, thus raising the motif of identity that is central to the plot. For these reasons I render the question literally, as an expression of surprise by Naomi and as a device that aligns Naomi's speech with Boaz's.

17. 'to me' is signalled again by the Q and can be explained and retained by the same reasoning as above in the note on v. 5.

18. *dābār* occurs first in the indefinite state to refer to the process that will ensue, and then in the definite state to refer to the issue that Boaz will resolve. The translation seeks to capture this sense through the use of English pl. and sg.

Form and structure

The narrator relates the events in Ruth 3 according to the pattern that configures those in Ruth 2. Together the chapters constitute a narrative diptych that reinforces the roles of the three characters as Ruth travels from the periphery of the community to its centre:

> Ruth and Naomi converse about securing a livelihood
>   (3:1–5; 2:1–2)
>   Boaz shows favour to Ruth (3:6–13; 2:3–13)
>   Boaz provides abundantly for Ruth (3:14–15; 2:14–18)
> Ruth returns with food and reports to Naomi
>   (3:16–18; 2:19–23)

Both chapters open with a scene that depicts the present precarious state of the two women and points to Boaz as the means of alleviating their plight. Ruth's decision to find a field in which to glean marks the two women as indigent (Ruth 2:2). Naomi's plan to find a place for Ruth to settle down reveals that they did not have a connection to the community (3:1). Boaz appears in each instance as the source of provision and connection, indirectly in Ruth 2:1 and directly in 3:2. Kinship appears prominently to define the relationship between the three. Boaz is a kinsman and close relative of Naomi (2:1; 3:2), and Ruth is the 'daughter' of Naomi (2:2; 3:1).

In both chapters Ruth departs and encounters Boaz outside the town (the field and the threshing floor respectively). The narration of the two encounters keeps the issue of identity squarely in view by employing a common plot structure (see the table below).

	The field (2:6–13)	*The threshing floor (3:3–13)*
Question	'Whose young woman is that?', v. 5	'Who are you?', v. 9
Response	'She is the young Moabite woman who returned with Naomi . . .', v. 6 'I am a foreigner', v. 10	'I am Ruth, your humble servant,' v. 9
Commendation	'Indeed, the entire town council knows you to be an admirable woman', v. 11b	'This, your latest act of devotion, is better than the first one . . .', v. 10b
Blessing	'May Yahweh repay you for what you have done . . .', v. 12	'Blessed are you by Yahweh . . . !', v. 10a

The repetition of key motifs, in complementary forms, binds the two encounters tightly together. In the field Boaz speaks of Ruth's receiving recompense from 'Yahweh, the God of Israel, under whose wings you have come for refuge' (2:12). At the threshing floor Ruth asks Boaz to spread his wing over her (3:9). In the field Boaz takes Ruth's part over against the 'young men' (*na'ărîm*, 2:9, 15–16). At the threshing floor he commends Ruth for choosing him instead of the 'young lads' (*baḥûrîm*, 3:10). In the field Ruth refers to herself ambivalently as Boaz's 'maidservant' and yet 'not even one' of his maidservants (*šipḥâ*, 2:13). At the threshing floor she refers to herself twice with the less-deprecating 'your humble servant' (*'āmâ*, 3:9).

A brief scene follows the dialogue in each chapter. Boaz provides Ruth with a copious amount of grain, which Ruth in turn takes back to Naomi (2:14–18; 3:14–15). In the field it is a surplus of roasted grain (2:14). At the threshing floor it is six portions of barley (3:15). In the field Boaz singles Ruth out for special attention (2:15–16). At the threshing floor, however, Boaz is concerned not to draw attention to Ruth's presence (3:14).

Both acts conclude with a scene between the two women that confirms the success of the endeavour (2:18–23; 3:16–18). Parallels in language continue with the addition of in-law terms alongside the kinship language: 'mother-in-law' (3:16–17; cf. 2:18, 19 [twice], 23) and 'my daughter' (3:16, 18; cf. 2:22). A parallel structure is also in evidence (see the table on p. 96).

	2:18–23	3:16–18
Report	(Ruth) carried (the barley) back to the village, v. 18	(Ruth) went back to her mother-in-law, v. 16a
Question	'Where did you glean today? Where did you work?', v. 19	'Who are you, my daughter?', v. 16b
Report	She told her mother-in-law about the man with whom she had worked, v. 19	She told her everything the man did for her, v. 16c
Quotation	'He also said to me, "Join my young men . . ."', v. 21	He said, 'You must not go back to your mother-in-law empty,' v. 17
Response	'It is a good thing, my daughter, for you to accompany his young women . . .', v. 22	'Sit tight, my daughter . . .', v. 18

In the common plot Naomi greets Ruth with a question upon her return, and the narrator reports that Ruth responded. Ruth elaborates by reporting what Boaz said, but in both instances the quotation appears to go beyond what Boaz is reported to have said during their encounter. Naomi subsequently responds by expressing her opinion about what has occurred. While Ruth 2 ends as Ruth 1 does, with a summary reference to harvest, no such summary appears here. Instead, the narrator signals an immediate resolution in the final act with Naomi's assertion that Boaz will take care of business.

The narrator further joins the field to the threshing floor by taking up, extending and redirecting key terms that occur in the previous chapter. The device cannot often be detected in translation, as the narrator makes skilful use of wordplays. The narrator reiterates these key terms via wordplay to reorient the broader motifs that configure the story. The scene begins with the repetition of terms that conclude the previous chapter:

> *Naomi* said to Ruth her daughter-in-law, 'It is a *good* thing, my daughter, for you to accompany his *young women* so you will not be harmed in another field.' So Ruth joined the *young women* of *Boaz*, gleaning until the end of the *barley* harvest and the wheat harvest. She stayed with *her mother-in-law*. (2:22–23)

> *Naomi her mother-in-law* said to her, 'My daughter, should I not try to find a place for you to settle down, so that it may go well with you? Now is not *Boaz* our kin – the man whose *young women* you have been associating with? Look, he is winnowing *barley* at the threshing floor tonight.' (3:1–2)

By pointedly referring to Boaz as 'our kin', Naomi reiterates and confirms the narrator's comment about Boaz from the previous scene: 'Naomi had a relative on her husband's side' (2:1). The use of slightly different terms, *môdā'* (2:1) and *môda'at* (3:2), differentiates the narrator's voice from Naomi's, while at the same time confirming the kinship bond that both variants express.

The root of *môda'at* (*yd'*, 'knowing') occurs four times as a verb in the present chapter, extending a single iteration in Ruth 2:11. Naomi tells Ruth to 'take note' of where Boaz lies down (v. 4). Boaz declares that the entire community knows Ruth to be an admirable woman (v. 11) but also expresses concern that no one know that she has come to the threshing floor (v. 14). Naomi concludes the act by advising Ruth not to do anything until she knows how things will play out (v. 18). The various subjects and senses of the verb, centring on a scene that takes place in the dead of night, intimate the difficulty of recognizing identities that are in flux within the story. Boaz commends Ruth for not knowing the community in the field (2:11), declares at the threshing floor that the community knows Ruth (3:11), but does not wish anyone to know that she has entered the communal space (3:14). Naomi counsels Ruth to gain knowledge of Boaz's space (3:4) and to wait for knowledge of what will happen through his efforts (3:18). A single iteration of *nkr* (recognize), which evokes Ruth's question in 2:10, reinforces the sense of ambiguity (3:14b) in the present scenario. In the field in the light of day and in the presence of many witnesses Ruth wonders why Boaz has recognized her. At the threshing floor at night she departs from a public space before anyone can recognize each other.

The narrator takes a similar tack with the repetition of *gō'ēl* (family redeemer). The previous chapter concludes with Naomi's announcement that Boaz is a family redeemer (2:20b). The root *g'l* (the consonants that signify the core concept) then occurs seven times in Ruth 3, as both noun and verb, as Ruth and Boaz confer on the threshing floor. Ruth identifies Boaz as a family redeemer (3:9). Boaz in response repeats the term six times in a few brief sentences (3:12–13). The naming, claiming and acknowledgment of a kinship bond thus constitutes the symbolic focus of the events in the chapter. By identifying Boaz as a family redeemer, Naomi claims him as kin (2:20; 3:2). Ruth implicitly does so when she appeals to Boaz on the threshing floor (3:9) and Boaz does the same by acknowledging the claim (3:12). Women at the periphery of the community claim the bond of kinship signified by *gō'ēl*, and a man at the centre affirms the claim.

The system configured by kinship operates by its own set of rules. Naomi qualifies her declaration that Boaz is a family redeemer by the disclosure that he is a relative: 'The man is a close relative [*qārôb*] of ours. He is one of our family redeemers' (2:20). 'Relative' and 'family redeemer' are thus rendered equivalent in Naomi's declaration and lead into her identification of Boaz as 'kin' (3:2). The qualifying term (*qārôb*) occurs again in Ruth 3:12 as Boaz ponders Ruth's proposal: 'Now it is indeed true that I am a family redeemer. But there is a family redeemer more closely related than I am' (*gō'ēl qārôb mimmenî*, 3:12). Here *qārôb* signifies both separation (from Boaz) and connection (through the priority of another's bond). In this way the narrator signals a new and ambivalent status for Boaz. Up to this point Boaz has been a welcoming but detached presence. Ruth's claim, however, now casts him as a member of her family circle. He is now both 'an eminent and powerful man' in the community, the family redeemer of a Moabite woman and more distantly related than another as yet unknown individual.

The narrator takes up other terms from the previous chapter to tie in associated motifs. First, Naomi declares that it is a 'good' thing that Ruth join Boaz's young women (2:22), and initiates the events of the next chapter by declaring her intent to see that things 'go well' for Ruth (3:1; both repetitions of the root *ṭwb*). Boaz, however, declares Ruth's possible redemption by the nearer relative as 'fine' (3:13), raising the question of what the good is within the context of competing social bonds. Secondly, Ruth's request that Boaz spread his wing over her (3:9) associates Boaz with Yahweh, 'under whose wings' (in the words of Boaz) Ruth has taken refuge (2:12). Boaz therefore becomes the one who both proclaims and embodies Yahweh's care and provision for Ruth. Finally, the narrator confirms Ruth as an appropriate partner for Boaz through the latter's declaration that all the village elders regard her as an 'admirable woman' (*'ēšet ḥayil*, 3:11). The Hebr. phrase raises Ruth in linguistic terms to an equivalency with Boaz, whom the narrator has introduced with the corresponding phrase *'îš gibbôr ḥayil* ('an eminent and powerful man', 2:1).

The motif of eating and drinking also links the chapters. In the field Boaz invites Ruth to eat and drink with his workers and provides a surplus that assures Naomi of his provision. At the threshing floor Ruth approaches Boaz when he lies down after eating and drinking, and the ensuing events again yield an abundance of food that sends a signal to Naomi. In both cases Boaz responds to the women's destitute condition with provision and promise.

The occurrence of two other terms links the events at the threshing floor to larger motifs that signal transformations in the plot and characters. First, Naomi begins the act by announcing her intention to find 'a place for (Ruth) to settle down' (*mānôāḥ*, 3:1), recalling the blessing that Naomi employs to dismiss Orpah and Ruth, that is, that Yahweh grant each of them a place to settle down (*mĕnûḥâ*) in the home of a husband (1:9). The first term (1:9) defines the end that will fill the emptiness of her daughters-in-law apart from her. The present term (3:1) signals a different trajectory of fulfilment for Ruth; the 'home of her husband' is located in Bethlehem rather than Moab.

Secondly, a third repetition of the thematic term *ḥesed* underscores that Ruth's devotion is the attribute that elicits Yahweh's blessing and confirms belonging. In the first act Naomi prays that Yahweh will reciprocate Orpah's and Ruth's devotion to her and her deceased men (1:8). Ruth, however, does not abandon Naomi but takes on the risky task of gleaning as a foreigner in the field outside Bethlehem. She returns with food for Naomi, who exclaims in response that Yahweh indeed has not abandoned his devotion to her and her deceased men (2:20). Now, at the threshing floor, Boaz declares that Ruth's request expresses an even greater act of devotion (3:10).

The conversations between Naomi and Ruth reveal that the initiative has passed from Ruth to Naomi. In the previous act happenstance and fortuitous circumstances lead Ruth to provision. In the present act Naomi devises a strategy that Ruth then carries out. As Ruth 3 opens, Ruth continues in deference and devotion to Naomi. Naomi, however, shifts from passivity to planning. In the first act she sought to send Ruth away. In the second, she responded to Ruth's request to glean with a terse 'go ahead, my daughter'. Now, however, she not only expresses her intent to find a good life for Ruth but moves to facilitate that happy outcome. Naomi, in short, now acts explicitly as a mother to Ruth.

The shift in Naomi's disposition has been signalled at the end of the previous act through understatement: she informs Ruth that Boaz is 'one of *our* family redeemers' (2:20). As the third act begins, Naomi is more direct: Boaz is '*our* kin' (3:2). The contrast with 2:1 is striking. There the narrator introduces Boaz as Naomi's 'relative on her husband's side . . . from the same clan as Elimelech'. There is no reference to Ruth. Naomi's declarations, however, extend the reach of kinship to include Ruth, signalling that Ruth the outsider is now expressly a member of the family.

The narrator underscores the unity of Ruth and Naomi through a patterned repetition that presents Ruth as completely compliant to Naomi's directives:

> Ruth to Naomi: 'Everything you have said to me, I will do'
> (v. 5)
> Narrator: '[Ruth] did everything her mother-in-law directed her to do' (v. 6)
>
> Boaz to Ruth: 'Everything you have said, I will do for you'
> (v. 11)
> Narrator: '[Ruth] told [Naomi] everything the man did for her'
> (v. 16)

The structure of the scheme connects Naomi and Boaz through Ruth. Ruth responds affirmatively to Naomi's words, and Boaz responds affirmatively to Naomi's words through Ruth. At this point it is important to return to a repetition discussed in the 'Notes on the text' above: both Naomi and Boaz enquire of Ruth's identity when she approaches them.

Startled awake in the dead of night, Boaz asks (v. 9), *mî 'āt*, 'Who are you?' Naomi greets Ruth with virtually the same question: *mî 'āt bittî*, 'Who are you, my daughter?' (v. 16). The questions foreground the issue of Ruth's identity, which, in the darkness, has undergone an extraordinary transformation. In the field and in the light of day she was Ruth the Moabite who, by the beneficence of Boaz, was invited into the village community. Now at the threshing floor, in the dead of night, she completes her journey to belonging by claiming the central figure of the community as her kin. It is noteworthy in this respect that Boaz's response to Ruth on that occasion contains the book's final occurrence of the verb *hālak* (to walk), which has been a thematic word throughout the story to this point (1:1, 7–8, 11, 16 [twice], 18–19, 21; 2:2 [twice], 3, 8, 9 [twice], 11). Boaz commends Ruth, who has not 'gone after' the young lads, whether poor or rich (3:10). After this, there is no more walking. The women have found security. The initiative passes to Boaz who, in the words of Naomi, 'will not rest until he resolves the matter' (3:18).

Comment

1–6

Naomi's newfound hope seems to energize her. She now concocts a plan to bring about a permanent arrangement between Ruth and Boaz. We are left to wonder exactly why Naomi does so or what kind of relationship she conceives. While Ruth's invitation to join the young women in the field is a good thing, the possibility of settling down with Boaz himself presents an even better outcome. How has Naomi interpreted Boaz's generosity? What motivates Boaz and on what basis should the women approach him? He seems to know a great deal about them (2:11). Has Ruth captured his fancy? Whatever his intentions, Naomi clearly believes that Boaz could use a push.

As noted above, Naomi's conversation with Ruth follows the pattern of the scene that opens the previous chapter but takes on a different tone. In 2:1–2 Ruth presents her plan to glean to Naomi, who responds with a curt response: 'Go ahead, my daughter' (2:2b). This time Naomi is the one with the plan. Whereas 'my daughter' is a perfunctory tag at the end of her response in 2:2, it is now the first thing she says when addressing Ruth. An expression of motherly concern for Ruth's well-being follows. Forms of the verbal phrase *yîtab l-* (it will be well with) signify a range of satisfying situations: safety (Gen. 12:13), freedom (Gen. 40:14), well-being (Jer. 7:23; 40:9; 42:6), long life (Deut. 4:40), material prosperity (Jer. 40:9), success (Deut. 6:18) and many children (Deut. 6:3).

Ruth's well-being will result in finding 'a place to settle down' (*mānôăh*, 3:1). Since a similar term has been used previously with reference to marriage (*měnûḥâ*, 1:9), and because marriage results in the plan now being hatched, it would appear that marriage is the 'settling down' that Naomi seeks for Ruth. This seems to receive support by the assumption that Naomi's reference to Boaz as 'our kin' presumes some form of levirate marriage. Yet Naomi does not specify, as she does in 1:9, that the settling down will be 'in her husband's home'. Moreover, Naomi says nothing about an obligation to provide an heir, and no biblical text mentions this within the scope of the redeemer's responsibilities. These factors leave open the possibility that Naomi is thinking of any kind of arrangement that will provide security for the women and give them access to the late Elimelech's property and the family's resources (Eskenazi and Frymer-Kensky 2011: 48–50). What *is* clear is that Naomi views Boaz as the key to the women's well-being.

The plan entails approaching Boaz at the threshing floor. Threshing floors were typically located just outside the village perimeter or town gate. They are associated in biblical literature with public or ritual activities. The king of Israel and Jehoshaphat sit together at the threshing floor at the gate of Samaria while prophets prophesy (1 Kgs 22:10). Mourning rites for Joseph take place at a threshing floor (Gen. 50:10–11). David sees the Angel of Yahweh at the threshing floor of Araunah the Jebusite and subsequently erects an altar there (2 Sam. 24:15–25; cf. 1 Chr. 21:18 – 22:1).

Naomi's reference to Boaz's winnowing barley seems chronologically out of place. The previous chapter concludes with the report that Ruth gleaned until the end of the barley and wheat harvests (2:23). Wheat ripens later than barley, and the wheat harvest took place at Pentecost, seven weeks after the barley harvest. If the ensuing events take place during the barley harvest – leading to the marriage of Ruth and Boaz – why would she continue gleaning until the end of the wheat harvest? A number of explanations have been proposed. On the basis of traditional farming practices in the Middle East today, Sakenfeld (1999a: 52) suggests that barley was saved and then threshed back-to-back with wheat. It is also possible that the vocalization of the consonantal Hebr. text is the result of confusion created by a wordplay between 'barley', *śě'ōrîm* (cf. 2:23), and 'gates', *śě'ārîm* (cf. 4:1, in the sg.). This has led to the proposal that the vowels should be changed to read 'winnowing at the gate' (Campbell 1975: 114, 117–119). Alternatively, 'barley' could have been chosen because it links, via wordplay, Ruth's appeal to Boaz during the barley harvest with the result of her appeal at the gate. A final possibility, again with narrative artifice in mind, is that the reference to the wheat and barley harvests in 2:23 draws attention to the fact that the supply of grain that Ruth and Naomi receive from the harvest will soon run out, prompting Naomi to concoct her plan (Eskenazi and Frymer-Kensky 2011: 47). When the harvest is over, there will be no more to glean. Then what?

Timing will be crucial. Ruth is to wait until after Boaz has lain down after eating and drinking. When referring to public activities, the phrase 'eating and drinking' generally refers to a festive meal (Gen. 24:54; 26:30; Exod. 32:6; Judg. 9:27; 1 Sam. 1:9; 30:16; 1 Chr. 12:39[40]; 29:22; Neh. 8:12; Zech. 7:6). The scenario, then, is of a communal feast celebrated to mark the harvest of grain, an occasion when food would be plenteous and wine would flow freely. Naomi directs Ruth to wait and make her move after the wine and food have had their effect on Boaz.

Boaz is not to know that Ruth is at the threshing floor until she is ready to reveal herself. Ruth is now numbered among the young women who work in Boaz's field, but she still has no secure place in the community. Hers and Naomi's survival will depend on her ability to distinguish herself from the rest of the women, and this will require a bold but careful plan. Naomi thus directs her daughter-in-law to do all that she can to ensure the maximum impact when the time comes: 'wash' . . . 'anoint' . . . 'dress up' . . . 'go down' (v. 3). The reference to anointing and dressing up is somewhat puzzling. While anointing with olive oil was common, the action here seems to refer to scented oil, an expensive commodity one would not expect two destitute women to have. 'Dressing up' is also puzzling, as one would not expect the women to possess more than one set of clothes. The verbal sequence of bathing, anointing, dressing can be explained with reference to an ANE literary trope that symbolizes a change in a character's state of affairs (Eskenazi and Frymer-Kensky 2011: 51). Ezekiel uses it to signify Yahweh's symbolic betrothal to Jerusalem (Ezek. 16:9–10). David washes, anoints and bathes when he learns that the child born to Bathsheba has died (2 Sam. 12:20). The sequence thus signals that Ruth's life is about to change.

Another four-verb sequence specifies how Ruth is to approach Boaz (v. 4): 'take note . . . go over . . . uncover . . . lie down'. Taken together, the verbs are sexually suggestive, comprising 'a roster of *double entendres*' (Campbell 1975: 132). Each occurs in a common idiom for sexual inter-course: *yādaʿ* ('know'; here 'take note'; e.g. Gen. 19:8, Num. 31:17–18, 35, Judg. 11:39); *bôʾ* ('come to'; here 'go over'; e.g. Gen. 6:4, 19:34, 38:8, 39:14); *šākab* ('lie'; e.g. Gen. 26:10, 30:15, 34:2, 39:7); and *gālâ* ('uncover'; e.g. Lev. 18:6, 20:11, Ezek. 22:10). The phrase 'uncover his feet' is par-ticularly suggestive, as 'feet' in the Hebr. text sometimes constitutes a euphemism for male genitalia (Judg. 3:24; 1 Sam. 24:3[4]; 2 Kgs 18:27; Isa. 7:20). In addition, the verbs *yādaʿ* (vv. 3–4, 11, 14, 18), *bôʾ* (vv. 4, 7 [twice], 14–17) and *šākab* (vv. 4 [three times], 7 [twice], 8, 13–14) occur with such frequency in the chapter as to constitute thematic words.

The suggestive language infuses Naomi's instructions with ambiguity. A place to settle down is the end, but by what means? If we follow where the suggestive language leads, the plan is seduction, perhaps predicated on the assumption that Boaz is attracted to Ruth. Thus Fewell and Gunn (1988: 78–79) see an entrapment scheme whereby a pregnant Ruth might bring 'a marriage or a pay-off' from a reputable man who will want to avoid a scandal. Other commentators assert that Naomi is telling Ruth to uncover herself next to Boaz, that is, to undress herself and lie down naked next to him (Nielsen 1997: 68–69, 75; van Wolde 1997a: 75–76; Carmichael 1977: 332–333). LaCocque (2004: 82–87) seeks to recover Ruth's virtue by explaining the scheme as a courageous gamble that has become necessary in order to ensure the continuation of Elimelech's line and the survival of her mother-in-law, and thus one instance of many biblical instances where doing something improper is required to bring justice or restoration. He thus characterizes Ruth's approach as 'an act of charity from the one that has no other resource to attain the world of a rich man than humbly to offer her own body' (86–87).

On the other hand, the presence of innuendo may be denied or viewed primarily as a device designed to raise suspense, allowing readers to see a more modest interchange. On this view, Ruth's elaborate preparation is intended to show respect to a potential benefactor or to enable her to put her best foot forward. So Bush (1996: 152–153, 155–156) views any sexual encounter as utterly implausible in the light of the characters' integrity, while Hubbard (1988a: 203–205) sees a plan to approach Boaz in private and discretely present him with the women's petition. It is also possible that the chapter presumes practices or customs that were apparent to the original audience but have since been lost. A study of Ruth 3 from the perspective of the Bowa people in Mali cautions that the tendency to see an erotic element at the threshing floor may be influenced to some degree by Western culture's highly sexualized view of marriage; 'the Western reader is unable to conceive of such a nocturnal context without sexuality playing a large role' (Dyk and Keita 2006: 31). The authors point to Bowa customs that present intriguing parallels to the scene at the threshing floor but that do not involve sexual intercourse.

Western predilections towards the erotic notwithstanding, the entire scenario appears to be crafted to elicit a sense of impropriety. However one understands Naomi's instructions, the plan she has in mind clearly breaches conventional norms (Eskenazi and Frymer-Kensky 2011: 48, 54). A woman lying down next to a man in the dead of night and uncovering *anything* below the waist invites certain conclusions, whether warranted or not. Adding to the air of sexual impropriety is the way the scenario evokes and plays off ethnic stereotypes. Naomi's plan casts Ruth in the role of the Moabite seductress. A Moabite woman approaching an esteemed Israelite elder, secretly and in the middle of the night, epitomizes Israelite anxiety about Moabite women's aggressive and dangerous sexuality (cf. Num. 25:1–3).

The plan and its execution is reminiscent of the story of Moabite origins, which also features scheming women, drinking, nocturnal sexual encounters initiated by the women and an overall undercurrent of forbidden sexuality (Gen. 19:30–38). That story results in the births of eponymous ancestors (Ammon and Moab, vv. 37–38). The present story will result in the birth of a dynastic ancestor. The former concerns a taboo

sexual encounter within the family; the present story suggests a forbidden sexual encounter with an outsider. Naomi's directions thus elicit
allusions and ambiguities that generate considerable tension. What are
the women up to and why? How should readers interpret what Naomi
says in the light of what the narrator has revealed about the women's
character and circumstances?

Naomi concludes on a note of confidence: 'He will tell you what to do.'
We are left to wonder why she knows how Boaz will respond. Does she
anticipate that this available young woman will prove irresistible to a man
sleeping off the effects of good wine and food? Or does she perceive Boaz
as a man of propriety who will appreciate the thoughtful and modest way
a destitute widow appeals to family responsibility? Whatever her thinking,
this last comment effectively transforms Ruth into a passive actor in
the drama. Naomi tells her what to do and when Ruth does it, Boaz tells
her what to do. Ruth's role in this act therefore stands in direct contrast
to her role in the previous act where she entered a dangerous space on her
own initiative. She now enters another dangerous space but this time at
Naomi's initiative. Ruth simply agrees to this task by promising to do
everything Naomi has said (v. 5). The narrator then confirms her obedience
with the report that she followed Naomi's instructions (v. 6).

7–9

Everything goes as planned (v. 7). The narrator begins the episode by
reporting that Boaz plays his part, connecting his actions to Naomi's
instructions by employing a four-verb pattern that echoes Naomi's instructions: 'ate . . . drank . . . was in a good mood . . . went over'. The narrator
then conveys Ruth's obedience by repeating the same verbs Naomi used
in her instructions ('went over', 'uncovered', 'lay down'; cf. v. 4a), adding
'in secret' to 'went over' (so, in my translation, 'crept over') to emphasize
the surreptitious nature of her mission. The noun *lā'ṭ*, 'secrecy', refers to
an action intentionally hidden from others (Judg. 4:21; 1 Sam. 18:22;
24:4[5]). 'Quietly' (TNIV, NLT) or 'softly' (ESV) are therefore somewhat mis-
leading translations, chosen to lessen the suggestion of scandal; Bush's
suggestion that the phrase refers to Ruth's uncovering Boaz's feet 'in such
a manner as not to disturb the sleeping man' (1996: 179) is a case in point.

Sometime later Boaz awakes with a start, for reasons the narrator does
not specify (v. 8). The Hebr. text, through the use of *hinneh* (look!),
conveys surprise as he rolls over and discovers a woman lying beside him.
The particle is often employed to bring the reader directly into a scene by
aligning the reader's sight with a character's. There is a playful irony in
the use of the exclamation. It is the middle of the night and probably very
dark. Boaz cannot see much of anything! The exclamation 'look – a
woman, lying at his feet!' calls to mind another surreptitious nocturnal

encounter. After reporting that Jacob entered the bridal tent to join the woman he thought was Rachel, the narrator simply says, 'When it was morning, look! She was Leah!' (Gen. 29:25).

As in the field, Boaz's first words with reference to Ruth are a question about her identity: 'Who are you?' (v. 9; cf. 'Whose young woman is that?', 2:5b). The answer to the question on the prior occasion is given by one of Boaz's workers, who identifies Ruth by her ethnicity and relationship with Naomi (2:6). On this occasion Ruth answers for herself. Now, for the first and only time in the story, she speaks her name and social status ('your humble servant'). With this, Ruth claims identity and personhood in her own right. She is no longer 'the young Moabite woman who returned with Naomi' (2:6).

'Your humble servant' (*'āmâ*) follows cultural codes that require acknowledgment of the addressee's higher social class, but this is a different term than Ruth uses in the field (*šiphâ*, 2:13). The reason that Ruth uses *'āmâ* instead of *šiphâ* is not clear, as the two terms are virtually synonymous. The use of *'āmâ* may be formulaic: the term occurs on the lips of women who bring a petition to a powerful male benefactor (1 Sam. 1:16; 25:24; 2 Sam. 20:17; 1 Kgs 1:13, 17; see Eskenazi and Frymer-Kensky 2011: 58–59). Alternatively, it may connote more dignity than *šiphâ* (Linafelt 1999: 37–38). Some interpreters have suggested that it marks Ruth as an eligible candidate for marriage or concubinage (Joüon 1953: 57; Hubbard 1988a: 211; Sasson 1989: 53, 80–81). Finally, we note that in the Hebr. text 'your humble servant' (*'ămātkā*) puns on the word for faithfulness (*'ămittekā*, 'your faithfulness') and so alludes to a salient attribute of Ruth's character; the two terms are identical in the consonantal text (*'mtk*). This suggests that the form of address has been chosen for stylistic reasons.

Whatever the case, Ruth's response portends a reconfiguration of relationships, for she not only names herself but Boaz as well. Her brief response takes the form of a symmetry that brackets an invitation within declarations of identity:

> I am Ruth, your humble servant.
>   You should spread your wing over your humble servant,
> For you are a family redeemer.

In response to Boaz's question Ruth identifies herself and Boaz in relation to each other and makes a request that will bind them together.

Ruth's declaration that Boaz is a family redeemer (*gō'ēl*) requires elaboration. Some interpreters claim that, in making the declaration, Ruth goes beyond Naomi's instructions (e.g. Hubbard 1988a: 212–213). Whereas Naomi informed Ruth that Boaz is 'one of our family redeemers' when Ruth returned from the field (2:20b), her instructions refer to Boaz only as 'our kin' (3:2). By claiming Boaz as a *gō'ēl*, Ruth appears to look beyond marriage to the redemption of property that falls principally within the family redeemer's purview. Is she communicating the intent of Naomi's instructions or has she misunderstood her mother-in-law (e.g. Berlin 1983: 90–91)? Has she taken the prerogative to expand the narrow scope of Naomi's goal to ensure that Naomi will be provided for as well (e.g. Hubbard 1988a: 212–213; cf. Sakenfeld 1999a: 75–77)? Biblical references to the *gō'ēl* nowhere include marriage to a deceased family member's widow among a family redeemer's responsibilities. How, then, are we to understand Ruth's declaration?

Based on the assumption that Ruth's invitation is a marriage proposal, many interpreters hold that she is appealing to some form of levirate marriage and seek to relate the practice to the duties of the *gō'ēl*. The biblical text restricts the practice to the brother of a deceased man who has died childless, obligating him to marry the widow and beget sons through her in order to 'perpetuate the name of his dead brother, that his name not be erased from Israel' (Deut. 25:6). The practice lies at the heart of the ancestral narrative of Judah (Gen. 38:1–30). It is generally argued that the situation in Ruth reflects an earlier and more expansive custom that was later restricted to the immediate family by the Deuteronomic legislation. (See the review in Bush 1996: 166–169.) Both the Deuteronomic law and the story of Tamar will be evoked later in the tale, the former by allusion through Boaz's declaration that he has taken Ruth as his wife in order to perpetuate the dead man's name over his property (4:7–10), and the latter through the townsfolk's blessing of Boaz's house (4:12).

A direct connection with levirate marriage in whatever form, however, is difficult to make. First, the purpose of levirate marriage as presented in the biblical text is the preservation of a patriarchal line. There is no mention, however, either in Naomi's instructions or in the conversation between Ruth and Boaz, of bearing sons or continuing the family line. Instead, Naomi explains her plan as a way to advance Ruth's well-being, and the conversation at the threshing floor focuses on how Boaz can formalize a relationship with Ruth. Secondly, Boaz is not strictly eligible in the light of the Deuteronomic legislation, as he is apparently not Elimelech's brother. Finally, as has been noted previously, the obligation to marry a widow nowhere appears in texts related to the *gō'ēl*. The responsibilities of the *gō'ēl* were directed towards the recovery or restoration of family members, property or honour rather than the perpetuation of the family line.

It is probable that the biblical legislation on levirate marriage reflects a specific instance of a broader sphere of social customs and practices. We possess limited knowledge of the range of Israelite cultural codes and customs and of their practice in various sociohistorical contexts. Biblical laws in particular do not constitute enacted legislation but rather reflect principles and ways of thinking that provided guidance and instruction to those given the authority to make decisions. In most civil cases town elders probably arrived at their decisions 'on the basis of a combination of overarching principle, common sense, and a well-preserved if perhaps spotty, probably orally transmitted, legal tradition' (Campbell 1975: 134; see also Sakenfeld 1999a: 59–61). Biblical texts may reflect salient or prominent activities undertaken by the gō'ēl but not necessarily the full scope of his obligations. Boaz, in other words, may not be a gō'ēl in the cases signified by biblical texts but may fulfil the role nevertheless. He has, moreover, already acted as a family redeemer in tangible ways by drawing Ruth into the village community and seeing that she is provided for (Beattie 1978: 44–45).

There are, to sum up, no known legal or social codes that obligate Boaz to marry Ruth or act as her redeemer. Naomi's plan is not contrived to get him to fulfil a legal responsibility he is shirking. Rather, the two women have been the recipients of his kindness and generosity. They know their benefactor is a relative. Now, at the end of the harvest season and facing the possibility that food may again grow scarce, they see the kinship bond they share with Boaz as the means to secure permanent well-being. Although the narrator keeps us in the dark about the intentions and particulars of Naomi's plan, it is evident that if Boaz is to become Ruth's provider and protector, he will do so of his own volition and not because he must. Ruth's appeal, so construed, challenges Boaz to move beyond words of blessings to become the agent of those blessings. In the field Boaz prayed that Ruth would receive reward and fair payment 'from Yahweh, the God of Israel, under whose wings you have come for refuge' (2:12). Now Ruth asks him to put his pious words into action and spread his wing over her, as if to say, 'Yahweh's protection is all very well, but what I really need is a man's protection' (Beattie 1978: 45).

Another possibility has been largely overlooked. That is, that Ruth's declaration that Boaz is a gō'ēl introduces a strategy by which Boaz may claim Ruth in marriage and at the same time defuse the scandal of her Moabite identity. Ruth surely recognizes that her Moabite ethnicity presents an impediment to any prospect of marriage to this eminent and powerful man. The social cost of marriage to a Moabite widow would be prohibitive. How can Ruth find her security with him, even if he is romantically inclined, in the face of this seemingly insurmountable obstacle? Ruth's claim that Boaz is a gō'ēl suggests a way that he may marry Ruth and in so doing actually enhance his reputation in the eyes of the community. By stepping into the role of a gō'ēl in order to marry Ruth, Boaz can cast the marriage as an admirable deed, performed to provide for the widow of a kinsman and preserve the assets of the family. Ruth, in other words, suggests a way to make a potentially scandalous marriage work by drawing on the basic social and moral conventions that define the role of the gō'ēl.

The symbolic import of Ruth's declaration strikes even deeper. What commentators have missed by focusing on the relationship between levirate

marriage and the role of the *gō'ēl* is that by identifying Boaz as a *gō'ēl*
Ruth claims him as *family*. While the social function of the *gō'ēl* remains
uncertain, the role is undertaken within the sphere of family structures
and for the benefit of those who share bonds of kinship. By identifying an
influential elder as a redeemer, Ruth announces that she is a member of
Boaz's family network. In so doing she attaches herself to an individual
who occupies the centre of town society.

In the field Boaz enquired about Ruth's identity and was told that she
was the Moabite woman who returned with Naomi (2:5–6). He now
enquires again, 'Who are you?' This time Ruth herself answers. She is 'your
humble servant'. She then identifies Boaz as a family redeemer. The intervening petition ('spread your wing') invites Boaz to take the step that will
unite her (the outsider) to himself (the insider) through the mediating
bond of marriage. In so doing Boaz will symbolically unite the two spheres
that configure the village of Bethlehem (and the concerns of post-exilic
Yehud): progeny and land. Ruth sets new possibilities before the Israelite
elder. By acknowledging her claim, Boaz affirms a family connection to
the erstwhile outsider and secures her place with him at the centre of the
community.

10–14a

Boaz leaves no doubt that he finds Ruth's proposal attractive – at least
initially. He responds effusively, blessing Ruth, agreeing to do all that she
has asked and acknowledging her family claim. Then he equivocates, dis-
closing that there is a family redeemer more closely related than he,
declaring that it will be fine if that one redeems her, and assuring her that
he will redeem her if the other claimant refuses. The sum of his response
articulates both an unqualified and enthusiastic willingness to take Ruth
as his wife and a qualified recognition of the social realities and protocols
that must be negotiated if the matter is to be concluded.

Boaz begins with a blessing. 'Blessed are you' responds textually both to
Naomi's pronouncement of blessing over Boaz (2:20) and to the greeting of
the field hands who hail him when he arrives at the field (2:4). The connection to Naomi's blessing is made by a virtual repetition of Naomi's blessing
('blessed are you' recalling 'blessed is he'). The connection with the workers'
blessing is made through an evocative wordplay: Boaz declares Ruth blessed
(*bĕrûkâ*) because she has not gone after the young men (*baḥûrîm*). Ruth
now joins Boaz as one of the characters in the story who receives a blessing.

Ruth receives a blessing because she has displayed extraordinary devotion
(*ḥesed*) to Boaz, specifically by choosing him over the young men of the
town. The exclamation suggests that Boaz, because of his age, has not
considered himself someone whom Ruth would look to as a partner.
'Whether poor or rich' reveals something of Boaz's view of Ruth and the

kind of relationship he expects to have with her. While many interpreters hold that he is commending Ruth for approaching a relative rather than any of the eligible bachelors in the village (thus ensuring Naomi's security as well as hers), the immediacy of the exclamation and Boaz's emphasis on the young men indicate that he has been labouring under a false assumption and is now delighted to learn otherwise. Ruth has chosen him over someone her own age. Boaz's generous response to Ruth's plight may have expressed more than detached nobility, but he has assumed that she would look to the wings of 'young men' for a permanent arrangement. This is why he declares her choice for him as even more laudable than the choice Ruth made earlier to stay with her mother-in-law, the first act of devotion to which Boaz alluded during their first meeting (2:11).

This marks the third mention of ḥesed (devotion), and it is Ruth who displays it. In the previous scene Naomi linked ḥesed and blessing, just as Boaz does here, when she acclaimed Yahweh for not forsaking the living or the dead (2:20). That and the present instance together look back to the first occurrence, when Naomi urged her daughters to leave her after the deaths of her husband and sons. At that time, Naomi prayed that Yahweh would show the same ḥesed to her daughters-in-law that they had shown to her (1:8). Although Orpah left, Ruth continued on with Naomi, confirming the full measure of devotion that elicits the praise of Boaz. Taken together, the three occurrences of ḥesed align Ruth's actions with Yahweh's: Yahweh is said to practise ḥesed in 2:20, Ruth is said to practise ḥesed here, and both practise ḥesed in 1:8.

What, in short, happens on the threshing floor and what exactly is Ruth asking of Boaz? How one understands the episode depends to a large extent on how one has construed, first of all, the whole of Boaz and Ruth's interactions from their initial encounter to the present moment, secondly, the intent and implementation of Naomi's plan for the evening, and thirdly, Ruth's declaration that Boaz is a gō'ēl. Did Boaz notice Ruth in the field because he found her attractive, and were his words calculated to discern her interest in him? If so, the surplus of grain that Ruth brought back to Naomi sent a message to the woman with whom Ruth was bound, to whom in a sense the young woman belonged (cf. 2:5). If this was the case, Naomi's plan seizes on Boaz's interest and sends a direct and un-ambiguous message of Ruth's availability and interest. Alternatively, was the interchange in the field a formal matter of protocols and provision, whereby a gracious village elder generously ameliorated the condition of a destitute relative and her foreign daughter-in-law? Taken this way, Naomi's plan can be viewed as an appropriate and decorous appeal for help on the basis of kinship bonds. If romantic attraction is the thread that leads Ruth to Boaz, the sexually nuanced language signals a possible sexual encounter. If, however, Naomi intends only for Ruth to approach Boaz discretely with an appeal for provision, then the encounter reflects codes and customs familiar to ancient readers but lost to modern ones.

Ruth's and Naomi's motives likewise can be discerned differently. Does Naomi have an ulterior motive in seeking a home for Ruth, knowing well that Ruth is her ticket to well-being, or is she selflessly looking out for Ruth's best interests? Does Ruth obediently carry out Naomi's instructions or does she misinterpret or intentionally alter the plan?

Upon her departure, Ruth responded to Naomi, 'Everything you have said to me, I will do' (v. 5). Now Boaz assures Ruth with the same words, 'Everything you have said, I will do for you' (v. 11). For the second time he refers to her as 'my daughter', corresponding to the two instances in which Ruth refers to herself as 'your humble servant' (v. 9). The familial language, in response to the social language Ruth employs, confirms Boaz's acknowledgment of the kinship bond Ruth has evoked by naming Boaz as a *gō'ēl* and the priority of that bond in defining his relationship to her.

Boaz then completes the elevation of Ruth's social status by declaring that the influential people of the town perceive her as an *'ēšet ḥayil*, an 'admirable woman'. The Hebr. phrase corresponds to that which introduces Boaz in 2:1. As noted in the commentary on 2:1, the masculine counterpart *gibbôr ḥayil* commonly denotes a warrior, although it broadly refers to someone with an exceptional ability to get things done (Gen. 47:6; Exod. 18:21; 1 Kgs 11:28). The feminine counterpart is epitomized by the exemplary wife in Prov. 31:10–31, whose salient attributes are initiative, diligence, energy and accomplishment. The sage praises the *'ēšet ḥayil* for her business savvy (vv. 13–14, 16, 18, 24) and effective management of her family and household (vv. 11–12, 15, 19, 27–28). 'She wraps her hips with strength and strengthens her arms' (v. 17); 'influence and honour are her clothing' (v. 25). The exemplary wife of Proverbs knows how to get things done and done well. She influences both events and people. The same can now be said of Ruth. Within the context of the story the appellation affirms that Ruth is an active agent, as fully able as Boaz to influence events and people. Within the symbolic matrix of the narrative the phrase renders Ruth the complement of Boaz and confirms that this outsider has now completed her journey to the centre of the community's life.

Presented as the view of the 'the entire town council' (lit. 'the whole gate of my people'), the epithet confirms that the community as a whole values Ruth and so anticipates the scene at the gate (4:1–12). The gate constituted the commercial and social centre of the community and the area at which elders of the village gathered to resolve disputes and render decisions. In biblical texts the phrase sometimes constitutes a metonym for the entire population of the town or is a metaphor for the institutions of justice and decision-making (e.g. Deut. 21:19; 22:15; Prov. 22:22; Amos 5:12, 15; Zech. 8:16). Here it probably refers to 'the legally responsible body of the town' (Campbell 1975: 124). Ruth's acceptance as an esteemed insider is not only affirmed by the powerful man to whom she has appealed but by all those who constitute the core of the community. She is now 'in'.

Then Boaz equivocates (vv. 12–13). He esteems Ruth and agrees to her plan – in principle. Social protocol, however, stands in the way and must be honoured. Ruth's declaration that Boaz is a *gō'ēl* has suggested a socially appropriate avenue by which this reputable village elder may marry a Moabite widow and at the same time enhance his standing as an honourable man. Boaz emphatically affirms Ruth's declaration, the family bond she appeals to and the possibility she advances, reversing normal syntax to accentuate his agreement (*gō'ēl 'ānōkî*, 'a family redeemer am I'). His choice of pr. appears to identify himself with Ruth even as his declaration to Ruth identified her with him. *'ānōkî* is the form of the first-person pr. customarily used when a person of lower class addresses someone of higher class, whereas the alternate form *'ǎnî* is utilized when speaking with someone of the same or lower class. Boaz thus places himself on Ruth's level, communicating, by an estimable title for Ruth and an unconventional address with reference to himself, that the two now share equivalent social space (Holmstedt 2010: 167, following Revell 1995: 199–217). Another nominative phrase follows (*gō'ēl qārôb*, 'a family redeemer, a close one') but, in contrast, distances Boaz from Ruth. While the two are in full agreement with each other, someone stands between them.

If the disclosure is surprising, what Boaz says next is completely confusing (v. 13). He wraps imperatives that direct Ruth to occupy his physical space around declarations that she may or may not occupy his social space as a result.

> A   Stay here for the night.
>   B   If he wants to redeem you when morning comes, fine
>   C   Let him redeem you.
>   B'   But if he is not interested in redeeming you,
>   C'   then I will redeem you, as Yahweh lives.
> A'   Lie here until morning.

Invitations to intimacy collide with declarations that things may not work out in the light of day. Does Boaz desire a romantic interlude or a sexual encounter? Or is he rather concerned that sending Ruth home alone, in the middle of the night, will put her in peril (cf. Song 5:7)? If, as we will learn shortly, Boaz is so concerned that no one discover Ruth's visit to the threshing floor, why does he not see to it that she departs now, in the dead of night, rather than heighten the risk by sending her away at dawn?

Boaz repeats the root for redemption (*g'l*) six times in these two verses, as if mulling over the implications, obstacles and prospects of Ruth's proposal. It may be that the flummoxed Boaz, now delighted to learn that Ruth desires him, is thinking out loud about how he can make the plan work and so take her as his wife. If the plan is to succeed, Boaz will have to work out a way to deal with an individual who is more closely related to Naomi and thus has the right of first refusal. It is possible that the nearer family redeemer, when presented with the opportunity, may decide to marry Ruth. If so, that would be that. Implementing Ruth's plan will entail some risk.

We return to the topic of levirate marriage and its bearing on our understanding of what Ruth proposes and Boaz agrees to. As noted in the comment on v. 9 above, no levirate obligation applies to Boaz when the situation is viewed in the light of the Deuteronomic legislation (Deut. 25:5–6) and the story of Tamar and Judah (Gen. 38:6–26). Furthermore, a levirate obligation does not fall within the sphere of a *gōʾēl*'s responsibilities as attested in biblical literature. There is no mention at this point in the story of a responsibility to a dead kinsman or continuing his line. The conversation is all about marriage between Ruth and Boaz. Ruth comes to Boaz seeking security, offers herself to him as an eligible partner and makes a proposal that will facilitate marriage without incurring social stigma.

It is important to keep in mind that the levirate legislation codifies a specific case that expresses a deeper social and moral sensibility, that is, the vital importance of maintaining the integrity and welfare of the family unit and its members. Technically speaking, *no one* is qualified to fulfil the levirate obligation for Ruth; her own brother-in-law is also deceased. The levirate legislation cannot, however, be viewed apart from the matrix of moral sensibilities that reinforced the kinship network of village society. Neither law nor custom obligates Boaz to take Ruth as his wife. Marrying Ruth will entail the same free choice and initiative on the part of Boaz that has characterized Ruth's decision to devote herself to Naomi.

To sum up, Ruth comes to Boaz at the threshing floor seeking a stable and permanent relationship that ensures a place and provision for herself and Naomi. Her Moabite ethnicity, however, presents a formidable barrier to that relationship. At the threshing floor she names Boaz her family redeemer and so suggests a way for him to marry her with honour. Boaz, however, realizes that taking this tack raises a complication, for the claim falls even more directly on a nearer kinsman. If this path is taken, the kinsman may decide to marry Ruth. That is the risk Boaz ponders as he contemplates Ruth's proposal.

14b–15

Ruth does not leave. Following Naomi's instructions, she does what Boaz tells her to do (cf. 3:4). The narrator now skilfully uses language to tie a number of threads together. First, we are told that Ruth got up 'before one person could recognize another'. The repetition of the root *nkr* (here, 'recognize') connects the current conversation to the previous one in the field, where Ruth said, 'Why have I found favour in your sight, that you would *notice* me, since I am a foreigner' (2:10)? As the darkness diminishes, only Boaz recognizes Ruth. Secondly, Boaz's concern that no one know that a woman (in particular *this* woman) has visited the threshing floor plays off Naomi's command to Ruth not to 'make yourself known to the man' (v. 3) and what Boaz has declared everyone knows about Ruth: she is an admirable woman (v. 11). Finally, the narrator contrasts what Boaz is thinking with what Boaz says to Ruth (v. 15) through two reports of direct speech. The first is an instance of interior speech that articulates Boaz's thoughts (cf. Gen. 20:11; Exod. 3:3; 1 Sam. 20:26; 2 Kgs 20:19). The second reports Boaz's directions to Ruth. The narrator presents the two speeches without comment or connection. We now find out why Boaz wants Ruth to leave early. Her presence at the threshing floor during the night will raise eyebrows at the very least. If she is discovered, the plan to present the marriage as an honourable act on behalf of a widow in the family is doomed to failure. This is especially the case if someone observes Boaz measuring out a large quantity of grain to Ruth and then sending her away, which will create the opposite effect. Boaz, after all, has a reputation to maintain. The words he speaks to Ruth are followed by the gift of grain. The narrator does not linger, and neither does Ruth. Three brief verbal phrases convey a sense of urgency that manifests Boaz's anxiety about the possibility of discovery: 'he measured . . . he put . . . he went back'.

16–18

The narrator continues the brisk tempo of the narrative with three verbal phrases that relate Ruth's return to Naomi: 'she went back . . . she said . . . she told'. Even though each of the verbs in the Hebr. text is in f. form, only the first and third refer to what Ruth says. The middle verb refers to Naomi and highlights her greeting: 'Who are you, my daughter?' As referenced in the note above on v. 16, the question in the Hebr. text echoes Boaz's startled query to the woman at his feet, 'Who are you?' Naomi's question therefore aligns her and Boaz with respect to Ruth, as both raise the fundamental question of her identity. The one who stayed and the one who returned both ask Ruth – now the bridge between the two – to identify herself, even as they identify her as kin: 'my daughter' (cf. vv. 1, 10–11).

Ruth's report to Naomi includes a single quotation that discloses new information: Boaz has sent the grain Ruth carries as a gift to Naomi. The quotation sets the information in relief, especially since it refers to something the narrator does not previously report. By doing so, the narrator reveals that Boaz is thinking about provision for Naomi as well. The arrangement will benefit both women. The gift may also be a signal to Naomi, the elder, with whom Ruth lives, in observance of social protocol. If the first gift of grain from the field was a nuanced signal of interest in

Ruth (2:18), then the copious amount Ruth brings back is an affirmative response to Naomi, whom Boaz may very well perceive as the one behind the whole plan. As marriages in this society were probably negotiated between males, convention would normally dictate that Boaz speak with the patriarch of the family. In this situation, however, all the males are dead. The last remaining member is Naomi who, as Ruth's mother-in-law, now stands in for the dead. The six measures of barley may thus be regarded as a gift that announces to the head of the household Boaz's request for marriage.

For Naomi, Boaz's gift and explanation communicate provision, fullness and restoration. Upon her return to the town, she had declared that she had left Bethlehem full and returned empty (1:21). Through the gift of grain Boaz announces the end of Naomi's emptiness. He therefore becomes for Naomi, as he has become for Ruth, the manifestation of Yahweh's unwavering devotion to the living and the dead (2:20). Ruth for her part functions as the mediator of the restoration and healing Boaz promises. Boaz and Naomi never meet directly in the narrative. Ruth is the link.

The grain Ruth carries thus announces a broader thematic reversal, from returning and emptiness to incorporation and well-being (Coxon 1989: 29). Some commentators view the grain as a symbol of the 'seed' Boaz promises, and thus portends the birth of a son (e.g. Linafelt 1999: 60–62; Fewell and Gunn 1990: 103). Yet as Eskenazi and Frymer-Kensky (2011: 67–68) note, barley and not seed is mentioned in this scene. They comment that 'the text's focus remains on bread – on household economy, not procreation'. This view is confirmed by the women of the village, who will speak of the birth of Ruth's son in terms of its import for Naomi (4:15). The symbolic and thematic focus here remains squarely on the restoration of Naomi's well-being and reintegration into the life of the community. By reporting Boaz's explanation for the grain when Ruth returns to Naomi, rather than at the threshing floor, the narrator keeps separate two crucial but related elements in the story. The conversation at the threshing floor takes place in a sexually charged atmosphere and is exclusively focused on prospects for marriage. Ruth's return to Naomi, however, evokes and completes the themes of faithfulness and fullness that configure the narrative as a whole. Ruth's return from gleaning, with a surplus of grain, earlier betokened the promise of restoration and plenitude for Naomi (2:19–23). Ruth's return from the threshing floor now announces the dawning of well-being and fullness for the women.

With the annunciation of fullness Ruth's work is done. Naomi tells her to 'sit tight' and let events take their course. At this point Naomi makes her own disclosure, although indirectly. That is, she knows Boaz better than she has let on to Ruth or the reader. Her previous references to Boaz have focused on his relationship to the two women: he is a kinsman and potential family redeemer. Now, however, she makes a comment regarding his personality. Naomi not only knows Boaz through a family connection;

she knows who he is as a person. Her response reveals two things about him. First, he knows how to get things done; he is a *gibbôr ḥayil* in deed as well as reputation. He will carry the matter through to its resolution. Secondly, he is determined. The matter will be settled in short order. The initiative now rests with Boaz, and Naomi also recedes into the background. The words spoken between the two women are the last they speak in the story. It remains only for Boaz to speak and the people of the town to answer.

Explanation

The book of Ruth offers a glimpse into the precarious lives of the poor in ancient Israel. Naomi's cry that she has returned to Bethlehem empty is not just a lament for the loss of her men (1:21). It is a cry of despair. She has nothing and no one except a Moabite daughter-in-law. The dire condition of the two women prompts Ruth to find a field in which to glean (2:2). The fact that she must do so reveals that no one in the village has stepped forward to help them. As a widow and a returnee, Naomi has no integral connection to the community. The loss of her men renders her empty not only because they are no longer with her but also because their absence renders her socially invisible. She returns to a place with property belonging to her deceased husband Elimelech (4:3) but evidently lacks the means to benefit from it. It may be that the plot of ground has lain fallow for so long that it no longer yields grain. More probable, however, is that someone else has been growing crops on the plot. In the subsistence economy of rural Judah, good cropland was too precious a commodity to waste. Rather than squander it, the likelihood is that a decision was made to continue farming it.

We do not even know if Naomi and Ruth have shelter. While systems for recording title to property are attested in urban settings in the ANE, we cannot assume the same for smaller, rural communities where decisions were generally made by village elders with the common good in mind; there was probably no courthouse in Bethlehem with a written deed to Elimelech's property. If we view the matter as the people of Bethlehem might have, we can appreciate the complicated situation Naomi might have faced when she returned unexpectedly. She and Elimelech had departed years before. Who knew if they would ever come back? In the light of their departure what good would it do to leave a house unoccupied? It is plausible to surmise that someone has moved in. Now, when Naomi returns, who is allowed to live in the house? The person whose husband owns it but abandoned it? Or the village family that has occupied it for years? It does not take much imagination to realize that, without a male advocate, Naomi might have found herself outside in more ways than one.

Biblical law codes established basic practices and protections that addressed the widow's economic and social vulnerability, as well as that of the poor in general. These followed a long legal tradition of care for the widow attested in Sumerian and Babylonian literature. While Mesopotamian law codes called for a variety of safeguards for the poor, the Israelite legal tradition is distinctive for protections that went beyond the others (Weinfeld 1995; D. L. Baker 2009; Pleins 2001: 51–54). Laws regulating the harvest were designed to ensure that the poor, including widows, would be able to acquire a minimal share of the produce. The corners of the fields were not to be harvested and the gleanings were to be left in the field. Likewise, vineyards and olive trees were not to be stripped bare, and fallen fruit was not to be gathered (Lev. 19:9–10; 23:22; Deut. 24:19–22). A portion of the third-year tithe was to be distributed to resident aliens, orphans and widows (Deut. 14:28–29; 26:12–13). The produce of fallow fields, vineyards and olive groves during sabbatical years was also reserved for the poor (Exod. 23:10–11). Other laws set in place protections from exploitation by the rich and powerful. Lending practices were regulated to prevent the rich from taking undue advantage of the poor (Exod. 22:25–27[24–26]; Deut. 15:7–11; 24:10–13, 17). Wages were not to be withheld from them (Deut. 24:14–15). Kidnapping for the purpose of enslaving was rendered a capital offence (Exod. 21:16; Deut. 24:7).

Stronger still were the prohibitions against oppressing the poor or depriving them of justice. The legal system was not to be turned against the poor so as to favour the interests of the rich (Exod. 23:3, 6). The commandment against oppressing the resident alien, widow and orphan (Exod. 22:21– 24[20–23]) stands out from the rest of the laws around it as the singular offence that prompts a direct response from Yahweh and so emphasizes his advocacy for the poor. A corresponding imperative in the wisdom tradition, also singular in expression, reinforces the notion. The sage declares that one must not oppress the poor, because Yahweh will take up their cause and crush those who crush them (Prov. 22:22–23). Yahweh is portrayed throughout the Old Testament as one who upholds the widow and orphan (Ps. 146:9) and renders justice on their behalf (Deut. 10:18; cf. Pss 72:12; 82:3; 140:12; Isa. 25:4). Prophetic texts confirm that these declarations are not mere rhetorical flourishes. Isaiah indicts the Jerusalem aristocracy for not advocating the cause of the widow and orphan (Isa. 1:23) and for plundering the poor and denying them their rights (Isa. 3:14–15; 10:1–2). Amos points to the oppression of the poor as the reason Yahweh has turned against the nation (Amos 2:7; 4:1; 5:11; 8:4– 7; cf. Jer. 2:34; Ezek. 22:29). Rendering justice for the widow and the orphan, therefore, does not just constitute a moral imperative but also a fundamental practice that reflects a divine priority.

Boaz's largesse to Ruth in the field and at the threshing floor give human expression to Yahweh's will and work on behalf of the powerless.

In both instances Boaz goes beyond what is expected and beyond what the law requires when he encounters a destitute widow. In the field he not only allows Ruth to glean but takes measures to see that she has more than enough to eat. He uses his power and standing to protect her so that she can work without being harassed or abused. At the threshing floor Boaz agrees to take Ruth the Moabite into his household and dignifies her by commending her character. In both cases he moves beyond charity to advocacy. He becomes the influential voice in the community who opens the way for the two widows to enjoy and participate in the life of the community. Boaz covers Ruth with his wing and offers her refuge, just as Yahweh does. He therefore embodies the care of Yahweh, the protector of the widow and orphan. Whereas laws and statutes define obligations, the story of Boaz and Ruth challenges God's people to go beyond the commandment and become agents of Yahweh's work to gain security and goodness for the powerless.

Even at that, Boaz does so only because the poor widow has approached him. Ruth 2 and 3 portray the distance that separates the widows' world from that of the eminent and powerful man. Boaz lives in a world of plenty, of eating and drinking. Naomi and Ruth live in an empty world, devoid of food and connection. Even though Boaz knows that the two women have come to the village and has been fully informed of their situation (2:11), they remain effectively outside his field of vision until Ruth enters his space (2:10). Only when she gets right next to him does he see her (3:8). After their night together, Boaz and Ruth return to different places: Boaz to the village; Ruth to her mother-in-law (3:15b–16a). Boaz, in short, lives in a secure and prosperous world, distant from the world inhabited by those who must live day by day.

Through Ruth, Naomi and Boaz the narrator juxtaposes the perspectives of the poor and the rich. The narrative illumines the invisibility of the poor, what measures they must sometimes take to make their presence and condition known, and what is called for from those who occupy a place at the centre. It is an invitation for upstanding members of the covenant community to move beyond charity and almsgiving and into the world of the powerless and excluded – to see and dignify them, come alongside them and, like Boaz, be the wings of Yahweh that cover them.

RUTH 4:1–22

Translation

4:1Boaz went up to the village gate and sat down there. Then, look! The very family redeemer of whom Boaz spoke was passing by! So he said, 'Come over here and sit down, Nobody Special!' He came over and sat down. 2Then he selected ten of the village elders and said, 'Sit down here.' They sat down. ³Then he said to the family redeemer, 'The parcel of the field belonging to our brother Elimelech: Naomi, the one who returned from the Field of Moab is selling it. ⁴I said to myself, "I should apprise you of this and say, 'Buy it publicly, in front of those sitting here, in front of the elders of my people.'" If you are going to redeem it, then do so. If you are not going to redeem it, then tell me and let me know, because there is no redeemer except you. And I am next.' Then he said, 'I will redeem it.'

⁵Then Boaz said, 'At the time you acquire the field from the hand of Naomi and from Ruth the Moabite, you also acquire the wife of the deceased, in order to perpetuate the name of the deceased over his estate.'

⁶The family redeemer said, 'I cannot redeem it for myself, as that may hurt my own estate. Redeem it for yourself. You have my right of redemption, because I cannot redeem it.'

⁷This was how it was done in earlier times in Israel to validate a matter concerning the redemption and transfer of property. One man would take off his sandal and give it to the other. This is how it was publicly attested in Israel. ⁸So the family redeemer said to Boaz, 'Acquire it for yourself,' and took off his sandal.

⁹Then Boaz said to the elders and all the people, 'You are witnesses today that I have acquired, from the hand of Naomi, everything that belonged to Elimelech, as well as to Chilion and Mahlon. ¹⁰I have also acquired Ruth the Moabite, the wife of Mahlon, as a wife for myself, to perpetuate the name of the deceased over his estate, so the name of the deceased may not be cut off from his brothers and from the gate of his rightful place. You are witnesses today.'

¹¹Then all the people at the gate, as well as the elders, said, 'We are witnesses. May Yahweh make the woman who is entering your house like Rachel and Leah who, between the two of them, built the house of Israel. Act powerfully in Ephrathah and gain renown in Bethlehem. ¹²May your house become like the house of Perez, whom Tamar bore to Judah, from the seed Yahweh will give you from this young woman.'

¹³So Boaz took Ruth in, and she became his wife. He went in to her. Yahweh granted her a pregnancy, and she bore a son.

⁴Then the women said to Naomi, 'Blessed be Yahweh, who has not allowed you this day to be without a family redeemer! May he gain renown in Israel! ¹⁵May he be someone who restores your life and provides for you in your old age. For your daughter-in-law, who loves you and is worth more than seven sons to you, has given birth to him.' ¹⁶Naomi took the child and held him to her breast. She became the one who took care of him. ¹⁷The neighbouring women gave him a name. They said, 'A son has been born to Naomi!' They called his name Obed. He is the father of Jesse father of David.

¹⁸This is the genealogy of Perez: Perez fathered Hezron. ¹⁹Hezron fathered Ram. Ram fathered Amminadab. ²⁰Amminadab fathered Nahshon. Nahshon fathered Salmon. ²¹Salmon fathered Boaz. Boaz fathered Obed. ²²Obed fathered Jesse. Jesse fathered David.

Notes on the text

4:1. *pĕlōnî ʾalmōnî*, 'a particular one, someone', occurs elsewhere only in 2 Kgs 6:8, where it refers to the unspecified location that an Aramean king chooses for his encampment, but which an Israelite prophet knows about, and in 2 Sam. 21:3, where it refers to a specific but undisclosed location. In both instances the phrase refers to a name known by the characters in the story but not divulged to the reader. 'Nobody Special' captures the combination of the vague and the specific expressed by the Hebr. phrase.

4. *wĕneged ziqney ʿammî*, 'in front of the elders of my people', stands in apposition to 'those sitting' (Holmstedt 2010: 188; see also D. W. Baker 2013: 890–891).

'If you are not going to redeem it'; the Hebr. text has a 3 m. sg. impf., *yigʾal*, 'he will redeem', but most translators follow multiple ancient versions and emend to a 2 m. sg. impf., *tigʾal*, 'you will redeem'. The 3 m. sg. makes little sense, while the 2 m. sg. fits the flow of speech. Sasson (1979: 118) proposed that the 3 m. sg. is a quick aside to the elders, but this would constitute a singular instance of the device and a significant disruption in what appears to be a focused address to the redeemer.

w'dʿ: the K is impf., 'so I will know', and the Q is juss., 'and let me know'.

5. The entire verse is fraught with difficulties. The first has to do with the phrase *ûmēʾēt rût hammōʾăbîyyâ ʾešet hammēt*, 'and (from?) Ruth the Moabite the wife of the deceased'. The mem in *ûmēʾēt* is difficult to account for. It may constitute the first element of a compound prep., of which *ʾēt* is the second. If so, the phrase signifies that the redeemer is acquiring the field from Ruth as well as from Naomi. This seems improbable in the light of the fact that Boaz has mentioned only Naomi as the seller (v. 3) and because a different phrase is used with reference to Naomi, *miyyad nāʿŏmî*, 'from the hand of Naomi'. Alternatively, the mem could be enclitic, rendering *ʾēt* as the direct object marker (Bush 1996: 216–217). If this is the case, the following phrase, 'the wife of the deceased', is ambiguous. The context of the declaration points to Ruth, but the grammatical antecedent points to Naomi. To resolve the confusion, most commentators (along with *BHS*) emend the text from *wmʾt* to *gmʾt*, thus rendering all that follows as the object of the main verb: '*also* Ruth the Moabite, the wife of the deceased, you acquire'. For reasons elaborated in the 'Comment' section, the emendation fits the general tone of Boaz's strategy and is therefore adopted here.

The second problem concerns a Q/K. The K is 1 com. sg. *knyty*, 'I acquire', which the Q reads as 2 m. sg. *knyth*, 'you acquire'. Who, in short, acquires Ruth at the sale of the field? If we follow the Q, Boaz is declaring that the redeemer will acquire Ruth as a wife when he redeems Elimelech's field, and thus links the redemption of property to the continuation of the patriarchal line. If we follow the K, however, Boaz declares that when Nobody Special redeems the property, Boaz will take Ruth as his wife, thus separating the issue of property from that of patriarchal continuity. Presumably, this means that a son born from the union of Boaz and Ruth will one day inherit the property that Nobody Special acquires (see Zevit 2005: 595–599). My translation follows the Q as the simpler rendering.

11. *waʿăśeh-ḥayil bě'eprātâ ûqĕrā'-šem bĕbêt laḥem*, 'act powerfully in Ephrathah and gain renown in Bethlehem'; the two elements in this compound are grammatically parallel: imp., object; prep., place-name object. For this reason some translators see them as an instance of synonymous parallelism (so TNIV, 'may you have standing in Ephrathah and be famous in Bethlehem'). On the basis of Boaz's prior declaration that he will perpetuate the name of the deceased, others take the first imp. as a reference to progeny (e.g. LaCocque 2004: 139; cf. NRSV, 'may you produce children in Ephrathah'). Furthermore, as the previous quotation indicates, many translators see the imperatives as extensions of the blessing. My translation recognizes *ḥayil* as a key signifier for both Ruth and Boaz that, in the context of the story, communicates energy, power and initiative – the ability to command attention and get things done. The LXX translator follows this line and, as I do, follows the imp. sense of the verbs. Understood in this way, the compound articulates the people's endorsement that Boaz continue to act as robustly and admirably in the community's life as he has at the gate.

Form and structure

Naomi's declaration that Boaz will not rest (3:18) leads immediately to a statement that Boaz went to the town gate. References to the town gate, with the elders assembled there, envelopes the process by which Boaz adroitly overcomes the obstacle represented by the nearer redeemer and receives public affirmation of his decision to marry Ruth (vv. 1, 11). The scene (vv. 1–12) comprises two sections that are divided by the narrator's explanation of the sandal ceremony (v. 7). The first reports a fast-paced exchange between Boaz and the nearer kinsman that results in the latter relinquishing his claim to Ruth and Elimelech's property (vv. 1–6). The second relates the ratification of Boaz's claim and the community's enthusiastic endorsement (vv. 8–12). The narrative then moves to a resolution with the reports of Boaz's marriage to Ruth and the birth of a son, whom the women of the town name and acclaim as Naomi's sustainer (vv. 13–17). The section concludes with a note that the son became the grandfather of David, which leads to the short genealogy that concludes the book (vv. 18–22).

Whereas Boaz and Ruth discuss marriage during the dark of night and with a concern that they not be seen together (3:14), the implementation of Boaz's plan takes place in the light of day and with a calculated intent to draw in many witnesses. Ruth 2 and 3 follow a common pattern that begins and ends with conversations between Ruth and Naomi and a plot propelled by the women. The final chapter, however, begins and ends with references to men, and the initiative shifts to Boaz. Ruth 3 and 4, moreover, display a plot sequence that aligns Naomi with Boaz. In Ruth 3 Naomi hatches a plan that depends on the element of surprise to enable Ruth to press the advantage and secure a promise of marriage from Boaz. The narrator reports the successful implementation of the plan by reporting Ruth's compliance with each point of the plan (3:6–7). Boaz's strategy in Ruth 4 also depends on the element of surprise, and the narrator confirms the compliance of both the elders and the nearer redeemer by reporting that everyone did just as Boaz directed. (' "Come over here and sit down, Nobody Special!" He came over and sat down . . . "Sit down here." They sat down' [vv. 1–2].)

Boaz, however, does not have the last word. One by one the main characters in the drama go silent. Ruth's final words merge with those of Boaz in 3:17 and promise plenitude: 'You must not go back to your mother-in-law empty.' Naomi's words are an admonition to wait and a declaration that Boaz will settle matters quickly (3:18). Boaz declares his intention to perpetuate patriarchal descent (4:10). The final words, then, are spoken by the community, first ostensibly by the men (townsfolk and elders, vv. 11–12) and lastly by the women (vv. 14–15, 17).

The men and women of Bethlehem invoke the name of Yahweh and speak of a blessed future both for Boaz, the one who Remained (vv. 11–12), and for Naomi, the one who Returned (vv. 14–15). Both acclaim the women's essential role of bearing children in ways that subtly challenge convention. The townsfolk speak of the importance of sons for continuing a 'name' that establishes one's reputation and of the 'seed', commonly associated with men, as a divine gift associated with a woman (v. 12). Their blessing lifts up patriarchal houses established by women with insider connections (Rachel and Leah) and an outsider (Tamar). The women who bless Naomi also speak ambiguously about the patriarchy (vv. 14–15). On the one hand, they point to Yahweh's faithfulness in seeing that she has a male, a family redeemer, and thus a connection to the social network. They also speak of the son who will restore and provide for her. On the other hand, they declare that one foreign woman is worth more than seven (Bethlehemite) sons, and they – not the men – determine the name of the newborn male.

The chapter as a whole, then, begins and ends with texts that ostensibly affirm the patriarchal system. Boaz games the system so as to present his marriage to Ruth as a perpetuation of the male line. The genealogy concludes the story by evoking the patrilineal structure that articulates the continuity of the system. Yet the men and the women of the town, who speak in the intervening text, muddle associations that configure the system. And despite the talk of perpetuating the name of the deceased (vv. 5, 10), the son born of the union of Ruth and Boaz is not identified, in the end, as Elimelech's or Mahlon's, but as the son of Boaz (v. 21).

Names constitute the thematic focus of the chapter. Seven iterations of *šēm* (name) in the Hebr. text of this last chapter (vv. 5, 10 [twice], 11, 14, 17 [twice]) complement seven instances at the beginning of the book (1:2 [four times], 4 [three times]). The repetitions link male identity, reputation, the remembrance of the dead, the birth of a new male and, in a singular instance, Yahweh's reputation. A cascade of personal and geographical names in the final chapter highlights the focal point of identity – Moab, Bethlehem, Ephrathah, Boaz, Naomi, Elimelech, Ruth, Chilion, Mahlon, Rachel, Leah, Tamar, Israel, Perez, Obed, Jesse, David – before the book comes to an end in an avalanche of names in the genealogy (vv. 18–22). There is even an exception that proves the identity role. Within this sea of names, the narrator renders anonymous the nearer redeemer ('Nobody Special') who refuses the widows their connection to property and incorporation into the social network.

The repetition of the names that begin the tale – Elimelech, Naomi, Mahlon and Chilion – punctuates the transformation of identities that has taken place during the course of the story. The names of the men are still associated with death (vv. 5, 10). Naomi, however, has passed from death to life, emptiness to fullness, and separation to belonging. The narrator employs participles to identify her, as well as Ruth, over against her men and the men of the town. Her men are 'the deceased' (*hammēt*, v. 11). She (rather than Ruth) is now characterized as 'the one who returned [*haššābâ*] from the Field of Moab' (v. 3; cf. 1:22; 2:6), as opposed to the elders of the community, who are 'the ones sitting' (or 'dwelling', or even 'remaining', *hayyōšĕbîm*, v. 4). Ruth, on the other hand, is no longer 'the Moabite who returned' with Naomi but is now 'the one entering' (*habbā'â*, v. 11).

In an ironic twist Elimelech, Chilion and Mahlon owe the survival of their names to Naomi and her Moabite daughter-in-law, whose initiative and devotion have made them visible again to the community. When Naomi arrived in Bethlehem, she declared bitterly that Yahweh had brought her back empty (1:21). Now the women of the city praise Yahweh for not allowing Naomi to be without a male advocate (4:14). She returned without sons and, at her advanced age, without hope of having sons (1:11–12). Now Yahweh has enabled Ruth to conceive and through her has given Naomi a son to provide for and restore her life in her old age.

Comment

1–6

The reader enters the scene at the gate knowing what the townspeople, and especially Nobody Special, do not. Boaz has been delighted by Ruth's proposal on the threshing floor and has acclaimed her as a worthy partner.

Her proposal has presented a strategy whereby Boaz can overcome the stigma of marrying a Moabite woman. By taking on the role of family redeemer, Boaz can marry Ruth and at the same time enhance his reputation as an honourable member of the community. The reader also knows, however, that the strategy comes with a risk. The appeal to kinship brings another individual into the picture, one more closely related to Elimelech, who by rights must be given the opportunity to step into the role of redeemer. The reader knows as well that Boaz has given Ruth and Naomi a pledge of good faith, a copious gift of barley that affirms his intention to carry the matter forward to completion. Finally, the reader knows that Boaz is not the kind of person who will rest while the matter remains unresolved. The only question that remains is how Boaz will bring the plan to fruition.

The scene associates the continuity of property with the continuity of kinship by evoking two Pentateuchal texts: legislation concerning the sale and redemption of property (Lev. 25:23–28) and levirate marriage (Deut. 25:5–10). The former addresses a circumstance in which the owner of property becomes impoverished, requiring him to sell his land. The legislation directs his next of kin (*gōʾălô haqqārōb ʾēlāyw*) to purchase the property so that it remains in the possession of the larger family unit. The redeemer or another purchaser then retains the property until the year of jubilee, when it reverts to the owner. The latter concerns a situation wherein 'brothers are living together' (Deut. 25:5) and one of the (married) brothers dies but has no sons. As in the legislation regarding land, the law is primarily concerned with ensuring continuity and family integrity. The law specifically declares that 'the wife of the deceased must not go outside, to become the wife of a stranger' (Deut. 25:5). Instead, a brother is to become her levir, that is, her husband in place of the brother, so that the firstborn of their union may 'perpetuate the name of his deceased brother' (Deut. 25:6). The legislation goes on to address a situation in which the brother refuses to perform the levirate obligation. In such a case a public hearing is required before the town elders, and if the brother continues to refuse, the widow is to spit in his face and remove his sandal.

The scene at the gate raises a number of questions when viewed against the backdrop of these two texts. By what right or protocol is Naomi selling Elimelech's land? What is she selling? The land itself or the right to till and harvest it? Has the land already been sold or is it being sold now? (The Hebr. verb allows for either.) Why does the removal of the sandal here signify the ratification of Boaz's acquisition of the property and wife of the deceased, as opposed to the refusal of the levirate obligation as in Deut. 25:8–10? How does the levirate legislation apply at all, since it explicitly addresses a situation between brothers who are living in proximity to each other? Neither Boaz nor the nearer kinsman is the brother of Elimelech, who has lived and died far away from the land. Most importantly, why does Boaz declare that the redemption of the field include marriage to the wife of the deceased, since a responsibility to take in the wife of a deceased relative nowhere appears within the purview of the family redeemer? (See the 'Comment' section regarding 3:7–9 above.) What does acquisition of the property and wife entail? Why does the nearer kinsman baulk at acquiring Ruth, and how would she impair his estate?

Various biblical texts present women holding property in trust for males (Num. 27:1–8; Josh. 17:3–6) and perhaps owning it outright (Josh. 15:18–19; 2 Kgs 8:1–6), but they are too few to draw anything more than tenuous conclusions. It may be that Elimelech sold the parcel in question when he departed for Moab, and Naomi, acting in his stead, is now seeking its redemption through a kinsman. Alternatively, Naomi could be putting the land up for sale now, and the nearer kinsman is being called upon to make a pre-emptive purchase so that the property does not pass to someone outside the family (cf. Jer. 32:7–15, 25). What is being sold, the property or its usufruct, is likewise unclear, as is the issue of what access Naomi may or may not have had to the property upon her return.

Boaz's declaration that the redemption of property includes an obligation to sire an heir through the widow has provoked a long and energetic conversation among interpreters. For the most part the conversation follows one of two main trajectories. One takes a developmental tack and posits that the social conventions and expectations that defined the role of the levir changed over time. That is to say, Ruth may reflect a loosening of practices that were more strictly observed in an earlier time (e.g. Zevit 2005: 581). The other tack views the cases depicted in biblical texts, whether legislation or narratives, as concrete instances of decision-making practices that reflect broader moral, religious or social sensibilities. Campbell summarizes succinctly:

> The basic principles underlying the Israelite use of the levirate practice are very much the same principles pertaining to redemption practice, and are in turn among the basic ones undergirding all Israelite law and custom . . . The fact that we can find no legal code which put the two together is probably irrelevant and as much due to the paucity of our sources as to any other cause. (Campbell 1975: 132–137)

The vast literature on this discussion has been summarized well by Bush (1996: 166–169, 211– 232) and Hubbard (1988a: 52–62).

My analysis of the narrative takes a cue from the common concern reflected by the texts on property redemption, levirate marriage and the responsibility of the family redeemer, that is, the cohesion and preservation of the kinship unit and its assets. The concern reflects a corporate sensibility that contrasts significantly with the individualism that configures Western societies. In the world of that day the integrity, continuity and well-being of the group determine individual identities, commitments and decisions. The sensibility is situated within a kinship matrix that is anchored by the patriarchal household (*bêt 'āb*) – the fundamental social unit in biblical Israel – and extends through expanding networks of relationships to the clan and the tribe. Kinship relationships overlap and intersect with others in village society, creating a social web that renders the well-being of the village dependent on well-being within and among families. Keeping the family and its resources intact, in short, is part and parcel of maintaining a harmonious communal life.

As noted above, biblical legislation reflects this sensibility and encodes it in the form of specific cases. Case law in the Old Testament, as in the ANE, was not oriented primarily towards deterring behaviour, as it is in many Western societies, but bends towards restoring social equilibrium and well-being. It was not sweeping in scope or abstract in expression but instead presented precedents rooted in real-life situations, which guided decisions made with the common good in mind. Law codes in short 'functioned as legal precedents intended to serve as references for settling cases, particularly difficult ones. Their purpose was illustrative and didactic; consequently, they are anything but complete and comprehensive' (Bush 1996: 168). Biblical laws in sum comprise specific instances of what were probably common moral and social norms that, in village contexts, enabled community leaders to think through conflicts so as to restore community well-being.

The scene at the gate does not feature lawyers citing laws to persuade a judge to rule in favour of their clients. Instead, we see a prominent member of the community hastily assembling an ad hoc group of village elders at the town gate, the communal gathering place, and just as hastily apprehending another villager and presenting a case that requires public decision and ratification. Although Boaz sets before the elders a situation that corresponds to aspects of biblical legislation, he does not quote chapter and verse. Rather, the entire procedure articulates a social and moral understanding that finds expression within the context of biblical case law. No particular legislative statute obligates Boaz or the nearer kinsman. Instead, Boaz presents a case before the assembled elders that requires a decision impinging on the common good.

Boaz raises two issues that jeopardize the assets of the house of Elimelech and therefore his clan: his land is being sold and his name may be lost. The sale of land, however construed, also brings to public view the fact that Naomi, his widow, is impoverished. The case therefore evokes a wider moral and social imperative that calls for *someone* within the larger kinship group to step forward. The imperative is succinctly expressed elsewhere: 'If any of your brothers sinks into poverty and can no longer support himself among you, you must uphold him as you would a resident alien or sojourner; he will live with you' (Lev. 25:35). Whether conceived particularly or generally, family must take care of family.

Boaz appears at the gate as a worthy candidate to take on this obligation. The narrator has introduced him as an eminent and powerful man
(2:1). As is evident during the harvest, he is a leading figure in the village,
with sufficient means to employ a crew of male and female workers
as well as a crew foreman. He does not miss much. Upon arriving in the
field, he notices a new person and, after exchanging pleasantries, reveals
that he knows about her (2:11). He directs and redirects the life and work
of the community that works his land and issues directives. He devotes
particular attention to the impoverished foreigner and forbids violence
and harassment, thus maintaining social harmony. At the threshing floor
he is thrown temporarily off stride and responds to Ruth's words with
a burst of emotion (3:10). Yet he quickly recovers his composure, sets a
discrete distance by a matter-of-fact reference to Ruth's potential marriage
to another, and resumes giving orders (3:13). Boaz is clearly a man who
knows how to get what he wants and possesses the social capital to
influence people and events (3:18).

Furthermore, the narrator has made the reader privy to the furtive conversation between Boaz and Ruth at the threshing floor. That conversation
is all about Ruth's proposal and Boaz's qualified acceptance. There is no
mention of Elimelech and Mahlon or of property. Perpetuating Elimelech's
line and preserving family assets is not even mentioned by the two
people who lie together in the darkness. Boaz's attention is fixed on this
woman who, to his delight, has approached him rather than the younger
men of the town. He speaks of her in terms that identify her as a worthy
partner, raises a complication that must be overcome if she is to become
his wife and tells her repeatedly to stay with him. Boaz is not concerned
about family continuity. He does not want land. He wants Ruth.

The conversation at the threshing floor lies in the background as Boaz
appears at the town gate, assembling a group of people who have no idea
what has occurred the night before. What the narrator has presented of
Boaz's character and of his recent conversation with Ruth suggests to the
reader a particular interpretation of the events that Boaz now orchestrates.
In private the conversation about a redeemer was all about Ruth. Now in
public the case Boaz sets before the elders is all about the redemption of
property and the perpetuation of Elimelech's line, with Ruth as an after-
thought and, as it turns out, a deal-breaker.

Put simply, the sale and redemption of the field is a clever ruse, a smoke-
screen thrown up to obscure Boaz's real objective: public affirmation for
his intention to marry the Moabite widow, with the enhancement of his
reputation as an honourable benefactor as an added benefit. Although the
outcome of the matter appears open, Boaz leaves little to chance. He begins
by catching the nearer kinsman off guard as he is passing by. He directs
him to sit down but does not divulge the reason. The man immediately
complies. The narrator names the nearer kinsman only as 'the family
redeemer', thereby identifying him as the obstacle that stands between

Boaz and Ruth (v. 1). Boaz, however, calls the man by an odd form of address: 'Nobody Special'. The name seems out of place and perhaps rude, akin to yelling, 'Hey you!' Interpreters have been puzzled by this. Boaz probably knows the man's name. Why would he summon him as though he were unknown? The answer to that question may be found on the level of narration. As noted in the 'Notes on the text', the name is a device that refers to someone whose name is known but not divulged to the reader. By utilizing this device, the narrator renders the man anonymous in contrast to Boaz, the man of eminence and power who is orchestrating events.

Boaz next selects a group of ten elders and directs them to sit. Impartiality may not necessarily be high on the list of qualifications. The elders also immediately comply. We are left to imagine what the redeemer is thinking as he sits and watches Boaz round up village leaders for who knows what purpose.

When everyone is in place, Boaz announces that Naomi is selling the parcel of the field that belongs to Elimelech (v. 3). The syntax of the Hebr. text puts the verb 'selling' squarely between 'parcel of the field belonging to our brother Elimelech' and 'Naomi, the one who returned from the Field of Moab', thus emphasizing the transaction. Boaz then disarms Nobody Special by feigning concern ('I said to myself, "I should apprise you of this"'), before flooding the unsuspecting kinsman with information: he should buy the field; he should decide whether or not to redeem it; he should inform Boaz of his decision; he has the right of first refusal; Boaz is next in line (v. 4). One senses that Boaz hardly takes a breath. The information comes at the redeemer with such rapid-fire staccato that he can scarcely take it in, let alone weigh his options.

As if to put more pressure on the man, Boaz emphasizes by repetition that what occurs is being done in full view of the whole community. Nobody Special's decision will be public: '*in front of* [Hebr. *neged*] those sitting here, *in front of* the elders of my people'. The decision that Nobody Special is called upon to make will be scrutinized by prominent elders, with whom Boaz identifies. The announcement introduces a matter that requires a thoughtful assessment of resources, possibilities and obligations. But Boaz does not allow for this. He puts the nearer kinsman on the spot in the public arena and presses him for a decision: 'If you are going to redeem it, then do so. If you are not going to redeem it, then tell me and let me know . . .' He ends with words that both isolate – 'there is no redeemer except you' – and associate – 'And I am next.' Nobody Special responds to Boaz's high-pressure assault on the spot with the terse affirmation 'I will redeem it.'

This is the moment Boaz has been waiting for. He has the nearer kinsman thinking about a transfer of property. He now shifts the focus drastically and declares that the acquisition of the property will also include the acquisition of a woman. Suddenly, women take the centre and property recedes in significance. Redemption now involves something completely different: perpetuating Elimelech's name by fathering an heir through the widow of the deceased. And a Moabite widow at that. Such weighty matters call for careful consideration.

At the threshing floor Boaz declared that the entire village council recognizes Ruth as a powerful woman (3:11). Now in front of the assembled elders Boaz intensifies the situation by fixing the nearer kinsman's perspective directly on her ethnic otherness. He emphasizes through word order her Moabite identity: 'and from Ruth the Moabite, you also acquire the life of the deceased' (v. 5). While the prospect of expanding his family by taking a relative's widow might give Nobody Special pause, the prospect of bringing a Moabite into his house introduces an added and unappealing dimension to the transaction.

Boaz is innovating. His declaration about the acquisition of Ruth presents a ruling that is reasonable within the framework of the community's shared values while at the same time advancing his objectives. The connection of property redemption with the marriage of the widow, in short, probably did not reflect a custom that was practised but since has been lost. If it did, the nearer kinsman would probably not have been surprised when Boaz announced it. Instead, it is a brilliant strategic move that employs the element of surprise and novelty to dispense with the nearer kinsman's claim. This is the reason for the hasty assembly and why Boaz does not make the declaration at the same time he announces the redemption of property. The whole plan depends on keeping the near kinsman back on his heels. Boaz has selected the elders. He speaks as one of them. He makes a declaration as an esteemed and concerned member of Elimelech's clan, in consonance with a common belief that caring for one's own is a fundamental good. Who can argue?

Certainly not Nobody Special, who now finds himself in a bind. What to do now? He has already agreed in the presence of the elders to redeem Elimelech's property. Now he faces an unattractive marriage that, to say the least, offers him little incentive. And an eminent leader presses him to decide here and now.

His response is predictable. Nobody Special offers a plausible excuse and backs out (v. 6). He communicates that his refusal is unequivocal by declaring 'I cannot redeem' at the beginning and end of his response. The reason he gives redirects the focus back to the subject of property. Commentators have generally taken Nobody Special's explanation at face value and have tried to discern the nature of impairment to his estate. Those who follow the K in v. 5 ('at the time you acquire the field . . . *I* will acquire the wife of the deceased') hold that the threat comes from the son, born from the union of Boaz and Ruth, who will one day lay claim to the property that Nobody Special has purchased (e.g. LaCocque 2004: 111–117; Linafelt 1999: 67–70). Following this line, the redeemer fears that he will not be able to recoup his investment in the property. Following the

Q (reading '*you* will acquire') leads to a similar interpretation of the nearer redeemer's refusal – fear of a wasted investment – in this instance the prospect of two additional mouths to feed with the result that one will eventually take the field back (e.g. Bush 1996: 210–233; Hubbard 1988a: 245–246).

There is another possibility, namely that the nearer kinsman's explanation is a face-saving move. Backed into a corner by Boaz's high-pressure tactics, he has agreed in a public forum to purchase the field, only to be confronted with a decree that he must also marry the Moabite widow of Mahlon to perpetuate the name of the deceased. We are led to wonder how much impact the acquisition of the field would have on Nobody Special's estate. Boaz has not even mentioned a purchase price, nor has Nobody Special asked for it – surely a strange omission if financial matters are foremost in his mind! His first response instead intimates that he has agreed to redeem the property in conformity with social protocol. Suddenly, he is being told that he must also marry a Moabite widow. How can he extricate himself? The answer that suggests itself immediately is to frame his decision in terms of property rather than to disclose his distaste for the idea of a Moabite wife. By claiming that he does not have the wherewithal to redeem the property in the light of this encumbrance, he can refuse with some measure of his honour intact.

It has all been an elaborate and brilliantly executed set-up. Boaz, who knows both the townspeople and how to get things done, has thought the matter through. Nobody Special had no idea what was coming when Boaz apprehended him at the town gate. He has been given no time to deliberate. Identified by his role (the redeemer) but not by his name, the one anonymous figure in a swirl of names, he has been used as a pawn in Boaz's plan to marry the Moabite woman and gain the approbation of his fellow townsfolk. In a flash Boaz has shrewdly swept away the one obstacle that stands in the way of his marrying Ruth, while at the same time presenting himself to all as the paragon of family values.

7–8

The narrator breaks into the story at this climactic moment with an aside. Interpreters have generally focused on explaining the content of the explanation, that is, what the aside reveals about customs in early Israel or the composition of the book. Campbell (1975: 148–149), for example, questions whether the aside is meant to refer to the distant past. He notes that the key term *lĕpānîm* (in earlier times) does not necessarily signify antiquity, as it can refer to something that happened either in the recent past (Job 42:11; Judg. 3:2; Neh. 13:5) or long ago (1 Chr. 9:20; Ps. 102:26). The point of the phrase in these instances has more to do with a radical change of circumstances than with evoking antiquity.

Much attention has been devoted to the sandal ceremony. As noted above, the removal of a sandal plays a symbolic role in the levirate legislation (Deut. 25:5–10) but in that case signifies the brother's refusal to fulfil his obligation to the widow. While the custom may have its origin in ANE practices, its meaning cannot be clearly ascertained in this instance. After surveying many alternatives, Carmichael (1977: 332–336) sees a link to the levirate legislation via Ruth's actions at the threshing floor. By uncovering Boaz's feet and requesting that he cover her, Ruth becomes Boaz's sandal. The redeemer's removal of his sandal then serves as a fitting complement. By removing his sandal, he rids himself of Ruth. The connection with Deut. 25:5–10, however, may be viewed in more direct terms. In both cases the removal of the sandal represents a refusal of a kinship responsibility. In the case of the levirate legislation the responsibility is clearly and unambiguously defined, and the kinsman's public refusal constitutes an incorrigible disposition worthy of public humiliation. In this case, however, the kinsman refuses for acceptable reasons and after initially assenting to a related responsibility. Public humiliation therefore does not appear to be a prominent element in the incident at the Bethlehem gate. The content of the narrator's words, in short, may simply serve to confirm that the transaction took place as dictated by social norms.

It is the striking break in the narration that draws our attention. The literary crafting of the aside and its strategic placement indicate that the interruption of the story is intended for rhetorical effect. Up to this point the narrator has been content simply to tell the story. There has been no commentary and no break in the flow of the story. The one exception, in which the narrator introduces Boaz (2:1), constitutes a relatively seamless transition from Naomi's return to Ruth's gleaning in the field. In contrast, the narrator's break in this instance suddenly diverts attention from the story to the voice narrating it, juxtaposing the world of the story and the reader's world.

The aside, in short, explicitly separates the world of Boaz and Bethlehem from the world of the reader and thus draws attention to the meaning of the proceedings for the reader's world. The reader presumably knows the levirate legislation (Deut. 25:5–10) and is alert to the allusion that Boaz's speech makes to it. The comment itself, however, takes the symbolic action of the legislation in a different direction, thereby alerting the reader that the thrust of the story itself is moving outside the parameters of legislation. The device thereby signals what will happen next. Boaz, although not technically qualified to fulfil the levirate role, will observe the spirit of the legislation in order to fulfil the greater end it addresses. He will redeem the property of the dead men and perpetuate the name of the deceased (Deut. 25:6). In so doing he will exemplify an expansive rather than restrictive approach to the law. The narrator's aside in other words evokes familiar legislation and, by mentioning a practice associated with another piece of legislation, draws attention to the interpretative elasticity Boaz employs to implement it.

9–12

The declaration Boaz makes to those assembled at the gate takes the form of a symmetry comprising four paired declarations (vv. 9–10):

A You are witnesses today
    B   that I have acquired, from the hand of Naomi,
        C   everything that belonged to Elimelech, as well as to Chilion and Mahlon.
    B' I have also acquired for myself
        C' Ruth the Moabite, the wife of Mahlon
            D   to perpetuate the name of the deceased over his estate
            D' so the name of the deceased may not be cut off from his brothers and from the gate of his rightful place.
A' You are witnesses today.

Two pairs of declarations are repetitive: 'you are witnesses'; 'I have acquired'. The other two bring together opposing elements. One utilizes names to set the insiders ('Elimelech, as well as Chilion and Mahlon') opposite the outsider, who now bears an insider epithet as well ('Ruth the Moabite, the wife of Mahlon'). The other brings together belonging ('to perpetuate the name of the deceased') and separation ('so the name of the deceased may not be cut off'). As a whole, the speech presents Boaz as the agent who bridges insider and outsider and mediates a new configuration that re-establishes fullness and continuity. By doing what someone else in the community has refused to do, he ensures that the community remains intact. Through him neither Elimelech nor his assets will be lost.

On the level of narration the declaration ties together the main threads of the story and resolves them. The family unit that left Bethlehem at the beginning of the story is now reunited (cf. 1:1–2); Elimelech, Naomi, Mahlon and Chilion reappear together in Boaz's speech as they did at first. The continuity of the *nāḥălâ* (estate) of Elimelech, the holdings that the family possesses, has been restored and will now be maintained. Elimelech's place in the community will be preserved. The faithful outsider, who has demonstrated devotion to the family she joined, has now been embraced and united with the faithful insider. Together they will bring about a good future.

'The gate of his rightful place' (*šaʿar měqômô*) occurs elsewhere in Deut. 21:19, where it refers to the equivalent of the modern courtroom. 'Gate' alone occurs throughout Deuteronomy as in a synecdoche for 'town'

(Deut. 12:18, 21; 16:11; 17:8; 18:6; 23:17[16]), while 'place' can also signify a town or place of residence (Campbell 1975: 151). The phrase must therefore refer in some way to Elimelech's position among the landholding elders of Bethlehem who supervised communal affairs. The absence of his voice in the decision-making body signifies an incomplete community. Boaz now represents Elimelech's voice as well as his own and so restores the place the latter vacated when he took his family to Moab. Bethlehem, not Moab, is Elimelech's rightful place. Now, through Boaz, Elimelech is back where he belongs, and wholeness returns to the community.

It comes as no surprise that the council of elders, hand-picked by Boaz, responds with enthusiastic agreement. 'All the people at the gate' join in (v. 11a). Evidently, a crowd has gathered to witness the deliberations. They now articulate the entire community's acceptance of the arrangement by declaring, 'We are witnesses.' Then they offer an extravagant blessing on the marriage and the children who will be born from it, saying nothing at all about the presenting issue Boaz has brought before them – the acquisition of the field and property of Elimelech and his sons! Either they see through Boaz's ruse or the elders have been in on it all along. Whatever the case, they bless the outcome Boaz has orchestrated. His marriage to a Moabite woman elicits public praise rather than social stigma.

The content and structure of the blessing (vv. 11b–12) complement the intricate symmetry of Boaz's declaration but speak of women rather than men:

> A May Yahweh make the woman who is entering your house
>   B like Rachel and Leah who, between the two of them,
>   C built the house of Israel.
>   D Act powerfully in Ephrathah
>   D' and gain renown in Bethlehem.
>   C' May your house become like the house of Perez,
>   B' whom Tamar bore to Judah, from the seed Yahweh will give you
> A' from this young woman.

Both Boaz and the people set a location (here Bethlehem and Ephrathah) and the concerns of men at the centre of their speeches, Boaz speaking of property and continuity and the townsfolk of power and renown. Boaz, for his part, associates these things with men, while the townsfolk associate them with women. The names of three women in the people's blessing (Rachel, Leah, Tamar) and one man (Perez) perfectly complement the names of three men (Elimelech, Mahlon, Chilion) and one woman (Ruth) in Boaz's declaration (vv. 9–10).

Structurally, the community's speech unites the building of the patriarchal household with the expansion of power and prestige by enclosing two imperatives ('act powerfully', 'gain renown') within two blessings

('May Yahweh make the woman who is entering your house like Rachel and Leah,' 'May your house become like the house of Perez'). A series of word pairs in the blessings create a tapestry of associations. Memories of ancestors (Rachel and Leah, Tamar and Perez), and evocations of tribal and national identity ('house of Israel', 'house of Perez'), attach identity to a sense of place (Ephrathah, Bethlehem). Most significant, however, are the references to Yahweh and Ruth that bracket the blessing. The towns-people begin by invoking Yahweh to make Ruth like Rachel and Leah, the two mothers of the nation. They conclude by invoking Yahweh to make Ruth's house like that of Perez. The two invocations contrast coming in with going out ('the woman who is entering your house' and 'the seed Yahweh will give you from this young woman'). As a whole, all the elements of the blessing tacitly affirm that marriage to an outsider, even to a Moabite, brings completion and the bestowal of divine favour.

Strangely, the people's enthusiastic affirmation erases Ruth's identity. She is 'the woman' (*hā'iššâ*) and 'this young woman' (*hanna'ǎrâ hazzô't*) in contrast to the personal names she brackets. Subtle cues, nevertheless, confirm her incorporation into the village community. She is, aptly, 'the one entering' (*habbā'â*). The women the townspeople acclaim, moreover, have significance not only as ancestral mothers but also exemplify the fusion of insider and outsider identities. Rachel and Leah were ethnic insiders but geographical outsiders (Gen. 28:1–5); they entered the land from outside but as members of the larger kinship network (Gen. 24:2–4). Tamar, on the other hand, was a geographical insider but an ethnic outsider; she lived in the land that Judah and his sons occupied but was evidently not a part of their family network. Finally, Ruth is both 'one who is entering your house' and one who will produce the 'seed' for a new and glorious house. The reference to 'seed' connects her with still another ancestral mother of mixed insider/outsider identity. After Hagar the Egyptian flees from the house of Abram, the angel of Yahweh meets her in the wilderness and announces that Yahweh will increase her seed (Gen. 16:10).

To sum up, the blessings of the elders and townspeople confirm the declaration of Boaz and laud his marriage to an outsider, while reminding the reader that the great families of Israel emanate from women of mixed identities. Their words intimate that Yahweh, through this union, will bring about something entirely new: the establishment of a new and prestigious house. The response as a whole, as Linafelt (1999: 72–76) has observed, ironically underscores how much the future that men desire is dependent on the bodies of women.

13–17

The terse narration of Boaz's marriage to Ruth and her subsequent pregnancy recalls the gathering of elders that begins the final act. At the gate Boaz selected ten of the village elders (4:2). Now he 'takes' Ruth (v. 13). And whereas the elders responded immediately and obediently at the gate, Yahweh now responds immediately and effectively when Boaz goes into Ruth, bestowing pregnancy and birth. The matter-of-fact tone of the report is surprising given the import of the event. Marriage and birth have been the end towards which the whole story has been progressing. They signify rest, security, belonging, continuity and provision – the main threads that tie the events together and motivate the characters.

This is the last time the names of Ruth and Boaz appear in the story itself. Though clipped, the narration nonetheless signals reciprocity. The Hebr. text utilizes two forms of the verb *bô'* (come into, enter) to link the two. The townsfolk have acclaimed Ruth as the one who comes into the house of Boaz (*habbā'â*, v. 11). Now Boaz goes into Ruth (*wayābō'*). Yahweh also responds to the blessing of the townspeople and the union of Boaz to Ruth they celebrated. Likewise, the note that Yahweh bestowed Ruth with pregnancy looks back to the people's acclamation of 'the seed Yahweh will give you from this young woman' (v. 12),

The blessing by the community women (vv. 14–15) extends the sense of completion by repeating the elements of the townspeople's blessing of Boaz at the gate (vv. 11–12): Ruth's worthiness ('worth more than seven sons'; cf. 'like Rachel and Leah', v. 11b); the birth of a son, an enhanced reputation: 'May he gain renown in Israel' (*wĕyiqqārē' šĕmô yisrā'ēl*; cf. v. 11c); Yahweh's part in providing a secure place within the community through the birth of a son ('May he be someone who restores your life'; cf. 'the seed Yahweh will give you', v. 12c).

There is, however, a significant difference between the two blessings. Boaz is the subject of the blessing bestowed at the gate, and the particulars express what a son means to men in the patriarchal system: reputation and progeny. Ruth, on the other hand, is the subject of the women's blessing, and the particulars express what the birth of a son means for women in this society: provision, status and security. For Boaz, in short, the birth of a son portends that he will live on through progeny and the perpetuation of his name. For Naomi, the son means a reconnection to the sustaining life of the community.

The full meaning of what Ruth means to Naomi can be adequately conveyed only through hyperbole. Naomi is without sons, but Ruth's devotion has accomplished more than many sons could offer. Boaz's 'acquisition' of Ruth along with Elimelech's property also brings Naomi into the community and with a fullness of life she did not have with Elimelech. Her husband did not possess the resources necessary to withstand the famine, but now through her Moabite daughter-in-law Naomi looks forward to a life that promises more than mere subsistence, in the house of an eminent and powerful man.

Wordplay and rhyming in the Hebr. text accentuate the meaning of Ruth and her son to Naomi. Repetitions of lamed and kaph connect the role 'your daughter-in-law' (*kalātēk*) will have in 'providing' (*ûlĕkalkēl*) 'for you' (*lāk*, twice) – and evoke *hālak* (go, walk), the thematic verb that threads the beginning section of the book. Rhyming reinforces the connection. 'The one who loves you' (*'ăhēbātek*) will bring support for 'your old age' (*'et-śêbātēk*).

The narrator does not directly report the birth of the child. Rather, the focus shifts to Naomi, who takes the child, just as Boaz took Ruth (v. 16; cf. v. 13), and holds him to her bosom in a display of maternal affection (cf. 1 Kgs 3:20). As the story closes, the narrator clothes the grandmother rather than the mother with maternal imagery. Here as well a sense of reciprocity infuses the narrative. The son will replenish and provide for Naomi in her old age, but Naomi cares for the child from his birth.

The women who live with Naomi have the last word (v. 17). The 'neighbouring women' (*haššĕkēnôt*) probably refer to the women of Boaz's extended family and those who lived in proximity. The term therefore carries with it a sense of space and relationship. Naomi would have accompanied Ruth to Boaz's household and to the complex of connected residential buildings in which the extended family lived. The women of the patriarchal household, along with those occupying other complexes in the vicinity, would have constituted the primary sphere of her relationships and interactions. The naming of Obed by these women probably refers to a naming ceremony in which the women of this residential complex named children (Meyers 1999b: 110–127). The unusual form of the declaration, 'a son is born to' (*yullad bēn l-*) resembles the reports of the births of ancestors in Genesis (4:26; 35:26; 46:22) and the public declaration of royal birth in Isa. 9:2. In the context of the story the women's proclamation of the son's birth to Naomi conveys their solidarity with Naomi, thus providing confirmation of her reintegration into the larger community.

The women proclaim the name of the child (Obed) after and not before they announce his destiny, a reversal of the naming sequence attested elsewhere (Eskenazi and Frymer-Kensky 2011: 92). The naming alludes suggestively to women's power in determining the identity and reputation that men prize so highly. In this respect the name 'Obed' (One Who Serves) is intriguing. It is a common name (1 Chr. 2:37; 11:47; 26:7; 2 Chr. 23:1) and is probably a shortened form of a theophoric name (e.g. Obadiah, 'One Who Serves Yahweh'). In one sense the name is apt: the child will serve Naomi and the community at large. Yet, given the role of social identities and classes in the book, the name takes on an ironic nuance: the son of the eminent and powerful man and his powerful wife is a servant. With the naming of Obed, the narrator brings the reader back to the world of men and thus to the concerns and structures that characterize it. The world of mother and daughter-in-law gives way, finally, to the story of father and sons that began the journey.

The last name in the narrative proper is David. The genealogical footnote closes the story by confirming the blessings at the gate in remarkable fashion. Ruth has indeed become like Rachel and Leah. She is the mother of a dynasty that will shape the nation's identity as profoundly as its tribal ancestors. Rachel and Leah tie the nation to its tribal past and to the kinship bonds that held the nation together. The grandson of Ruth, however, will inaugurate a comprehensive transformation that will result in a very different nation – one in which loyalties are redefined, bonds redirected to the centralizing structures of monarchy, and fundamental theologies relocated to a temple and a city. Tribal Israel originates in Rachel and Leah. The kingdom of Israel originates in Ruth.

18–22

The story has concluded fittingly with the narrator's report that Obed was the grandfather of David. At first glance the genealogy looks like it has been tacked on. Primarily for this reason the preponderance of critical scholarship throughout the twentieth century regarded the genealogy as an addition by a later editor. It is difficult to know if this was the case or not, as the apparent discontinuity may reflect more of a modern literary disposition than an ancient one. Although different in form, the genealogy complements the narrative in significant ways. As has long been noted, it echoes the naming of father and sons that begins the book (1:1–3) and so constitutes the second segment of an inclusio that situates the story of the women within the world of men (Bertman 1965: 166–167). In addition, it extends the story's focus on Boaz rather than Elimelech and so confirms the association between David and the former that must have been preserved in Israel's memory. Most importantly, it casts the whole book as an ancestral narrative on a par with those of Abraham and Jacob (Nielsen 1997: 7). Genealogies follow the stories of Israel's ancestors in Genesis (25:12–18; 35:23–29; 36:1–40), rounding off the narratives and anticipating new ones. They also function as structuring devices in Genesis, demarcating the beginnings and endings of patriarchal cycles, so that the narratives in a sense fill out the genealogies (J. W. Wright 2003: 347–349). The genealogy that concludes Ruth, therefore, is an integral part of the book, functioning as the narrative precursor to David in much the same way that the stories of the patriarchs in Genesis serve as the narrative precursor to Moses.

The genealogy has been edited for literary effect. It comprises ten generations, too few a number to cover the span of time from the patriarchal period to the period just before the monarchy. On the basis of ten-member schemes in Amorite royal genealogies Sasson (1989: 178–184) draws attention not only to the corresponding number in the Ruth genealogy but also to its structure, which privileges the first, seventh and tenth names (Perez, Boaz and David, respectively) and situates an equal number of names before and after the exodus (Nahshon being the hinge that combines both). The scheme may also explain why the genealogy begins with Perez and not Judah, the eponymous tribal ancestor. Perez has just been mentioned in the elders' blessing of Boaz (4:12). Beginning the genealogy with Perez preserves the numerical symmetry while also connecting the genealogy organically with the narrative.

The narrative and the genealogy interpret each other in various ways. First, the genealogy provides a tacit endorsement of the prohibited marriage between Boaz the Israelite and Ruth the Moabite. If not a match made in heaven, it certainly is one that leads to extraordinary heights. Secondly, as Eskenazi and Frymer-Kensky have observed (2011: 92–94), the story of Naomi and Ruth provokes the reader to interpret all genealogies differently. Their story reveals how much the work and participation of women contribute to forging the link between the males. This leads to a fuller view of all genealogies, one that views them not just as links in a male chain but also as witnesses to stories that speak of the value and virtue of women as well as men.

At the symbolic level the juxtaposition of story and narrative destabilizes the entire patriarchal system. Ruth begins with the naming and deaths of men (1:1–5). It ends with the naming of men and the extension of their names through their progeny. The book opens with men who have no future. It ends with men who have a glorious future. The intervening story reveals that this extraordinary transformation has not been due primarily to the efforts of men but because of the faithfulness of women, specifically one who enters from outside the system. Taken on its own, the genealogy indicates that the links that render social continuity are those that bind males to each other in a network of names. In the light of the story, however, we now see that the ties that bind the past to the future are those that women make within the network. Patriarchs fret about sons and the future. Matriarchs make sons and make the future.

The story also unmasks the network of names – the patriarchal system that is constructed on it – as a fiction. The perpetuation of Elimelech's name and property lie at the heart of the community's concerns and of the appeal Boaz makes at the gate. The genealogy discloses, however, that the name the larger community remembers is not that of Elimelech but Boaz! Elimelech's name has not been perpetuated through progeny after all. The genealogy therefore pulls the rug out from under the entire system. The clash between genealogy and story, finally, makes a hermeneutical point. Ruth's story has demonstrated why Mosaic commandments cannot be understood or implemented in their strict sense. Times and customs change. Circumstances arise that require creative interpretation of the Torah. Hospitality and devotion trump legalism.

Explanation

The story of Ruth as a whole opposes law with narrative, a fixed identity with a flexible identity, and a rigid hermeneutic with an expansive one.

The final chapter uses narrative to demonstrate that laws and command-ments are not ends in themselves but rather serve the ends of Yahweh's redemptive purposes. Boaz does not bend the people towards strict obser-vance of the commandments. Rather, he bends legislation towards the end of welcoming those who have entered the covenant community but have no place.

The legislation and law codes of the Pentateuch are embedded in narrative contexts. In many cases laws are situated within and explained by the story of a particular event. Legislation for the observance of Passover and the Feast of Unleavened Bread (Exod. 12:1–28) stands between Moses' warning that Yahweh will slay the firstborn of Egypt and the account of that event (Exod. 11:1–10; 12:29–32). A large and well-formed unit of laws (20:1 – 23:33) interrupts the account of the covenant-making at Sinai (19:1–25; 24:1–18). Deuteronomy makes a connection between law and narrative by joining the law code at the centre of the book (Deut. 12:1 – 26:15) to narrative sections (1:1 – 3:29; 34:1–12), connected by exhortations to faith-fulness and obedience (4:1 – 11:32; 26:16 – 33:29).

The location of legislation within narrative contexts leads the reader to view the application of laws and commandments within the context of God's saving works and Israel's faithful response. Laws arise out of and advance God's redemptive purposes. They provide concrete ways for God's people to live out their faith, to express devotion and offer thanksgiving and praise. Laws organize and define the ordered community Yahweh established in the wilderness. They are embedded deeply within the life of the people.

Christ demonstrated the hermeneutical relationship between law and narrative when challenged on his perceived failure to observe the Sabbath commandment (Mark 2:23–28). At issue was his failure to chastise his hungry disciples from picking some kernels of grain and eating them. Since this occurred on a Sabbath day, a group of Pharisees accused them of breaking the commandment. The accusation derived from a strict and inflexible understanding of the law. Jesus, however, responded by directing his accusers to Israel's narrative, specifically to an episode that occurred when David was fleeing from Saul (1 Sam. 21:1–6). On that occasion David transgressed the law by requesting and receiving bread that had been presented to God and was meant only for the priests (Lev. 24:5–9). After reminding his listeners of the passage, Jesus remarks, 'The Sabbath was made for humanity, not humanity for the Sabbath' (Mark 2:27). Three things are noteworthy in this passage. First, Christ set a narrative text in opposition to a commandment. Secondly, he implied that sustaining life takes priority over the strict application of the commandment; both David and the disciples broke commandments in order to assuage hunger. Thirdly, he commented on the role of the law: laws are made to serve people, not the other way around.

Narrative texts throughout the Old Testament stand in tension with commandments. The stories of Rahab and the Gibeonite envoys provide vivid illustrations (Josh. 2:1–24; 6:17–18, 22–25; 9:1–27). The stories relate two accounts of Canaanites whose lives were spared by Joshua in direct violation of commandments that required Israel to wipe out the peoples of the land (Deut. 7:2b; cf. Exod. 23:33a; Deut. 20:16–17). Immediately following an exhortation to meticulous observance of the commandments (Josh. 1:8–10) the narrator reports that Israelite spies enter the land, where they are taken in and protected by a Canaanite prostitute named Rahab. In return for her protection the spies promise to spare her and her family from the slaughter that awaits the inhabitants of Jericho. Joshua himself makes good on the promise when the Israelites take the town and massacre the entire populace. Both the spies and Joshua break commandments that directly apply to the situation. Yet there is no hint of reproach or rebuke, and Yahweh continues to fight for Israel in the ensuing campaigns of conquest.

The scenario is repeated when Gibeonite emissaries present themselves as emissaries of a far-off city and persuade Joshua and the Israelite leaders to make a treaty with them. The Gibeonites too are spared, even though they constitute an entire enclave of indigenous people. This is a much more egregious breach of the commandment. Yet again, there is no rebuke. Remarkably, both Rahab and the Gibeonites gain renown in the larger narrative. Rahab appears as the mother of Boaz in the genealogy of Jesus (Matt. 1:5) and is lifted up as a paragon of faith by New Testament writers (Heb. 11:31; Jas 2:25). Gibeon becomes a revered shrine. David deposits the ark of the covenant there, before taking it to Jerusalem (1 Chr. 16:37–40; 21:29), and Solomon sacrifices there and receives an endowment of wisdom (1 Kgs 3:3–14; 2 Chr. 1:3–13).

The common thread in these and similar narratives is the extension of mercy and grace to those excluded or condemned by the relevant commandments. Both Rahab and the Gibeonites acclaim Yahweh's supremacy and mighty acts (2:9–13; 9:9–10), align with God's people and receive life rather than death. Indeed, as Robert Polzin (1980: 85–91) has noted, Israel itself is constituted by God's gracious disposition; Israel is no more deserving of the gift of the land than the indigenous peoples are of being spared. Commandments are not the be-all and end-all of life with God. Rather, a vision of God's saving work provides the hermeneutical key for determining if and how laws are implemented.

The scene at the Bethlehem gate, and indeed the entire book of Ruth, presents a sophisticated elaboration of this idea. Boaz makes creative use of laws and legal conventions to welcome a faithful foreigner into the covenant community. In so doing he directly overrides both commandments and convention. The consequence is the blessing and reintegration of a member of the community, the restoration of communal well-being, new life and a new future. The concluding genealogy reveals what no one in the story can know: the transgression of legal and social boundaries has set in motion a transformation that will change the very fabric of the nation and result in new theological vistas in the form of a monarchy, a temple and a holy city.

It turns out, then, that conversion plays a prominent role in the message of Ruth after all, albeit not entirely along the lines of traditional interpretation. Ruth resists the idea that membership in the covenant community is restricted to those who can trace a bloodline to the nation's ancestors and that walls must be erected to keep ethnic others safely outside. It presents an alternative vision that recalls the heart of the covenant tradition, that is, that Israel is a community constituted by covenant rather than by genetics. Israelite identity, in other words, is ultimately volitional, not innate. One becomes an Israelite by the decisions one makes to live in devotion to Israel's God and to display the devotion to others that lies at the heart of the commandments. Ruth reveals that Israel's internal walls have gates, and it establishes the means by which outsiders may pass through them to unite with those who bear the blessing of Abraham. Ruth the Moabite confesses Israel's God, exemplifies covenant devotion and, in due course, receives the blessing of Yahweh and a standing among Israel's ancestors.

As a corollary, Ruth also contests a rigid interpretation of the commandments. Ruth's welcome by the residents of Bethlehem stands in opposition to the unequivocal commands of Moses. Does Ruth, then, negate the Mosaic commandment? This would seem the logical conclusion to draw if the laws are to be taken literally. As the commentary has revealed, however, the narrator of Ruth directs us away from a literal interpretation of the commandments and towards an interpretation tuned to the intent of the law. The import and application of commandments, as demonstrated allusively through Boaz's declarations at the gate, must be discerned not in the particulars but in the focus of the commandment as it impinges on lived experience.

A pattern emerges upon examination of the biblical proscriptions against intermarriage. Each instance directly links the proscription to admonitions not to worship or serve other gods. Moses warns Israel against worshipping other gods and declares that making covenants with the peoples of the land will lead Israel to prostitute itself, sacrifice to other gods and intermarry, which will in turn lead sons and daughters to prostitute themselves (Exod. 34:11–16). The linkage is made even more directly in Deut. 7:2–4, where Moses explicitly prohibits making covenants and intermarrying with the peoples of the land, 'for that would turn your children from following after me and they would serve other gods'. Later Joshua admonishes the Israelites not to intermingle with the nations of Canaan and not to invoke, swear by, serve or bow down to their gods (Josh. 23:7), and declares that intermarrying will result in the nation's obliteration (23:12). The pattern continues in the report of Solomon's marriages to foreign wives, which references the Deuteronomic commandment before informing the reader that his wives turned his heart after other gods, leading him to worship them and, particularly, to build altars to the gods of the Moabites and Ammonites on the outskirts of Jerusalem (1 Kgs 11:1–8).

Intermarriage, in the relevant texts, therefore points beyond itself to the imperative that Israel devote itself exclusively and wholeheartedly to Yahweh. Solomon is condemned not so much for marrying foreign women as for turning his heart towards their gods, which opens the door to the worship of their gods within Israel. Intermarriage, in short, functions as a metaphor in the commandment just as it does in the narrative. Apostasy is the focus of these commandments, with intermarriage serving as a salient metaphor for the failure to preserve the nation's internal boundaries – boundaries that are configured by exclusive devotion to Yahweh. Reading the proscriptions of intermarriage in the light of Ruth clarifies a misreading of their true purpose and focus. Their intent is to charge Israel, in the strongest terms, to guard against the influence of the surrounding nations; specifically, to prevent outside deities from entering the community's life and worship. Turning to other gods, the proscriptions clearly state, threatens the exclusive devotion to Yahweh that defines the nation and thus threatens its very existence. The proscriptions against intermarriage in sum are directed towards keeping foreign *gods* out, not necessarily foreign *people* out.

In a similar yet broader sense Ruth also contests a literalistic interpretation of commandments invoked to validate social systems that diminish the worth and standing of women, the poor, the immigrant and others on the periphery. Set within a world that revolves around the position, perspective and power of men, this story about immigrant women brings into view the hardship endured by those who do not have access to the resources enjoyed by the community. In the devotion and initiative of Ruth it illustrates the rich contributions that those on the periphery can make to a nation that welcomes them. And in the hospitality and initiative of Boaz the narrative offers a glimpse of what the world can be when Yahweh's ways are honoured.

The book of Ruth expresses the heart of the biblical vision. The consequences of Ruth's faithfulness extend beyond the confines of the book. As the genealogy suggests and the townspeople intimate, her decisions and actions initiate a new beginning in Israel's story. With the establishment of David's kingdom, Israel will be completely redefined and reconstituted, and Yahweh's work in and through Israel will assume an entirely different trajectory. Yahweh will bless both king and dynasty, settle in Jerusalem and engage the powers and political systems that shape the world. This social and theological transformation will begin with Yahweh's gift of sons in response to the initiative and devotion of devalued women: Ruth's son, the forefather of the dynastic monarch, and Hannah's, the kingmaker who will set events in motion (1 Sam. 1:1–28). The new trajectory that begins with Ruth points beyond the near horizon, to an even more profound reconstitution of the covenant people, inaugurated by the faith of Mary, another childless woman, which will see Ruth's vision fully realized through the kingdom established by Jesus Christ, great David's greater Son.

BIBLIOGRAPHY

COMMENTARIES ON RUTH

Adutwum, O. (1998), 'Ruth', in W. R. Farmer, A. Levoratti, D. L. Dungan and
   A. LaCocque (eds.), *International Bible Commentary*, Collegeville:
   Liturgical Press, 566–571.
Auld, A. G. (1985), *Joshua, Judges, and Ruth*, DSBS, Philadelphia: Westminster.
Block, D. I. (1999), *Judges, Ruth*, NAC, Nashville: Broadman & Holman.
Bowen, N. R. (2009), 'Ruth', in G. R. O'Day and D. L. Petersen (eds.),
   Theological Bible Commentary, Louisville: Westminster John Knox,
   97–99.
Bush, F. (1996), *Ruth/Esther*, WBC, Nashville: Thomas Nelson.
Campbell Jr., E. F. (1975), *Ruth*, AB, New York: Doubleday.
Chisholm Jr., R. B. (2013), *A Commentary on Judges and Ruth*, Kregel
   Exegetical Library, Grand Rapids: Kregel Academic.
Eskenazi, T. C., and T. Frymer-Kensky (2011), *Ruth*, JPSBC, Philadelphia:
   Jewish Publication Society.
Farmer, K. A. R. (1998), 'The Book of Ruth', in *NIB* 2:891–246.
Fentress-Williams, J. (2012), *Ruth*, Abingdon Old Testament Commentary,
   Nashville: Abingdon.
Fischer, I. (2001), *Rut*, HTKAT, Freiburg: Herder.
Franke, J. R. (ed.) (2005), *Joshua, Judges, Ruth, 1–2 Samuel*, ACCS, Downers
   Grove: InterVarsity Press.
Gafney, W. C. M. (2010), 'Ruth', in H. R. Page Jr. and R. C. Bailey (eds.),
   *The Africana Bible: Reading the Scriptures from Africa and the African
   Diaspora*, Minneapolis: Fortress, 249–254.
Gray, J. (1986), *Joshua, Judges, and Ruth*, NCB, rev. ed., Grand Rapids:
   Eerdmans.
Hamlin, J. E. (1996), *Surely There Is a Future: A Commentary on the Book
   of Ruth*, ITC, Grand Rapids: Eerdmans.
Hubbard Jr., R. L. (1988a), *Ruth*, NICOT, Grand Rapids: Eerdmans.
Joüon, P. (1953), *Ruth*, Rome: Pontifical Biblical Institute.
Köhlmoss, M. (2010), *Ruth*, ATD, Göttingen: Vandenhoeck & Ruprecht.
LaCocque, A. (2004), *Ruth*, tr. K. C. Hanson, CC, Minneapolis: Fortress.
Lee, E. P. (2012), 'Ruth', in C. A. Newsom, S. H. Ringe and J. E. Lapsley (eds.),
   Women's Bible Commentary, 3rd ed., Louisville: Westminster John
   Knox, 142–149.
Levine, A.-J. (1992), 'Ruth', in C. A. Newsom and S. H. Ringe (eds.), *Women's
   Bible Commentary*, 2nd ed., Louisville: Westminster John Knox, 74–84.

Linafelt, T. A. (1999), 'Ruth', in T. A. Linafelt and T. K. Beal, *Ruth & Esther*, Berit Olam, Collegeville: Liturgical Press, ix–90.

Matthews, V. H. (2004), *Judges & Ruth*, NCBC, Cambridge: Cambridge University Press.

Nielsen, K. (1997), *Ruth*, OTL, Louisville: Westminster John Knox.

Roop, E. F. (2002), *Ruth, Jonah, Esther*, Believers Church Bible Commentary, Scottdale: Herald.

Sakenfeld, K. D. (1999a), *Ruth*, IBC, Louisville: John Knox.

Sasson, J. M. (1989), *Ruth: A New Translation with a Philological and Formalist-Folklorist Interpretation*, 2nd ed., Sheffield: Sheffield Academic Press.

Yee, G. A. (2014), 'Ruth', in G. A. Yee, H. R. Page Jr. and M. J. M. Coomber (eds.), *The Old Testament and Apocrypha*, Fortress Commentary on the Bible, Minneapolis: Fortress, 351–359.

Younger Jr., K. L. (2002), *Judges/Ruth*, NIVAC, Grand Rapids: Zondervan.

Zakovitch, Y. (1999), *Das Buch Rut: Ein jüdischer Kommentar*, SBS 177, Stuttgart, Katholisches Bibelwerk.

Zenger, E. (1992), *Das Buch Ruth*, ZBK 8, Zürich: Theologischer Verlag.

OTHER WORKS

Achenbach, R., R. Albertz and J. Wöhrle (eds.) (2011), *The Foreigner and the Law: Perspectives from the Hebrew Bible and the Ancient Near East*, Beihefte zur Zeitschrift für Altorientalische und Biblische Rechtsgeschichte 16, Wiesbaden: Harrassowitz.

Adams, S. L. (2014), *Social and Economic Life in Second Temple Judea*, Louisville: Westminster John Knox.

Adler, R. (1999), *Engendering Judaism: An Inclusive Theology and Ethics*, Boston: Beacon.

Alter, R. (1981), *The Art of Biblical Narrative*, New York: Basic.

Anderson, A. A. (1978), 'The Marriage of Ruth', *JSS* 23:171–183.

Aschkenasy, N. (1986), *Eve's Journey: Feminine Images in the Hebraic Literary Tradition*, Philadelphia: University of Pennsylvania Press.

———— (1994), 'Language as Female Empowerment in Ruth', in Kates and Reimer 1994: 111–124.

———— (2007), 'Reading Ruth Through a Bakhtinian Lens: The Carnivalesque in a Biblical Tale', *JBL* 126:437–453.

———— (2010), 'From Aristotle to Bakhtin: The Comedic and the Carnivalesque in a Biblical Tale', in H. Liss and M. Oeming (eds.), *Literary Construction of Identity in the Ancient World: Proceedings of the Conference Literary Fiction and the Construction of Identity in Ancient Literatures*, Winona Lake: Eisenbrauns, 265–281.

Assmann, J. (1997), *Moses the Egyptian: The Memory of Egypt in Western Monotheism*, Cambridge, Mass.: Harvard University Press.

Atkinson, D. (1983), *The Message of Ruth: The Wings of Refuge*, BST,
    Leicester: Inter-Varsity Press; Downers Grove: InterVarsity Press.
Bachrach, Y. (1973), *Mother of Royalty: An Exposition of the Book of Ruth
    in Light of the Sources*, tr. L. Oschry, New York: Feldheim.
Bailey, R. C. (1995), 'They're Nothing but Incestuous Bastards: The Polemical
    Use of Sex and Sexuality in Hebrew Canon Narratives', in F. F. Segovia
    and M. A. Tolbert (eds.), *Reading from This Place*, vol. 1: *Social
    Location and Biblical Interpretation in the United States*, Minneapolis:
    Fortress, 121–138.
Baker, D. L. (2009), *Tight Fists or Open Hands? Wealth and Poverty in Old
    Testament Law*, Grand Rapids: Eerdmans.
Baker, D. W. (2013), 'Explicative Waw', in G. Khan (gen. ed.), S. Bolokzy,
    S. E. Fassberg, G. A. Rendsburg, A. D. Rubin, O. R. Schwarzwald and
    T. Zewi (eds.), *Encyclopedia of Hebrew Language and Linguistics*,
    Leiden: Brill, 1:890–892.
Bal, M. (1987), *Lethal Love: Feminist Literary Readings of Biblical Love
    Stories*, ISBL, Bloomington: Indiana University Press.
Bar-Efrat, S. (1980), 'Some Observations on the Analysis of Structure in Biblical
    Narrative', *VT* 30:154–174.
Barth, F. (1994), 'Enduring and Emerging Issues in the Analysis of Ethnicity',
    in H. Vermeulen and C. Govers (eds.), *The Anthropology of Ethnicity:
    Beyond 'Ethnic Groups and Boundaries'*, Amsterdam: Het Spinhuis, 11–32.
Barth, F. (ed.) (1969), *Ethnic Groups and Boundaries: The Social Organisation
    of Culture Difference*, London: Allen & Unwin.
Bauckham, R. (1997), 'The Book of Ruth and the Possibility of a Feminist
    Canonical Hermeneutic', *BibInt* 5:29–45.
Beattie, D. R. G. (1971), 'Ketibh and Qere in Ruth IV 5', *VT* 21:590–594.
—— (1974), 'The Book of Ruth as Evidence for Israelite Legal Practice',
    VT 24:251–267.
—— (1977a), *Jewish Exegesis of the Book of Ruth*, JSOTSup 2, Sheffield:
    JSOT.
—— (1977b), 'A Midrashic Gloss in Rt 2.7', *ZAW* 89:122–124.
—— (1978), 'Ruth III', *JSOT* 5:39–51.
—— (1999), 'Ruth, Book of', in J. H. Hayes (ed.), *Dictionary of Biblical
    Interpretation*, Nashville: Abingdon, 426–428.
Bechtel, L. (1991), 'Shame as a Sanction of Social Control in Biblical Israel:
    Judicial, Political, and Social Shaming', *JSOT* 49:47–76.
Bellis, A. O. (2007), *Helpmates, Harlots, and Heroes: Women's Stories in the
    Hebrew Bible*, 2nd ed., Louisville: Westminster John Knox.
Berger, Y. (2009a), 'Ruth and the David–Bathsheba Story: Allusions and
    Contrasts', *JSOT* 33:433–452.
—— (2009b), 'Ruth and Inner-Biblical Allusion: The Case of 1 Samuel 25',
    JBL 128:253–272.
Berlin, A. (1983), *Poetics and Interpretation of Biblical Narrative*, Sheffield:
    Almond.

—— (1994), 'Ruth and the Continuity of Israel', in Kates and Reimer 1994: 55–64.

Berman, J. (2007), 'Ancient Hermeneutics and the Legal Structure of the Book of Ruth', *ZAW* 119:22–38.

Bernstein, M. J. (1991), 'Two Multivalent Readings in the Ruth Narrative', *JSOT* 50:15–26.

Berquist, J. L. (1993), 'Role Dedifferentiation in the Book of Ruth', *JSOT* 57:23–37.

—— (1995), *Judaism in Persia's Shadow: A Social and Historical Approach*, Minneapolis: Fortress.

—— (2006), 'Constructions of Identity in Postcolonial Yehud', in Lipschits and Oeming 2006: 53–89.

—— (2008), 'Resistance and Accommodation in the Persian Empire', in R. A. Horsley (ed.), *The Shadow of Empire: Reclaiming the Bible as a History of Faithful Resistance*, Louisville: Westminster John Knox, 41–58.

—— (ed.) (2007), *Approaching Yehud: New Approaches to the Study of the Persian Period*, SemeiaSt 50, Atlanta: Society of Biblical Literature.

Bertman, S. (1965), 'Symmetrical Design in the Book of Ruth', *ZAW* 84:165–168.

Bialik, H. N., and Y. H. Ravnitzky (1992), *The Book of Legends: Legends from the Talmud and Midrash*, tr. W. G. Braude, New York: Schocken.

Bird, P. (1997), *Missing Persons and Mistaken Identities: Women and Gender in Ancient Israel*, OBT, Minneapolis: Fortress.

Black, J. (1991), 'Ruth in the Dark: Folktale, Law and Creative Ambiguity in the Old Testament', *Literature and Theology* 5:20–36.

Block, D. I. (2008), 'Ruth 1: Book of', *DOTWP&W* 672–687.

Boer, R. (2003), 'Terry Eagleton: The Class Struggles of Ruth', in *Marxist Criticism of the Bible*, London: T. & T. Clark, 65–86.

Borowski, B. (2002), *Agriculture in Iron Age Israel*, Boston: American Schools of Oriental Research.

Bos, J. (1988), 'Out of the Shadows: Genesis 38; Judges 4:17–22; Ruth 3', *Semeia* 42:37–67.

Brady, C. M. M. (2013), 'The Conversion of Ruth in Targum Ruth', *Review of Rabbinic Judaism* 16:133–146.

Braulik, G. (1996), 'Das Deuteronomium und die Bücher Ijob, Sprichwörter, Rut: Zur Frage früher Kanonizität des Deuteronomiums', in Erich Zenger (ed.), *Die Tora als Kanon für Juden und Christen*, Herders biblische Studien 10, Freiburg: Herder, 61–138.

—— (1999), 'The Book of Ruth as Intra-biblical Critique on the Deuteronomic Law', *AcT* 19:1–20.

Brenner, A. (1983), 'Naomi and Ruth', *VT* 33:385–397.

—— (2005), *I Am . . . Biblical Women Tell Their Own Stories*, Minneapolis: Fortress.

—— (2010a), 'From Ruth to the "Global Woman": Social and Legal Aspects', *Int* 64:162–168.

—— (2010b), 'From Ruth to Foreign Workers in Contemporary Israel: A Case Study in the Interaction of Religion, Politics, and the Economy', in R. Boer (ed.), *Secularism and Biblical Studies*, Oakville, Conn.: Equinox, 178–191.

Brenner, A. (ed.) (1993), *A Feminist Companion to Ruth*, FCB, Sheffield: Sheffield Academic Press.

—— (1999), *Ruth and Esther*, Second Series, FCB, Sheffield: Sheffield Academic Press.

Brett, M. G. (ed.) (1996), *Ethnicity and the Bible*, Leiden: Brill.

Bridge, Edward J. (2011), 'Self-Abasement as an Expression of Thanks in the Hebrew Bible', *Bib* 92:255–273.

Briggs, R. (2010), *The Virtuous Reader: Old Testament Narrative and Interpretive Virtue*, Grand Rapids: Baker Academic.

Brueggemann, W. (1986), 'The Costly Loss of Lament', *JSOT* 36:57–71.

Butler, J. T. (2012), 'Ruth in Two Canons', in F. Bridger and J. T. Butler (eds.), *Conversations at the Edges of Things: Reflections for the Church in Honor of John Goldingay*, Eugene: Pickwick, 14–26.

Callahan, S. N. (2012), 'But Ruth Clung to Her: Textual Constraints on Ambiguity in Ruth 1:14', *TynB* 63:179–197.

Campbell Jr., E. F. (1974), 'The Hebrew Short Story: A Study of Ruth', in H. N. Bream, R. D. Heim and C. A. Moore (eds.), *A Light unto My Path: Old Testament Studies in Honor of Jacob M. Myers*, Philadelphia: Temple University Press, 83–101.

—— (1989–90), 'Naomi, Boaz, and Ruth: Ḥesed and Change', *ASB* 105:64–74.

—— (1999), 'Ruth Revisited', in S. L. Cook and S. C. Winter (eds.), *On the Way to Nineveh: Studies in Honor of George M. Landes*, ASOR Books 4, Atlanta: Scholars Press, 54–76.

Capsi, M. M., and R. S. Havrelock (1994), *Women on the Biblical Road: Ruth, Naomi, and the Female Journey*, Lanham, Md.: University Press of America.

Carasik, M. (1995), 'Ruth 2,7: Why Was the Overseer Embarrassed?', *ZAW* 107:493–494.

Carmichael, C. M. (1977), 'A Ceremonial Crux: Removing a Man's Sandal as a Female Gesture of Contempt', *JBL* 96:321–336.

—— (1980), 'Treading in the Book of Ruth', *ZAW* 92:248–266.

Carroll R., M. D. (2003), 'Widow', in *DOTP* 890–892.

—— (2011), 'Aliens, Immigration, and Refugees', in J. B. Green (gen. ed.), J. E. Lapsley, R. Miles and A. Verhey (eds.), *Dictionary of Scripture and Ethics*, Grand Rapids: Baker, 53–58.

—— (2013), 'Welcoming the Stranger: Toward a Theology of Immigration in Deuteronomy', in J. S. DeRouchie, J. Gile and K. J. Turner (eds.), *For Our Good Always: Studies on the Message and Influence of Deuteronomy in Honor of Daniel I. Block*, Winona Lake: Eisenbrauns, 441–461.

—— (2014), *Christians at the Border: Immigration, the Church & the Bible*, Grand Rapids: Brazos.

Childs, B. S. (1979), *Introduction to the Old Testament as Scripture*, Philadelphia: Fortress.

Chyutin, M. (2011), *Tendentious Hagiographies: Jewish Propagandist Fiction BCE*, LSTS, London: T. & T. Clark.

Claassens, L. J. M. (2012), 'Resisting Dehumanization: Ruth, Tamar, and the Quest for Human Dignity', *CBQ* 74:659–674.

Coetze, M. W. (2011), 'The Concept of *yr't Yahweh* as Wisdom Motif in the Book of Ruth', *Journal for Semitics* 20:176–191.

Cohen, S. J. D. (1999), *The Beginnings of Jewishness: Boundaries, Varieties, Uncertainties*, Berkeley: University of California.

Cohn, R. L. (1994), 'Before Israel: The Canaanites as Other in Biblical Tradition', in L. J. Silberstein and R. L. Cohn (eds.), *The Other in Jewish Thought and History: Constructions of Jewish Culture and Identity*, New York: New York University Press, 74–90.

Coxon, P. W. (1989), 'Was Naomi a Scold? A Response to Fewell and Gunn', *JSOT* 45:25–37.

Craghan, P. W. (1989), 'Esther, Judith, and Ruth: Paradigms for Human Liberation', *BTB* 12:11–19.

Crowell, B. L. (2009), 'Postcolonial Studies and the Hebrew Bible', *CBR* 7:217–244.

Davies, E. W. (1981), 'Inheritance Rights and the Hebrew Levirate Marriage', *VT* 31:138–144, 257–268.

—— (1983), 'Ruth IV 5 and the Duties of the *Go'el*', *VT* 33:231–234.

Davies, P. R. (2008), *Memories of Ancient Israel: An Introduction to Biblical History – Ancient and Modern*, Louisville: Westminster John Knox.

—— (2010), 'Urban Religion and Rural Religion', in J. Barton and F. Stavrakopoulou (eds.), *Religious Diversity in Ancient Israel and Judah*, London: T. & T. Clark, 104–117.

Day, L. (1998), 'Power, Otherness, and Gender in the Biblical Short Stories', *HBT* 20:109–127.

Day, L., and C. Pressler (eds.) (2006), *Engaging the Bible in a Gendered World: An Introduction to Feminist Biblical Interpretation in Honor of Katherine Doob Sakenfeld*, Louisville: Westminster John Knox.

Dearman, J. A. (2005), 'Moab, Moabites', in *DOTHB* 705–707.

Donaldson, L. E. (1999), 'The Sign of Orpah: Reading Ruth Through Native Eyes', in Brenner 1999: 130–144.

Dube, M. (2001), 'Divining Ruth for International Relations', in A. K. M. Adam (ed.), *Postmodern Interpretations of the Bible: A Reader*, St. Louis: Chalice, 67–79.

Dyck, J. E. (1996), 'The Ideology of Identity in Chronicles', in Brett 1996: 89–116.

Dyk, J. W., and S. Keita (2006), 'The Scene at the Threshing Floor: Suggestive Readings and Intercultural Considerations on Ruth 3', *BT* 57:17–32.

Erbele-Küster, D. (2002), 'Immigration and Gender Issues in the Book of Ruth', *Voices from the Third World* 25:32–39.

Eskenazi, T. C. (1992), 'Out of the Shadows: Biblical Women in the Postexilic Era', *JSOT* 54:25–43.

—— (2006), 'The Missions of Ezra and Nehemiah', in Lipschits and Oeming 2006: 509–529.

Exum, J. C. (1993), *Fragmented Women: Feminist (Sub)versions of Biblical Narratives*, Valley Forge, Pa.: Trinity.

—— (1996), *Plotted, Shot and Painted: Cultural Representations of Biblical Women*, JSOTSup 215, Sheffield: Sheffield Academic Press.

Fenton, S. (2003), *Ethnicity*, Cambridge: Polity.

Fewell, D. N., and D. M. Gunn (1988), ' "A Son Is Born to Naomi!": Literary Allusions and Interpretation in the Book of Ruth', *JSOT* 40:99–108.

—— (1989a), 'Boaz, Pillar of Society: Measures of Worth in the Book of Ruth', *JSOT* 45:45–59.

—— (1989b), 'Is Coxon a Scold? On Responding to the Book of Ruth', *JSOT* 45:39–43.

—— (1990), *Compromising Redemption: Relating Characters in the Book of Ruth*, LCBI, Louisville: Westminster John Knox.

Fisch, H. (1982), 'Ruth and the Structure of Covenant History', *VT* 32:425–437.

Fischer, I. (1999), 'The Book of Ruth: A "Feminist Commentary to the Torah?" ', in Brenner 1999: 24–49.

Forget, G.-D. (2010), 'Navigating "Deuteronomistic History" as Cultural Memory', *R&T* 17:1–12.

Gage, W. A. (1989), 'Ruth upon the Threshing Floor and the Sin of Gibeah: A Biblical-Theological Study', *WTJ* 51:369–375.

Gillmayr-Bucher, S. (2007), ' "She Came to Test Him with Hard Questions": Foreign Women and Their View on Israel', *BibInt* 15:135–150.

Glover, N. (2009), 'Your People, My People: An Exploration of Ethnicity in Ruth', *JSOT* 33:293–313.

Geoghegan, J. C. (2006), *The Time, Place, and Purpose of the Deuteronomistic History: The Evidence of 'Until This Day'*, BJS, Providence, R.I.: Brown University Press.

Gordis, R. (1974), 'Love, Marriage, and Business in the Book of Ruth: A Chapter in Hebrew Customary Law', in H. H. Bream, R. D. Heim and C. A. Moore (eds.), *A Light unto My Path: Old Testament Studies in Honor of Jacob M. Myers*, Philadelphia: Temple University Press, 241–264.

Goulder, M. (1993), 'Ruth: A Homily on Deuteronomy 22–25?', in H. A. McKay and D. J. A. Clines (eds.), *Of Prophets, Visions, and Wisdom of Sages: Essays in Honour of R. Norman Whybray on His Seventieth Birthday*, JSOTSup 162, Sheffield: Almond, 307–310.

Gow, M. (1992), *The Book of Ruth: Its Structure, Theme and Purpose*, Leicester: Apollos.

Grant, R. (1991), 'Literary Structure in the Book of Ruth', *BSac* 148:424–441.

Grant-Henderson, A. L. (2002), *Inclusive Voices in Postexilic Judah*, Collegeville: Liturgical Press.

Grätz, S. (2007), 'The Second Temple and the Legal Status of the Torah: The Hermeneutics of the Torah in the Books of Ruth and Ezra', in G. Knoppers and B. M. Levinson (eds.), *Pentateuch as Torah*, Winona Lake: Eisenbrauns, 273–287.

Green, B. (1982), 'The Plot of the Biblical Story of Ruth', *JSOT* 23:55–68.

Greenstein, E. L. (1999), 'Reading Strategies and the Story of Ruth', in A. Bach (ed.), *Women in the Hebrew Bible*, New York: Routledge, 211–231.

Grossman, J. (2007), ' "Gleaning Among the Ears" – "Gathering Among the Sheaves": Characterizing the Image of the Supervising Boy (Ruth 2)', *JBL* 126:703–716.

Gruen, E. S. (2009), 'Kinship Relations and Jewish Identity', in L. I. Levine and D. R. Schwartz (eds.), *Jewish Identities in Antiquity: Studies in the Memory of Menahem Stern*, Texts and Studies in Ancient Judaism, Tübingen: Mohr Siebeck, 101–116.

Gunkel, H. (1913), 'Ruth', in *Reden und Aufsätze*, Göttingen: Vandenhoeck & Ruprecht, 65–92.

Hals, R. M. (1969), *The Theology of the Book of Ruth*, Philadelphia: Fortress.

Halton, C. (2012), 'An Indecent Proposal: The Theological Core of the Book of Ruth', *SJOT* 26:30–43.

Hawk, L. D. (2011), 'Cast out and Cast off: Hagar, Leah, and the God Who Sees', *Priscilla Papers* 25:9–13.

Hoffmeier, J. (2009), *The Immigration Crisis: Immigrants, Aliens, and the Bible*, Wheaton: Crossway.

Holmstedt, R. D. (2010), *Ruth: A Handbook on the Hebrew Text*, BHHB, Waco: Baylor University Press.

Hubbard Jr., R. L. (1988b), 'Ruth iv 17: A New Solution', *VT* 38:293–301.

——— (1997), '*Ganzheitsdenken* in the Book of Ruth', in H. T. C. Sun and K. L. Eades (eds.), *Problems in Biblical Theology: Essays in Honor of Rolf Knieriem*, Grand Rapids: Eerdmans, 192–209.

——— (2007), 'The Structure of the Book of Ruth', *JSS* 52:179–180.

——— (2008), 'Kinsman-Redeemer and Levirate', in *DOTWP&W* 378–383.

Huffmon, H. B., F. A. Spina and A. R. W. Green (eds.) (1983), *The Quest for the Kingdom of God: Studies in Honor of George E. Mendenhall*, Winona Lake: Eisenbrauns.

Hunter, A. (1981), 'How Many Gods Had Ruth?', *SJT* 34:427–436.

Hurvitz, A. (1983), 'Ruth 2:7: "A Midrashic Gloss"?', *ZAW* 95:121–123.

Hutchinson, J., and A. D. Smith (1996), 'Introduction', in J. Hutchinson and A. D. Smith (eds.), *Ethnicity*, Oxford: Oxford University Press, 3–14.

Hyman, R. T. (1983), 'Questions and the Book of Ruth', *HS* 24:17–25.

——— (1984), 'Questions and Changing Identity in the Book of Ruth', *USQR* 39:189–201.

Irwin, B. P. (2008a), 'Removing Ruth: *tiqqune sopherim* in Ruth 3:3–4?', *JSOT* 32:331–338.

—— (2008b), 'Ruth 3: History of Interpretation', *DOTWP&W* 693–700.

Jobling, D. (1993), 'Ruth Finds a Home: Canon, Politics, Method', in J. C. Exum and D. J. A. Clines (eds.), *The New Literary Criticism and the Hebrew Bible*, JSOTSup 143, Sheffield: JSOT, 125–139.

Johnson, W. M. (1995), 'Ethnicity in Persian Yehud: Between Anthropological Analysis and Ideological Criticism', in *SBLSP 1995*, Atlanta: Scholars Press, 177–186.

Johnston, D. (2009), 'Setting the Book of Ruth in Its Literary Context with Special Reference to the Epilogue of the Book of Judges', *IBS* 27:156–162.

Jones III, E. A. (2014), '"Who Are You, My Daughter [מי את בתי]?", A Reassessment of Ruth and Naomi in Ruth 3', *CBQ* 76:653–664.

Kates, J. A., and G. T. Reimer (eds.) (1994), *Reading Ruth: Contemporary Women Reclaim a Sacred Story*, New York: Ballantine.

Ketchum, J. (2010), 'The Goel Custom in Ruth: A Comparative Study', *ResQ* 52:237–245.

King, P. J., and L. E. Stager (2001), *Life in Biblical Israel*, Louisville: Westminster John Knox.

Knoppers, G. N. (2001), 'Intermarriage, Social Complexity, and Ethnic Diversity in the Genealogy of Judah', *JBL* 120:15–30.

Koosed, J. L. (2011), *Gleaning Ruth: A Biblical Heroine and Her Afterlives*, Columbia: University of South Carolina.

Korpel, M. C. A. (2001), *The Structure of the Book of Ruth*, Assen: Van Gorcum.

Kruger, P. A. (1984), 'The Hem of the Garment in Marriage: The Meaning of the Symbolic Gesture in Ruth 3:0 and Ezek. 16:9', *JNSL* 12:79–86.

—— (2009), 'Nonverbal Communication and Narrative Literature: Genesis 39 and the Ruth Novella', *BN* 141:5–17.

Kunin, S. D. (1999), 'Israel and the Nations: A Structuralist Survey', *JSOT* 83:19–43.

Kwakkel, G. (2010), 'Under Yahweh's Wings', in A. Labahn and P. Van Hecke (eds.), *Metaphors in the Psalms*, BETL, Leuven: Peeters, 141–165.

Kwok, P.-L. (2004), 'Finding a Home for Ruth: Gender, Sexuality, and the Politics of Otherness', in R. M. Fowler, E. Blumhofer and F. F. Segovia (eds.), *New Paradigms for Bible Study*, London: T. & T. Clark, 135–154.

LaCocque, A. (1990), *The Feminine Unconventional: Four Subversive Figures in Israel's Tradition*, Minneapolis: Fortress.

Landy, F. (1994), 'Ruth and the Romance of Realism, or Deconstructing History', *JAAR* 62:285–317.

Lapsley, J. E. (2006), 'Seeing the Older Woman: Naomi in High Definition', in Day and Pressler 2006: 102–113.

—— (2011), *Whispering the Word: Hearing Women's Stories in the Old Testament*, Louisville: Westminster John Knox.

Larkin, K. J. A. (1996), *Ruth and Esther*, OTG, Sheffield: Sheffield Academic Press.

Lau, P. H. (2009), 'Gentile Incorporation into Israel in Ezra-Nehemiah', *Bib* 90:356–373.

—— (2011), *Identity and Ethics in the Book of Ruth: A Social Identity Approach*, BZAW 416, Berlin: de Gruyter.

—— (2012), 'Back Under Authority: Towards an Evangelical Postcolonial Hermeneutic', *TynB* 63:31–144.

Lee, E. P. (2006), 'Ruth the Moabite: Identity, Kinship, and Otherness', in Day and Pressler 2006: 89–101.

Leggett, D. A. (1974), *The Levirate and Go'el Institutions in the Old Testament, with Special Attention to the Book of Ruth*, Cherry Hill, N.J.: Mack.

LeMon, J. M. (2010), *Yahweh's Winged Form in the Psalm: Exploring Congruent Iconography and Texts*, OBO 242, Fribourg: Academic; Göttingen: Vandenhoeck & Ruprecht.

Leneman, H. (2010), 'More Than the Love of Men: Ruth and Naomi's Story in Music', *Int* 64:146–160.

Levine, B. A. (1983), 'In Praise of the Israelite *Mišpāḥâ*: Legal Themes in the Book of Ruth', in *The Quest for the Kingdom of God: Studies in Honor of George E. Mendenhall*, Winona Lake: Eisenbrauns, 95–106.

Levine, E. (1976), 'On Intra-familial Institutions of the Bible', *Bib* 57:554–559.

Lim, T. H. (2011), 'How Good Was Ruth's Hebrew? Ethnic and Linguistic Otherness in the Book of Ruth', in D. C. Harlow, M. Goff, K. J. Hogan and J. S. Kaminsky (eds.), *The 'Other' in Second Temple Judaism: Essays in Honor of John J. Collins*, Grand Rapids: Eerdmans, 101–115.

Linafelt, T. (2010), 'Narrative and Poetic Art in the Book of Ruth', *Int* 64:118–129.

Lipschits, O., and M. Oeming (eds.) (2006), *Judah and the Judeans in the Persian Period*, Winona Lake: Eisenbrauns.

Loader, J. A. (1994a), 'Of Barley, Bulls, Land and Levirate', in F. G. Martínez (ed.), *Studies in Deuteronomy: In Honour of C. J. Labuschagne on the Occasion of His Sixty-fifth Birthday*, VTSup 53, Leiden: Brill, 389–401.

—— (1994b), 'Yahweh's Wings and the Gods of Ruth', in I. Kottsieper, J. van Oorschot and D. Römheld (eds.), *'Wer ist wie du, Herr, unter den Göttern?' Studien zur Theologie und Religionsgeschichte Israels. Für Otto Kaiser zum 70. Geburtstag*, Göttingen: Vandenhoeck & Ruprecht, 389–401.

Loretz, O. (1960), 'The Theme of the Ruth Story', *CBQ* 22:391–399.

—— (1977), 'Das Verhältnis zwischen Rut-story und David-Genealogie im Rut-Buch', *ZAW* 89:124–126.

McCarthy, C. (1985), 'The Davidic Genealogy in the Book of Ruth', *PIBA* 9:53–62.

McKinlay, J. E. (1999), 'A Son Is Born to Naomi: A Harvest for Israel', in Brenner 1999: 151–157.

McNutt, P. M. (1999), *Reconstructing the Society of Ancient Israel*, LAI, Louisville: Westminster John Knox.

Malamat, A. (1968), 'King Lists of the Old Babylonian Period and Biblical Genealogies', *JAOS* 88:163–173.

Maldonado, R. D. (1995), 'Reading Malinche Reading Ruth: Toward a Hermeneutics of Betrayal', *Semeia* 72:91–109.

Mangrum, B. (2011), 'Bringing "Fullness" to Naomi: Centripetal Nationalism in the Book of Ruth', *HBT* 33:62–81.

Manor, D. (1984), 'A Brief History of Levirate Marriage', *ResQ* 27:129–142.

Martin, M. W. (2008), 'Betrothal Journey Narratives', *CBQ* 70:505–523.

Masenya, M. J. (2004), 'Struggling with Poverty/Emptiness: Rereading the Naomi–Ruth story in African-South Africa', *JTSA* 120:46–59.

—— (2009), ' "Impoverished on Harvesting Ground": Ruth 3 and African Women in an HIV-Positive South Africa', in D. Hopkins and M. Lewis (eds.), *Another World Is Possible: Spiritualities and Religions of Darker Global Peoples*, Oakville, Conn.: Equinox, 134–141, 356–357.

—— (2010), 'Is Ruth the *'ēšet ḥayil* for Real? An Exploration of Womanhood from African Proverbs to the Threshing Floor (Ruth 3:1–13)', *SHE* 36, Suppl, 253–272.

Matthews, V. H. (2009), 'The Determination of Social Identity in the Story of Ruth', in E. Dutcher-Walls (ed.), The *Family in Life and Death: The Family in Ancient Israel*, LBC, London: T. & T. Clark, 16–27.

Merrill, E. H. (1985), 'The Book of Ruth: Narration and Shared Themes', *BSac* 142:130–141.

Meyers, C. (1988), *Discovering Eve: Ancient Israelite Women in Context*, New York: Oxford University Press.

—— (1991), ' "To Her Mother's House": Considering a Counterpart to the Israelite *Bêt 'āb*', in D. Jobling, G. T. Sheppard and P. L. Day (eds.), *The Bible and the Politics of Exegesis: Essays in Honor of Norman K. Gottwald on His Sixty-fifth Birthday*, Cleveland: Pilgrim, 39–51.

—— (1993), 'Returning Home: Ruth 1.8 and the Gendering of the Book of Ruth', in Brenner 1993: 85–115.

—— (1999a), 'Guilds and Gatherings: Women's Groups in Ancient Israel', in P. H. Williams Jr. and T. Hiebert (eds.), *Realia Dei: Essays in Archaeology and Biblical Interpretation in Honor of Edward F. Campbell Jr. at His Retirement*, SPHS 23, Atlanta: Scholars Press, 154–184.

—— (1999b), ' "Women of the Neighborhood" (Ruth 4.17): Informal Female Networks in Ancient Israel', in Brenner 1999: 110–127.

Milgrom, J. (2000), *Leviticus 17–22*, AB, New York: Doubleday.

Milne, P. (1986), 'Folktales and Fairy Tales: An Evaluation of Two Proppian Analyses of Biblical Narratives', *JSOT* 34:35–60.

—— (1988), *Vladimir Propp and the Study of Structure in Hebrew Biblical Narrative*, Sheffield: Almond.

Moffat, D. P. (2013), *Ezra's Social Drama: Identity Formation, Marriage and Social Conflict in Ezra 9 and 10*, LHB/OTS 579, London: Bloomsbury.

Moor, J. de (1984, 1986), 'The Poetry of the Book of Ruth', *Or* 53:262–283; 55:16–46.

Moore, E. (2008), 'Ruth 2: Ancient Near Eastern Background', *DOTWP&W* 687–683.

Moore, M. (1997), 'Two Textual Anomalies in Ruth', *CBQ* 59:234–243.

———— (1998), 'Ruth the Moabite and the Blessing of Foreigners', *CBQ* 60:203–217.

Myers, J. M. (1955), *The Linguistic and Literary Form of the Book of Ruth*, Leiden: Brill.

Nash, M. (1998), *The Cauldron of Ethnicity in the Modern World*, Chicago: University of Chicago Press.

Neusner, J. (1993), *The Mother of the Messiah*, Harrisburg: Trinity.

Newsom, C. A. (1989), 'Woman and the Discourse of Patriarchal Wisdom: A Study of Proverbs 1–9', in P. L. Day (ed.), *Gender and Difference in Ancient Israel*, Minneapolis: Fortress, 142–160.

Niditch, S. (1985), 'Legends of Wise Heroes and Heroines', in D. A. Knight and G. M. Tucker (eds.), *The Hebrew Bible and Its Modern Interpreters*, Philadelphia: Fortress, 445–463.

Noll, K. L. (2007), 'Deuteronomistic History or Deuteronomic Debate? (A Thought Experiment)', *JSOT* 31:311–345.

Novick, T. (2011), 'Wages from God: The Dynamics of a Biblical Metaphor', *CBQ* 73:708–722.

O'Kane, M. (2010), 'The Iconography of the Book of Ruth', *Int* 64:130–145.

Osgood, S. J. (1992), 'Women and the Inheritance of Land in Early Israel', in G. J. Brooke (eds.), *Women in the Biblical Tradition*, SWR 31, Lewiston: Mellen, 29–52.

Ostriker, A. (1994), 'The Redeeming of Ruth', in A. Ostriker (ed.), *The Nakedness of the Fathers: Biblical Visions and Revisions*, New Brunswick: Rutgers University Press, 169–175.

———— (2002), 'The Book of Ruth and the Love of the Land', *BibInt* 10:343–358.

Ozick, C. (1989), 'Ruth', in C. Ozick (ed.), *Metaphor and Memory*, New York: Knopf, 260–264.

Panthakan, P. (2010), 'Double *Ḥesed* of God in Naomi's Life (Ruth 1:19–22)', *Asian Journal of Pentecostal Studies* 13:20–39.

Pardes, I. (1992), *Countertraditions in the Bible: A Feminist Approach*, Cambridge, Mass.: Harvard University Press.

Parker, S. B. (1988), 'The Birth Announcement', in L. Eslinger and G. Taylor (eds.), *Ascribe to the Lord: Biblical and Other Essays in Memory of Peter C. Craigie*, JSOTSup 67, Sheffield: JSOT, 133–149.

Phillips, A. (1986), 'The Book of Ruth – Deception and Shame', *JJS* 37:1–17.

Pleins, J. D. (2001), *The Social Visions of the Hebrew Bible: A Theological Introduction*, Louisville: Westminster John Knox.

Plum, K. F. (1989), 'Genealogy as Theology', *SJOT* 1:66–92.

Pohl, C. D. (1999), *Making Room: Recovering Hospitality as a Christian Tradition*, Grand Rapids: Eerdmans.

Polzin, R. (1980), *Moses and the Deuteronomist: A Literary Study of the Deuteronomistic History*, New York: Seabury.

Porten, B. (1977), 'Theme and Historiographic Background of the Scroll of Ruth', *GCA* 6:69–78.

——— (1978), 'The Scroll of Ruth: A Rhetorical Study', *GCA* 7:23–49.

Prinsloo, W. S. (1980), 'The Theology of the Book of Ruth', *VT* 30:33–41.

Rao, N. (2009), 'The Book of Ruth as a Clandestine Scripture to Sabotage Persian Colonial Agenda: A Paradigm for a Liberative Dalit Scripture', *Bangalore Theological Forum* 41:144–134.

Rashkow, I. (1993), 'Ruth: The Discourse of Power and the Power of Discourse', in Brenner 1993: 26–41.

Rauber, D. F. (1974), 'Literary Values in the Bible: The Book of Ruth', in K. R. R. Gros Louis, with J. S. Ackerman and T. S. Warshaw (eds.), *Literary Interpretations of Biblical Narratives*, Nashville: Abingdon, 163–176.

Rebrera, B. (1987), 'Translating Ruth 3:16', *BT* 38:234–237.

Rendsburg, G. (1999), 'Hebrew Philological Notes', *HS* 40:27–32.

Revell, E. J. (1995), 'The Two Forms of First Person Singular Pronoun in Biblical Hebrew: Redundancy or Expressive Contrast?', *JSS* 40:199–217.

Rutledge, D. (1996), *Reading Marginally: Feminism, Deconstruction, and the Bible*, BibIntSer 21, Leiden: Brill.

Sakenfeld, K. D. (1985), *Faithfulness in Action: Loyalty in Biblical Perspective*, OBT, Philadelphia: Fortress.

——— (1999b), 'Ruth 4: An Image of Eschatological Hope', in M. A. Farley and S. Jones (eds.), *Liberating Eschatology: Essays in Honor of Letty Russell*, Louisville: Westminster John Knox, 55–67.

——— (1999c), 'The Story of Ruth: Economic Survival', in P. H. Williams Jr. and T. Hiebert (eds.), *Realia Dei: Essays in Archaeology and Biblical Interpretation in Honor of Edward F. Campbell Jr. at His Retirement*, SPHS 23, Atlanta: Scholars Press, 215–227.

——— (2001), 'At the Threshing Floor: Sex, Reader Response, and a Hermeneutic of Survival', *OTE* 15:164–178.

——— (2003a), *Just Wives: Stories of Power and Survival in the Old Testament and Today*, Louisville: Westminster John Knox.

——— (2003b), 'Naomi's Cry: Reflections on Ruth 1:20–21', in B. A. Strawn and N. Bowen (eds.), *A God So Near: Essays on Old Testament Theology in Honor of Patrick D. Miller*, Winona Lake: Eisenbrauns, 129–143.

Sasson, J. M. (1978a), 'A Genealogical "Convention" in Biblical Chronography?', *ZAW* 90:171–185.

——— (1978b), 'The Issue of *Ge'ullah* in Ruth', *JSOT* 5:52–64.

——— (1978c), 'Response to D. R. B. Beattie's "Ruth III"', *JSOT* 5:49–51.

——— (1987), 'Ruth', in R. Alter and F. Kermode (eds.), *The Literary Guide to the Bible*, Cambridge, Mass.: Belknap, 321–328.

Saxegaard, K. M. (2001), ' "More Than Seven Sons": Ruth as Example of the Good Son', *SJOT* 15:257–275.

——— (2010), *Character Complexity in the Book of Ruth*, FAT, Tübingen: Mohr Siebeck.

Schipper, J. (2012), 'The Syntax and Rhetoric of Ruth 1:9a', *VT* 62:642–645.

Sheehan, J. F. X. (1973), 'The Word of God as Myth: The Book of Ruth', in R. J. Clifford and G. W. MacRae (eds.), *The Word in the World: Essays in Honor of Frederick L. Moriarty, S. J.*, Cambridge: Weston College, 35–43.

Shepherd, D. (2001), 'Violence in the Fields? Translating, Reading, and Revising in Ruth 2', *CBQ* 63:444–463.

Siquans, A. (2009), 'Foreignness and Poverty in the Book of Ruth: A Legal Way for a Poor Foreign Woman to be Integrated into Israel', *JBL* 128:443–452.

——— (2012), 'Israel braucht starke Frauen und Männer: Rut als Antwort auf Spr 31, 10–31', *BZ* 56:20–38.

Smith, A. D. (1986), *The Ethnic Origins of Nations*, Oxford: Basil Blackwell.

——— (1999), *Myths and Memories of the Nation*, Oxford: Oxford University Press.

——— (2003), *Chosen Peoples: Sacred Sources of National Identity*, Oxford: Oxford University Press.

——— (2004), *The Antiquity of Nations*, Cambridge: Polity.

Smith, M. S. (2004), *Memories of God: History, Memory, and the Experience of the Divine in Ancient Israel*, Minneapolis: Fortress.

——— (2007), '"Your People Shall Be My People": Family and Covenant in Ruth 1:16–17', *CBQ* 69:242–258.

Smith-Christopher, D. L. (1994), 'The Mixed Marriage Crisis in Ezra 9–10 and Nehemiah 13', in T. C. Eskenazi and K. H. Richards (eds.), *Second Temple Studies*, JSOTSup 175, Sheffield: Sheffield Academic Press, 243–265.

——— (1996), 'Between Ezra and Isaiah: Exclusion, Transformation, and Inclusion of the "Foreigner" in Postexilic Biblical Theology', in Brett 1996: 117–142.

Sparks, K. L. (1998), *Ethnicity and Identity in Ancient Israel: Prolegomena to the Study of Ethnic Sentiments and Their Expression in the Hebrew Bible*, Winona Lake: Eisenbrauns.

Spina, F. A. (2005), *The Faith of the Outsider: Exclusion and Inclusion in the Biblical Story*, Grand Rapids: Eerdmans.

Stahlberg, L. D. (2008), 'Modern Day Moabites: The Bible and the Debate about Same-Sex Marriage', *BibInt* 16:442–475.

Sternberg, M. (1998), *Hebrews Between Cultures: Group Portraits and National Literature*, ISBL, Bloomington: Indiana University Press.

Sutskover, T. (2010), 'The Themes of Land and Fertility in the Book of Ruth', *JSOT* 34:283–294.

The Bible and Culture Collective (1995), 'Structuralist and Narratological Criticism', in *The Postmodern Bible*, New Haven: Yale University Press, 70–118.

Thompson, M. (1993), 'New Life Amid the Alien Corn', *EvQ* 65:197–210.

Thompson, T., and D. Thompson (1968), 'Some Legal Problems in the Book of Ruth', *VT* 18:79–99.

Tiessen, N. (2010), 'A Theology of Ruth: The Dialectic or Countertestimony and Core Testimony', *Direction* 39:255–264.

Tollers, V. L. (1990), 'Narrative Control in the Book of Ruth', in V. L. Tollers and J. Maier (eds.), *Mapping of the Biblical Terrain: The Bible as Texts*, Lewisburg, Pa.: Buckness University Press, 252–259.

Trible, P. (1978), *God and the Rhetoric of Sexuality*, OBT, Philadelphia: Fortress.

Ulrich, D. (2008), 'Ruth 4: Person', *DOTWP&W* 700–703.

VanGemeren, W. A. (1997), 'Ruth: Theology of', in *NIDOTTE* 4:1153–1157.

Waard, J. de, and E. A. Nida (1992), *A Translator's Handbook on the Book of Ruth*, 2nd ed., UBS Handbook Series, London: United Bible Societies.

Wajdenbaum, P. (2011), *Argonauts of the Desert: Structural Analysis of the Hebrew Bible*, Copenhagen International Seminar, Oakville, Conn.: Equinox.

Waltke, B. K., and M. O'Connor (1990), *An Introduction to Biblical Hebrew Syntax*, Winona Lake: Eisenbrauns.

Weinfeld, M. (1995), *Social Justice in Ancient Israel and in the Ancient Near East*, Minneapolis: Fortress.

Weisberg, D. B. (2009), 'Character Development in the Book of Ruth', in H. Ellens (ed.), *Probing the Frontiers of Biblical Studies*, Eugene: Pickwick, 33–36.

Weiss, D. (1964), 'The Use of *qnh* in Connection with Marriage', *HTR* 57:243–248.

Wendland, E. R. (1988), 'Structural Symmetry and Its Significance in the Book of Ruth', in P. C. Stine (ed.), *Issues in Bible Translation*, UBSMS 3, London: United Bible Societies, 30–63.

Westbrook, R. (1977), *Property and the Family in Biblical Law*, JSOTSup 113, Sheffield: Sheffield Academic Press.

Westermann, C. (1999), 'Structure and Intention of the Book of Ruth', tr. F. J. Gaiser, *WW* 19:285–302.

White, H. (1987), *The Content of the Form: Narrative Discourse and Historical Representation*, Baltimore: Johns Hopkins University Press.

Williams, J. G. (1982), *Women Recounted: Narrative Thinking and the God of Israel*, BLS 6, Sheffield: Almond.

Wilson, R. (1977), *Genealogy and History in the Biblical World*, New Haven: Yale University Press.

Wojcik, J. (1985), 'Improvising Rules in the Book of Ruth', *PMLA* 100:145–153.

Wolde, E. van (1997a), *Ruth and Naomi*, tr. J. Bowden, Macon, Ga.: Smith & Helwys.

——— (1997b), 'Texts in Dialogue with Texts: Intertextuality in the Ruth and Tamar Narratives', *BibInt* 5:1–28.

Wong, W. C. (1999), 'History, Identity and a Community of Ḥesed: A Biblical Reflection on Ruth 1:1–17', *AJT* 13:3–13.

Wright, G. R. H. (1986), 'The Mother-Maid at Bethlehem', *ZAW* 98:56–72.

Wright, J. W. (2003), 'Genealogies', *DOTP* 345–349.

Yee, G. A. (2009), ' "She Stood in Tears Amid the Alien Corn": The Perpetual Foreigner and Model Minority', in R. C. Bailey, T.-S. Benny Liew and F. F. Segovia (eds.), *They Were All Together in One Place? Toward Minority Biblical Criticism*, SemeiaSt, Atlanta: Society of Biblical Literature, 119–140.

Yoder, C. R. (2003), 'The Woman of Substance (אשת חיל): A Socioeconomic Reading of Proverbs 31:10–31', *JBL* 122:427–447.

Zerubavel, E. (2003), *Time Maps: Collective Memory and the Social Shape of the Past*, Chicago: University of Chicago Press.

Zevit, Z. (2005), 'Dating Ruth: Legal, Linguistic, and Historical Considerations', *ZAW* 117:574–600.

Ziegler, Y. (2007), ' "So Shall God Do . . .": Variations of an Oath Formula and Its Literary Meaning', *JBL* 126:59–81.

Zornberg, A. (1994), 'The Concealed Alternative', in Kates and Reimer 1994: 65–81.

INDEX OF SCRIPTURE REFERENCES

INDEX OF AUTHORS

INDEX OF SUBJECTS